Cherokee Sister

Cherokee Sister

The Collected Writings
of Catharine Brown, 1818–1823

CATHARINE BROWN

Edited and with an introduction
by Theresa Strouth Gaul

University of Nebraska Press
Lincoln and London

LIBRARY OF CONGRESS
Cataloging-in-Publication Data
Brown, Catharine.
Cherokee sister: the collected
writings of Catharine Brown,
1818–1823 / Catharine Brown, Theresa
Strouth Gaul.
pages cm. — (Legacies of
nineteenth-century American
women writers)
Includes bibliographical references.
ISBN 978-0-8032-4075-9 (pbk.: alk
paper) 1. Brown, Catharine, 1800?–
1823—Diaries. 2. Brown, Catharine,
1800?–1823—Correspondence.
3. Cherokee women—Tennessee—
Biography. 4. Cherokee Indians—
Missions—Tennessee—History—
19th century. 5. Brainerd Mission—
History—19th century. I. Gaul,
Theresa Strouth. II. Title.
E90.B87A3 2014
973.04975570092—
dc23   2013027957

Set in Adobe Caslon Pro
by Laura Wellington.
Designed by A. Shahan.

Contents

PART 2. NINETEENTH-CENTURY
REPRESENTATIONS OF CATHARINE BROWN

Illustrations

Acknowledgments

Profuse thanks go to the following: for financial support during the completion of this project, TCU's Research and Creative Activities Fund, Dean Andrew Schoolmaster, and former English Department chair Brad Lucas; for archival information and support, archivists and librarians at Houghton Library, Chattanooga Public Library, the Cornwall Historical Society, and especially Jessica Steytler at the Congregational Library; for administrative assistance, Merry Roberts and Lynn Herrera; for invaluable research, editing, and proofreading assistance, Jennifer Bauer-Krueger, Chelsea Smith, Kourtney Kinsel, Lisa Thomas, and Wendy Williams; for much needed and appreciated feedback on drafts, Elizabeth Flowers, Ann George, Desirée Henderson, Charlotte Hogg, Karen Steele, and Aleisa Schat; for offering advice and answering questions, Faith Barrett, Josh Bellin, Laura Mielke, Robert Dale Parker, Alexandra Socarides, and Hilary Wyss; for collegial support and encouragement, Jennifer Putzi, Rebecca Sharpless, Elizabeth Stockton, Nicole Tonkovich, Linda Hughes, Sarah Robbins, and my colleagues in the TCU English Department; for mentoring, support, encouragement, collaboration, and sharing of editing expertise, Sharon M. Harris; for belief, balance, and humor, Dave, Simon, and Sadie.

Statement of Editorial Method

This edition attempts to balance readability with adherence to currently accepted editing practices. To this end, the following editorial principles have guided the preparation of the volume.

Letters

Brown's letters survive in a variety of forms. Of the thirty-two letters in this volume, nineteen of the letters were included in Rufus Anderson's *Memoir of Catharine Brown, a Christian Indian of the Cherokee Nation.* Of those nineteen, three were also published in nineteenth-century periodicals, three were published in Elias Cornelius's *The Little Osage Captive*, and nine of them exist in manuscript today. Of the thirteen letters in this volume that were not included in *Memoir*, four have never been published before, and the remaining nine were published in nineteenth-century periodicals; none of these nine has been reprinted since their original periodical printings, and only one of the nine exists in manuscript today. Of the total of fourteen letters existing in manuscript, eleven are written in Catharine Brown's hand; the others are handwritten copies of her letters.

In this volume, the earliest version of each letter functions as the source text for the transcriptions provided. The following hierarchy was followed to determine the source: (1) manuscript in Brown's hand; (2) manuscript copy by another hand; (2) periodical publication; (3) version in *The Little Osage Captive*; (4) version in *Memoir*.

Letters that were printed in *Memoir* appear in *Cherokee Sister* twice, once in part 1 and once in part 2 in the reprinting of *Memoir*. The choice to duplicate their printing in the volume was made for several reasons. First, it is the editor's contention that when Brown's letters are read as *letters* and in relation to her other letters rather than in relation to

Anderson's framing and interpretation in *Memoir*, new interpretations may emerge. Printing all of Brown's known letters together in a "collected letters" edition therefore enables readers to encounter her letters with a focus and concentration on her authorship and employment of epistolary conventions. Second, presenting the transcriptions based on the earliest remaining sources of Brown's letters (part 1) in the same volume with the versions printed in *Memoir* (part 2) allows readers to make comparisons between the two. These comparisons can potentially be meaningful, especially between Brown's handwritten letters and the edited, printed versions. See the introduction for further discussion of these points.

All letters are introduced by a headnote providing information that includes the name and location of the recipient and a list of the source texts. If the letter exists in manuscript, the word *manuscript* is followed by the abbreviated archive name; if the letter was published in a periodical, the title and date of publication are provided; and if the letter was published in *The Little Osage Captive* or *Memoir*, the title is given.

Editing of Manuscripts

The manuscripts used in the preparation of this volume are held by Yale University Library, Chattanooga Public Library, Houghton Library, and the Congregational Library. That last collection of documents appears to consist of the specific source materials Rufus Anderson collected and used when preparing *Memoir*.

The manuscripts of Brown's letters and the manuscript fragment of her diary, which is a copy from the original prepared by the missionary Laura Potter after Brown's death, are in generally good condition. There are few holes or tears, and illegibility tends to result from conditions described below. Brown's handwriting shows marked improvement in fluidity during the period she was writing letters. When evidence exists of the passage of letters written in Brown's hand through the mail (e.g., the recipient's address, the return address, and the postage amount appearing in the area of the folded outer page functioning as an envelope), the information is given in the first note for the letter. Words in brackets in the note help to clarify what information is present (e.g., [return address:], [postage:], [address:]). When the manuscript does not provide such information or for letters that were copied in another's hand, mailing information is not given.

Manuscripts, whether in Brown's hand or another's, were edited with the goal of rendering transcriptions as close to the original as possible given the limitations of print to capture the idiosyncrasies of handwriting. Misspellings and irregular punctuation and capitalization are retained. Words inserted above the line are represented ∧in this way.∧ Words struck through with a single line are represented in this way. Underlined words appear in this way. [Words in brackets] indicate partially obscured or illegible words that the editor has reconstructed based on contextual clues. [Words in brackets?] indicates reconstructions that are less certain.

To enhance readability and consistency, the following changes were made to the formatting of the manuscript letters: regularized indentations of paragraphs and inserted indentations when they were not present but it is clear the previous paragraph has ended (because the remainder of the line remains blank); regularized dates to right margin in italics, closing and signature to left, and name of recipient at the bottom of the letter, when given, to left margin in small caps; and regularized dash length and spacing on either side of dashes.

Brown seems to have used the same character for the upper- and lowercase "c." Whichever character seemed appropriate for the word (e.g., uppercase for Christian, Christmas) has been used. Like other writers of her era, Brown sometimes connected two words in her script; these have silently been separated. Mr., Mrs., and Dr., which sometimes have letters raised above the line or underlined and sometimes contain a period, are regularized to the form given at the beginning of this sentence. "Th" or "rd" when following a date (e.g., 5th) are brought level with the line of type rather than raised above it, as are patronymic prefixes.

In the transcription of the diary, made from the manuscript copy written out by Laura Potter, indentations have been regularized for each entry. Some of the entries are followed by several long dashes; these are omitted. Other dashes are regularized in length, as are the spaces on either side of the dash. Potter's handwriting does clearly distinguish between the upper- and lowercase "c." She consistently renders *christian* with a lowercase letter, which is reproduced in the transcription here.

[Illegible] indicates a word that is not readable in the manuscript. When a word is not legible because it has been canceled by means of a line drawn through it, it is rendered as [illegible]. In some cases, rather than canceling a word, writers used their fingers to wipe away the ink. They sometimes then wrote over this area of the paper. If the illegibility of a word or character(s) stems from such blotting, it is also represented by [illegible] and additionally described in a note. If the condition of the paper—for example, a hole or tear—creates the illegibility, an explanatory note explains the cause. If the illegibility is due simply to difficulty in reading the handwriting, no note is given. Other noteworthy aspects of the manuscripts will be described in notes.

The manuscripts used in preparing this volume have a variety of extraneous markings on them, not in Brown's hand, that seem to postdate the writing and receipt of the letter. These markings include the notations of the recipients of the letters (such as the date of receipt) as well as markings presumably made by Anderson as he prepared *Memoir*, such as lines in the margin, slash marks, and boxes with writing covered over by x's. These marking have not been reproduced or noted here (except in a few unusual cases), since the goal of this volume is to present Brown's letters as she wrote them, not as they were manipulated by later readers.

Editing of Print Sources

In part 1, when representing letters having *Memoir* as their source, the following changes were made in order to create a consistency of format between all letters: removed title for letter, regularized placement of closing and signature, and eliminated typographical conventions of book publication such as the italicizing of place and date and the use of all capitals for the first words of letters. "Th" or "rd" when following a date (e.g., 5th) are brought level with the line of type rather than raised above it.

When representing letters having periodicals as their source, the following changes were made: removed headlines; regularized the positions of dates, closings, and signatures, as well as paragraph indentations; and eliminated typographical conventions of periodical publication such as the italicizing of place and date and the use of all capitals for signatures and the first words of letters. "Th" or "rd" when following a date (e.g., 5th) are brought level with the line of type rather than raised above it.

When printed letters do not include the name of the recipient, the designation given the recipient in the header is taken from other print publications, when available. When letters that appeared in periodicals were introduced by editorial comments, these comments are given in a note.

The letters printed in Elias Cornelius's *The Little Osage Captive* do not include precise dates, salutations, or subscriptions. This information is taken from *Memoir* in these cases.

The publication information for items in part 2 is given either in a headnote above the title of the work or in the reproduced title page. Original spellings in these items, even misspellings, have been retained.

Some discussion of the text used to prepare the edition of *Memoir* is in order. There were at least eleven reprintings of *Memoir* in the nineteenth century. The most widely cited editions are the first two, both published in 1825 (first edition—Boston: S. T. Armstrong, and Crocker and Brewster; New York: J. P. Haven; second edition—Boston: Crocker and Brewster; New York: J. P. Haven). They differ in only relatively minor ways; for example, a description of a Cherokee mission school is cut from the conclusion of the second edition. Other editions were printed in Glasgow and London in 1825; Cincinnati and York PA, in 1827; and Boston, New York, and London in 1828.

The next most widely disseminated version was printed by the American Sunday School Union in 1831 and was reprinted several times at later dates (1832, 1838, 1855). This edition differs from the 1825 editions more substantively. It includes a number of added footnotes and an appendix at the end of the book, which provide additional information on members of Catharine Brown's family and missionaries, offer a description of a mission school examination, give background information on

Arkansas missions, and explain developments in Cherokee literacy (such as George Guess's syllabary and the printing of the *Cherokee Phoenix*)—all of which occurred after Brown's death. The footnotes and appendix seem to be geared toward apprising readers in 1831 of developments in the Cherokee Nation and American Board missions since the book's initial publication in 1825.

This volume relies on the first edition as the source text, since it is the version published nearest in time to Brown's life and reviewed widely in the periodical press. In addition, it was preserved nearly intact through later editions, which only augmented rather than altered it.

The only changes made here to the 1825 edition are the removal of chapter descriptions from the beginning of chapters (they are preserved in the table of contents), the removal of extraneous spaces between words and end punctuation marks that appear to be typographical errors, and setting Brown's subscription on a separate line from the last sentence of the letter.

Abbreviations

ABCFM American Board of Commissioners for Foreign Missions
BJ Joyce B. Phillips and Paul Gary Phillips, eds., *Brainerd Journal: A Mission to the Cherokees, 1817–1823* (Lincoln: University of Nebraska Press, 1998).
CBP Catharine Brown Papers, Congregational Library
CBC Catharine Brown Correspondence, Chattanooga Public Library
CM William G. McLoughlin, *Cherokees and Missionaries, 1789–1839* (New Haven CT: Yale University Press, 1984).
HLVC Herman Landon Vaill Collection, Yale University Library
Memoir *Memoir of Catharine Brown*

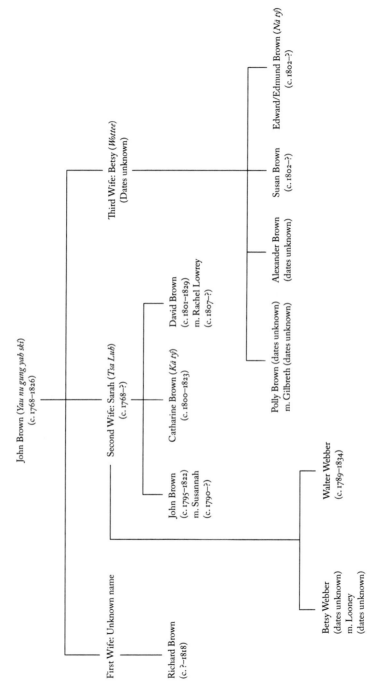

Fig. 1. Brown family tree.

Cherokee Sister

"Then raising herself in the bed & wiping a tear, that was falling from her eye, she with a sweet smile began to relate what God had done for her soul while upon that sick bed."

Page 115

Fig. 2. Frontispiece illustration to Rufus Anderson's *Memoir of Catharine Brown*. Reprinted by permission of DeGolyer Library, Southern Methodist University, Dallas, E90.B87 A5.

Editor's Introduction

The diary and letters of Catharine, will rank high as
specimens of fine epistolary writing. The simplicity of the
style, and the natural amiableness and ardent piety which
breathe through every sentence, not only interest the feelings,
but excite the admiration for the talents of the writer.

"LITERARY AND SCIENTIFIC"
Zion's Herald, Feb. 2, 1825

In the frontispiece illustration to the second edition of *Memoir of Catharine Brown, a Christian Indian of the Cherokee Nation* (1825), the memoir's subject, Catharine Brown (1800?–1823), reclines on her deathbed.
Dressed in a nightcap and gown and lying on a four-poster bed bor-
dered by curtains, Brown shows no visual traces of her Cherokee identity except for the shading that slightly darkens her face. A large, open
book—presumably a Bible—rests on the bedcovers, signifying Brown's
conversion to Christianity and acquisition of literacy. Near the bed, a
female missionary leans over a writing desk, pen in hand, raptly listen-
ing to Brown's words, a scene that illustrates the memoir's depiction of
Brown's dictation of her final letter when she was too physically weak-
ened by consumption to write.

Significantly, the missionary writes down Brown's spoken words, thus
placing Brown's cultural productions within a tradition of as-told-to
narratives penned by white writers who transcribed American Indian
oral transmissions. Yet Catharine Brown was a letter writer and diarist whose writings had been published in scores of religious periodicals and were admired by many. The illustration's effacement of Brown's
authorial agency and its reduction of her to a supine object of white
representation make it a fit visual metaphor for textual renderings of

Brown following her death and the ways scholars have interpreted her for nearly all of the intervening two centuries. Presenting Brown's oeuvre of thirty-two letters and a diary for the first time, *Cherokee Sister: The Collected Writings of Catharine Brown, 1818–1823* puts the pen back in her hand. In doing so it makes available the writings of what is arguably the earliest Native woman author of published, self-written texts in the United States.[1]

When a teenage girl named Kā tý enrolled at the Brainerd Mission School in the Cherokee Nation, she could not have imagined that six years later she would gain a degree of renown in religious circles far away in New England. Renamed Catharine by her missionary teachers, she quickly distinguished herself with her academic progress and piety. The Brainerd Mission School, where Brown was educated, was part of a larger effort of the American Board of Commissioners of Foreign Missions (ABCFM), an organization made up largely of Congregationalists and Presbyterians, to evangelize "heathen" peoples both within the United States and abroad. Putting into practice the U.S. government's policy of "civilizing" American Indians at the very moment the government and general public were beginning to doubt the efficacy of such programs and turn toward Indian removal as a solution to "the Indian question," American Board missionaries constructed a network of schools in the Cherokee Nation to enact their goals of educating and evangelizing. Some Cherokees welcomed the schools with the view that educating their children in Western ways was a vital strategic move in retaining their autonomy and their lands.

Beginning in 1818, only months after Brown's enrollment at the Brainerd Mission School, New England religious publications began regularly printing missionary-authored accounts describing her experiences, academic progress, and religious development. Like many individuals in the nineteenth century, Brown corresponded with a variety of people, and because of her celebrated status as the first American Board Cherokee convert to Christianity, many of her letters made their way into print. Through the missionary accounts and the publication of her letters, Brown became a familiar figure and author in the columns of religious periodicals, which dominated magazine print culture in New England during this period and contributed to a broader "evangelical culture, developed discursively through print, that had missionary endeavor at its heart."[2] Already by September 1818, only eight months after her introduction to the reading public in the *Panoplist*, a missionary writer simply assumed his readers' familiarity with Brown as a reason he need not say more about her: "Much has been put before the public respecting this promising girl. I need not for this reason, trouble you with a detailed account of the wonderful dealings of God with her."[3] With only approximately a two-month lag time between the occurrence of an event in Brown's life and its report in a northern periodical, readers might have felt something of what viewers of reality shows experience today: the unfolding of a person's character and experiences over real time.

Many readers felt quite compelled by Catharine Brown's story as it developed in periodicals, following her through her enrollment in the school in 1817, conversion and baptism in 1818, assumption of the role of missionary teacher in 1820, and death from tuberculosis in 1823. In addition to the evidence provided by the sheer number of articles mentioning her, periodicals printed letters testifying to her profound effects on readers. One reader of the *Religious Remembrancer* explained, "The effect produced by the sight of the *writing of an Indian*, has been considerable. I put it into the hands of a person who is a stranger to religion, and probably never before heard of missionary exertions. He returned it with eyes filled with tears, unable to make one remark. Several times during the afternoon, his eyes were filled to overflowing; and a mournful shade of thought crossed the brow of this hitherto thoughtless character."[4] Her letters also reportedly provoked people to charitable acts. After having Brown's letters read aloud to them, members of an organization voted to contribute their yearly budgetary allotment for wine to the Brainerd Mission School, and three hundred schoolchildren donated sixty dollars.[5] As late as several years after her death, an article arguing for the efficacy of civilizing programs among American Indians used her letter writing as evidence of the success of such efforts, claiming that letters Brown wrote had "gone to every corner of our country, and thus, though dead, she yet speaketh."[6] Poems memorializing her life continued to appear in print throughout the 1820s.

Missionaries recognized how effective her demonstration of extraordinary piety could be in reaching unbelievers and rebutting the increasing belief that Native Americans could not become civilized, which threatened to lessen support for missionary endeavors. The American Board decided to publish a memoir about her life, and its assistant secretary Rufus Anderson assembled the materials for *Memoir of Catharine Brown, a Christian Indian of the Cherokee Nation* in the year following her death, with the book appearing in print in 1825.[7] Anderson's portrayal of Brown resonated with readers and disseminated her life story over the seas and across decades. Widely reviewed and excerpted in periodicals at the time of its publication, *Memoir* sold 2,500 copies within six months of its release.[8] The development and growth of an evangelical print culture and readership combined with changes in the publishing industry, which included new printing technologies that allowed for successive editions of a book as well as changes in the distribution capabilities of the book trade, brought *Memoir* to more readers than would have been possible even a couple of decades earlier.[9] At least ten subsequent editions of *Memoir* appeared in the years after its initial publication, including editions in Glasgow and London, a French translation, and reprintings by the American Sunday School Union, which distributed inexpensive publications to the hundreds of thousands of children attending Sunday schools throughout the country.[10] Barry O'Connell has provocatively speculated that *Memoir* reached more readers and disseminated images of Native Americans more widely than James Fenimore Cooper's *The Last of the Mohicans*.[11] The narrative was also reprinted at least three times in the twentieth century.

To the extent that she has been remembered at all by a few specialists in Cherokee studies or Native studies, Brown's place in history and literature has been conserved through *Memoir of Catharine Brown*; indeed all recent scholarship about her uses the biography as its central, and often sole, source.[12] This fixation with *Memoir* testifies more to the material durability of the book as an artifact and the scholarly establishment's privileging of the book over other genres and media than to *Memoir*'s primary significance in considering Brown's cultural positioning in the early nineteenth century. *Cherokee Sister* redirects critical attention to Brown's own writings and, in doing so, makes visible new interpretations of her importance. When reading through the constricted lens of *Memoir*, earlier scholars treated Brown as a docile and dominated victim of missionaries, someone who represented the tragic fate of Indians who abandoned their identities to assimilate to white ways. In contrast, when read through the lens proffered by her writings and broader developments in the fields of Native and literary studies, Brown emerges as an agent, a leader, a figure of enduring Cherokee resilience and adaptability, and—importantly—a writer.

An oft-overlooked contemporary of Native activists and leaders like William Apess (Pequot), Black Hawk (Sauk), and prominent Cherokee men including Elias Boudinot, John Ridge, and John Ross, Brown has not shared in the critical attention afforded other early Native writers in recent decades. Apess and Samson Occom (Mohegan) have seen a sustained critical interest, epitomized by the publication of editions of their collected works. Scholarly editions of writings by John Johnson (Mohegan), Jane Johnston Schoolcraft (Ojibwe), Elias Boudinot, E. Alice Callahan (Muskogee), Sarah Winnemucca (Paiute), and Zitkala-Ša (Dakota) make their literary contributions available for scholarly and classroom study. Yet despite the extent of Brown's written oeuvre—which, at thirty-two recovered letters and a diary, accords her status, after Occom and Johnson, as the most prolific Native writer before the late 1820s—she has been virtually excluded from the emerging canon of Native writers in the United States, even from works focusing on Native women writers.[13]

Brown is long overdue recognition alongside other Native individuals who crafted public personae in the service of their peoples on the stage provided by early nineteenth-century U.S. print culture. As a woman whose writings gained an audience and held meaning for readers, Brown additionally merits attention along with other American women writers who employed the genres of life writing. Informed by scholarship in Native studies, Cherokee studies, and religious studies—the fields wherein Brown has heretofore attracted the most, albeit modest, amount of scholarly attention—*Cherokee Sister* positions Brown at the nexus of literary considerations of women and Native writers and the genres of biography, autobiography, epistolary writings, and diary writing. The title of the volume highlights the nationalist, gendered, and religious aspects of the epistolary project that occupied Brown's pen during the last five years of her life.

Cherokee Sister: The Collected Writings of Catharine Brown, 1818–1823 brings together a range of textual representations of Brown's life and introduces them to new audiences. The volume presents for the first time a scholarly edition of her collected writings, comprising thirty-two letters and a diary. Some of these writings are printed here for the first time; some are appearing for the first time since their original publication in periodicals in the early nineteenth century; and others were previously accessible only within the pages of Anderson's biography. In addition to her letters and diary, the volume includes reprintings of other nineteenth-century publications related to her life, such as the missionary drama *Catharine Brown, the Converted Cherokee* (1819), poems printed in periodicals, and an annotated edition of *Memoir of Catharine Brown*. The inclusion of these materials allows the reader to consider Brown's writings in relation to missionary discourses and to engage with the variety of genres—biography, drama, and poetry—testifying to her cultural import in the early nineteenth century.

This introduction establishes some of the many contexts with which readers need to be familiar in order to generate meaningful interpretations of Brown's writings. First, I focus on Brown's life and the contexts of Cherokee history and Cherokee-Euro-American contacts during the colonial and early republican eras of U.S. history. Merging biographical information with scholarship from Native studies, religious studies, and other fields, these backgrounds orient readers' attention to the complicated negotiations Brown enacted as a Cherokee woman and Christian convert living in the politically fraught era preceding Cherokee removal. Next I offer literary frameworks—including scholarship on letters, diaries, biographies, and early Native writings—for engaging with Brown's writings and others' writings about her. These frameworks forward an interpretation of Brown's work that emphasizes her agency as a writer working within the epistolary and diary-writing conventions of her time and a Cherokee woman working on behalf of her Nation by writing into existence a cross-racial and transnational network of supporters.[14]

"My beloved people": Early Life and Cherokee Contexts

When Brown was born at the turn of the nineteenth century, she entered into a rapidly transforming cultural, social, and political milieu.[15] Cherokees had already experienced more than a century of contact with European colonists, a period marked by conflict, warfare, treaty making, and, to an unusual degree, adaptability. As Daniel Heath Justice (Cherokee) explains, Cherokee people in particular have a "long history of intermarriage, adaptation, and innovative accommodation": "Cherokees have always met geopolitical and social challenges squarely with whatever tools and strategies were available at the time."[16] The period after the American Revolution brought with it near devastation, as Cherokees suffered brutal retaliations by American forces for their alliance with the British, reducing their population by as much as one-third. By the time Cherokees reached a permanent peace with the United States in 1794, they had ceded over half their land in treaties and been displaced from traditional hunting territories and sacred towns. In return for land cessions and their promise of loyalty to the United States, Cherokees understood that they were guaranteed the boundaries of their landholdings and the right to self-governance. Yet for the next four decades, Cherokees found themselves fighting to maintain their sovereignty and homeland in the East. During the period of Brown's life, tensions with Euro-Americans were strained by controversies over the U.S. government's failure to uphold the Hopewell Treaty of 1785, which defined Cherokee land boundaries, and the increasing numbers of white settlers moving into the Cherokee Nation. Seeking respite from the steady encroachment of white settlers into tribal lands, some Cherokees began moving to Arkansas as early as 1782, and there was a steady influx into the area after 1795. The federal government encouraged migration, making offers of western land in exchange for land cessions in the Southeast.[17] The vast majority of Cherokees, however, resisted the government's persuasions and remained in their homeland.

With implementation in the 1790s of the U.S. government's "civilization" policy toward American Indians, which held out the promise of citizenship if they assimilated into white society, the pace of change in Cherokee life accelerated. A "new multicultural Cherokee world" resulted, in the historian Tiya Miles's words, one that displayed the "persistence of Cherokee cultural ways" as well as "the adoption of Euro-American practices in a context of U.S. colonialism and coercive surveillance."[18] Cherokees shifted their decentralized political structures toward consolidation at the national level in order to better protect landholdings, and aspects of day-to-day life also altered, with some Cherokees beginning to live in log cabins on isolated homesteads, practice agriculture with Western implements, dress in Western clothing, and adopt other Western ways, including slaveholding and patriarchal social relations. The religious historian Joel W. Martin, who has published the largest body of scholarship on Brown to date, characterizes her as "a privileged member of the slave-owning, propertied, politically powerful Cherokee elite," an identity that exemplifies many of these changes.[19]

But in other, equally important ways, Brown's life was rooted in Cherokee tradition. Brown's parents, John (Yau nu gung yah ski) and Sarah (Tsa luh), raised her near the village of Creek Path in what is now northeastern Alabama. In addition to her brothers, John and David, Brown had a number of half-siblings, resulting from John's two other marriages (one of them concurrent) and Sarah's one previous marriage.[20] The children of Cherokee mothers and fathers who may have been Euro-American or biracial, John and Sarah nonetheless spoke no English and raised their children to practice Cherokee spiritual beliefs and passionately engage with Cherokee history. In the only preserved family reminiscence of the period of Brown's childhood, her brother David (ca. 1801–29) remembered:

In the Cherokee Nation, I sprung, and was there reared up in the habits of my country; of course my parents are heathen. Yaenugvyaski, my honoured father, early taught me the religion of my ancestors. Many times did he relate to me, while sitting in some solitary retreat, the wars with Europeans, and the wrongs and losses sustained by them. My fond mother too, when I was quite young, often sung for me a mournful song, commemorative of the death of some of my valiant forefathers, who fell in the arms of death while defending the rights of our country. Importunate was she to inform me of the injuries done to her countrymen, and often invoked the Great Spirit to destine her son to aid the return of peace and gladness in all the dwellings of Tsalagi [Cherokees].[21]

John and Sarah's defense of Cherokee rights was probably prompted not only by memories of the retaliatory depredations of American troops on Cherokee villages during and after the Revolutionary War, but also by the Chickamauga resistance movement of the late eighteenth century, which originated in the vicinity of Creek Path, where they lived. Creek Path was one of the Lower Towns in the Chickamauga region, which emerged as a locus of Cherokee power and resistance in the wake of the Revolution. John Brown was a respected Lower Town leader; upon first meeting him, missionaries noted that "he manifested a very discerning mind" and that "perhaps there are few among the natives better informed or more inteligent than this man."[22]

We have little information about Brown's first sixteen years. A scrap of paper attributed to Brown's sister Polly Gilbreath offers a few tantalizing details: "Very little intercourse with whites. ^Some white near [home]; [illegible] class.^ Saw some travelling company. Was noticed as very amiable. Lived a while with Mrs. Coody—learned to talk english here, Attended school a short time. Also another school short time—when a child—forgot all but her letters before going to Brainerd. Sent for by Mrs. McD."[23] Mrs. Coody (Jane [Jenny] Ross Coody) and Mrs. McD (Anna [Annie] Shorey McDonald) were the sister and grandmother, respectively, of the future principal chief John Ross. Coody's husband was Euro-American, as was McDonald's. In these bicultural homes emanating from several generations of intermarriages of white men and Cherokee women, Brown gained familiarity with Western ways; as another source commented, "She had learned much of the habits & manners of the whites. I believe what she knew of letters & of civilized life, she obtained at Mr. Ross & Coody's."[24] Another source suggests that her facility in English was gleaned from U.S. citizens passing through the Nation or the family's African American slaves: "She learnt to talk english of Slaves and travelers when quite young she could spell in words of three letters This she learnt of a white man who staid a while at her fathers."[25] The multicultural world Brown inhabited shaped the young woman and imparted to her skills and knowledge that prepared her for her future experiences. Her time with McDonald may have particularly set her on a course toward the Brainerd school, since McDonald's husband, John, sold his property to the American Board as the site for the mission.[26]

Colonial violence intersected directly with Brown's life when her father and half-brother Richard (the son of her father from another marriage) joined U.S. troops led by General Andrew Jackson to put down a Creek resistance movement that comprised the so-called Creek War (1813–14). As many as six hundred Cherokees volunteered to fight; among them, John and Richard Brown earned the ranks of captain and colonel, respectively.[27] One legacy of the Brown men's service in the war was Jackson's lasting respect; he felt a personal affection for Richard, who later became president of the National Committee, and kept in contact with John long past the conclusion of the conflict.[28]

Hundreds of U.S. soldiers encamped near the Browns' home in Creek Path during this period of military conflict, and the family suffered thefts of "livestock, corn, farm tools, rails, boards, whiskey, and money"; on one occasion, soldiers burned down their chimney.[29] Brown herself was reportedly menaced with rape when hundreds of U.S. soldiers camped near the home during the Creek War. Anderson obliquely mentions this event, referring to "temptations to which she was exposed" and how she "once even forsook her home, and fled into the wild forest, to preserve her character unsullied" (173).[30] The details of this story, which Anderson states are not "proper" to recount in *Memoir* (173), provide a fuller glimpse of this frightening episode in Brown's life:

> Every stratagem which intrigue could invent, had been used in vain to seduce her by ₐsome ofₐ the officers & men when our army was stationed near there during the Creek war—An officer full bent on his diabolical purpose, promised her marriage, she spurned

his proposals & told him to go to his own wife & children (for it seems he had a wife & several children) that she would not disgrace herself in that manner; he afterwards offered her a bribe of $500. which she spurned with disdain & to get clear of him run off & took shelter in the wild forest. . . . She had taken shelter in the hut of a half breed near Dittoe's landing from the pursuit of this ruffian (for I know no softer name by which he can be called) where one evening she with others was amusing themselves in friendly chit chat under the shady bowers of the towering forest near the hut when suddenly she sprang up & to use my informants language, darted like a patridge into the thicket, all were astonished at this unexpected & unaccountable movement of hers, & while they were endeavouring to account for it the mistory was [illegible] solved by the approach of the officer before alluded to, who had found out her retreat & persued her—when he offered my informant a bribe if he would put her into his possession— He also stated that in order to secure herself from him she went to Brainard & put herself under the care of the missionaries.[31]

Framed by its Euro-American teller as a foiled seduction narrative, the story, when read as one of attempted rape, provides insight into how the violence of U.S. incursions into Native lands extended to the sexual harassment and assault of Cherokee women, a "form of sexual imperialism that was part of colonization."[32] It also provides another suggestive reason for Brown's enrollment at Brainerd: she may have sought the very real bodily protection the school could offer her in a time of social and political upheaval.

As the story of Brown's sexual peril suggests, the transformations Cherokees experienced during this era had particular kinds of consequences for women like her and her mother, Sarah. Historical scholarship on Native women has paid particular attention to women as "crucial participants in the ongoing struggle for the survival of Indian cultures and communities."[33] Cherokee women tend to be viewed as particularly adept at maintaining traditional identities and culture while adapting to changing circumstances, acting as "negotiators of change," to cite the title of Nancy Shoemaker's influential essay collection. As Sarah Hill writes in her examination of Cherokee basket making, "Women bridged differences ... [as they] neither abandoned Cherokee customs nor denied white influences. They did not merge passively into new identities nor hold intractably to old ones. Rather, they engaged fully in the complexities of change."[34]

Cherokee women had traditionally possessed high degrees of sexual freedom and social, economic, and political power, especially when compared to Euro-American women of the same era. Cherokee society operated according to principles of harmony and balance, with men and women performing distinct yet complementary roles in a "system of gender reciprocity and equivalence."[35] As Carolyn Ross Johnston explains in her study of Cherokee women, their "close association with nature, as mothers and producers, served as a basis of their power within the tribe, not as a basis of oppression."[36] Cherokee women farmed, gathered food, and maintained domestic spaces, while men hunted. Social order emerged and was maintained through clans. In this matrilineal society, women owned the property, improvements to properties, and agricultural fields. They participated in political councils and exerted their opinions in political matters, and some held respected ranks, such as "war woman" or "beloved woman." "They were neither subordinate nor superior to men; the Cherokee division of labor based on one's sex did not imply hierarchy, but equality," Johnston concludes.[37]

The changes occurring in the colonial period and its aftermath, however, altered their roles and place in society. Women experienced diminished economic power and autonomy as they were excluded from the eighteenth-century deerskin economy, which assigned economic value in trade with Euro-Americans to Cherokee men's traditional role as hunters.[38] Because of this, Cherokee women may have been to some extent more open to the U.S. government's civilization program of the late eighteenth century, hoping it would validate their traditional realm of agricultural labor.[39] In addition, Cherokees' nineteenth-century movement toward consolidating power in a national government, which disempowered towns and clans, compromised traditional sources of women's status. Cherokee laws as they emerged in the 1820s preserved women's rights to own property but excluded women from formal political processes and legislated, for the first time, limits on their sexual and marriage practices.[40]

Scholars have typically viewed Native women's status as deteriorating due to colonization.[41] Agrarian capitalism, which the U.S. government's civilization program pushed Cherokees to adopt, assigned dominance over home and land to men and therefore elevated patriarchy, concomitantly disempowering women.[42] The U.S. civilization program provoked "a restructuring of power relations. . . . The space of the 'domestic' in Cherokee life—within homes, on farms, and even within the national leadership—was undergoing dramatic rearrangement and reinterpretation," argues Miles.[43] Even within this context, however, scholars such as Johnston and the historian Theda Perdue, author of a large body of scholarship on Cherokees, have insisted on recognizing the "cultural persistence" of gender roles and "the durability of gender conventions."[44] Johnston registers the diversity of the experience of change as well as resistance to it within the Cherokee community in her argument that modifications in gender roles were not as all-encompassing as past historians have argued.[45] She argues that the most significant changes regarding gender in the Cherokee Nation during this period were the emergence of differing models of womanhood and new disagreements about gender roles. While for elite, educated, and biracial women there may have been a transformation in gender roles tending toward patriarchy, for the majority of Cherokees who were full-blooded and/or traditionalist, little changed.[46] And even among acculturated women, Johnston argues, "Cherokee women were central in asserting Cherokee nationalism and cultural autonomy. They creatively accepted those aspects of the civilization program that made their domestic tasks easier, such as using spinning wheels, but the majority rejected the injunctions to become subordinate to men and resisted attempts to diminish their power."[47]

"The dear missionaries": Education, Conversion, and Missionary Contexts

Catharine Brown and American Board missionaries first encountered each other at the Brainerd Mission in 1817, when Brown was around seventeen years of age. Based in New England, the American Board established schools in the Cherokee Nation with U.S. government funding and used literacy as a means of inculcating "civilized" values and Christian conversion. Missionary teachers strove to accomplish nothing less than a complete reorientation of Cherokee students into model Euro-American citizens: students were to study dutifully, behave obediently and chastely, and abjure Cherokee pastimes, sports, and religious rituals. Missionaries particularly enforced conformity to Euro-American gender roles: boys were taught to work in the fields and girls carried out domestic duties. While the American Board mission schools stand as predecessors and models for the later Native American boarding schools that caused immeasurable trauma and pain to generations of children, Martin points out that it is important "to avoid anachronistically equating Brainerd with later models." Martin emphasizes that there was a crucial difference between these early schools and later ones: Cherokee leaders chose to invite the American Board missionaries into the Nation, encouraged them to open more and more schools, and enrolled their children in the schools.[48] The fact that Cherokees had not been conquered shaped their response to Christianity; as Martin explains, "Cherokees had the power to decide for themselves."[49] Indeed the missionaries who came to the Cherokee Nation hoped "to impress their faith on the Cherokees, but they found instead a social world where Cherokee cultural ways persevered and Cherokee community agendas predominated."[50]

Some Cherokees embraced the education missionaries offered. Their recognition of the dynamics that had been transforming their culture and practices for centuries led them to desire the skills that would allow them—and their children—to participate economically and politically in the world that surrounded them. They recognized that the younger generations needed English language and literacy skills to navigate their context and, crucially, that gaining a Western education for their children could become a key strategy in their ongoing fight to retain their landholdings. Cherokee leaders concluded that the schools would be "of great advantage to the nation" (173), and the respected principal chief Pathkiller reportedly told "his people wherever he goes that schools are very good for them."[51] Missionaries recorded Cherokee parents' eagerness to enroll students at the mission schools, the numbers of students they had to turn away, and the numerous requests for new schools throughout the Nation.

At the same time, many Cherokees distrusted missionary influences and resisted missionary efforts to varying degrees. Perhaps the most obvious resistance can be measured by the fact that most Cherokees did not enroll their children in the schools, and most Cherokees did not convert. Some who did enroll their children soon removed them, and those who did convert oftentimes did not maintain their new religion for very long.[52] At its height in 1825, the American Board operated eight schools in the Cherokee Nation, educating from 200 to 250 students, with 882 students enrolled over the period 1817–33; notably the ABCFM recorded only about 167 Cherokee converts from the whole population (not just students) in the period through 1830.[53] Yet in important ways Cherokees and missionaries crafted a partnership during the period of Brown's education—a functional partnership directed toward different goals, but a working alliance nonetheless.[54]

At the time she traveled the one hundred miles to enroll at the school, Brown already "understood & spoke the English language considerably well, on plain familiar subjects" but "could barely spell words of ˄three letters˄ ~~two syllables~~."[55] She took to her studies eagerly, quickly improving her literacy skills, and soon advanced to study geography, astronomy, natural history, and history. Her baptism in January 1818 came less than a year after her arrival, granting her the status of the first Cherokee convert of the American Board. Brown's conversion and subsequent identity as a "Christian Indian" has proved an obstacle to some scholars, who dismissed her as a mere missionary pawn who abjured her Native identity and therefore did not deserve serious consideration as a Native writer.[56] Such understandings insist upon an ahistorical, essential, and unchanging opposition of American Indian and Euro-American peoples. As Martin explains, Native people responding to the conflict between opposing cultures were often seen as having only two possible responses: concession (usually called assimilation) or resistance.[57] Individuals who embodied identities combining aspects from opposing sides of the cultural divide—most particularly individuals like Brown, who were categorized as "Christian Indians" or "writing Indians"—were viewed as, in effect, "self-canceling oxymorons," alienated from their tribal cultures, communities, and identities.[58]

Scholarship in Native studies over the past several decades has thoroughly critiqued this perspective and prepared readers to recognize Brown as a far more complex figure than previously acknowledged. Led by Native scholars, the field has generated a number of key terms—*survivance, intellectual sovereignty,* and *communitism* among them—that emphasize the concept of Indian agency, defined in its simplest terms as Native people's "capacity to play an active role in shaping history."[59] Agency could be exerted through resistance but also through strategies that were key to survival in an often violent colonial context, such as negotiation and acculturation. Justice defines acculturation with a positive valance as "the adaptation of certain Eurowestern ways into a larger Cherokee context, thus changing some cultural expressions while maintaining the centrality of Cherokee identity and values."[60] Such scholarship opens up the possibility of seeing that some Indian people may have deployed Christianity to stave off colonialism's most dire effects and conserve Native communities. By situating Native people in history as actors negotiating complicated historical, political, and social contexts, recent scholarly work emphasizes "the creative way native men and women appropriated, used, reinterpreted, modified, and reinvented Christianity." As Martin concludes, conversion "can connote survival, not surrender—not erasure, but rather renewal."[61]

Though the missionaries viewed her conversion in 1818 as confirmation that "her views of the world are changed" (248), Brown more likely displayed a blending of Christian and Cherokee beliefs in her conversion and subsequent religious practices. Perdue notes that praying in nature and fasting, two of Brown's activities that caused some concern to the missionaries, were traditional Cherokee routes to spiritual enlightenment.[62] Further evidence of the complexity of her religious development rests in a missionary's recounting of Brown's description of a dream, "a powerful source of knowledge" in Cherokee culture.[63] The dream reveals the combining of Cherokee and Christian religious elements in her emerging spiritual identity at a key turning point in her religious development:

> In my sleep I tho't I was travelling, & came to a hill that was almost pirpendicular. I was much troubled about it, for I had to go to its top, & knew not how to get up. She said she ~~had~~ ∧saw∧ ~~seen~~ the steps where others had gone & tried to put her feet in their steps; but found she could not ascend in this way, because her feet slipped—Having made several ∧un∧successful attempts to ascend, she became very weary, but although she succeeded in getting near the top, but felt in great danger of falling. While in this distress ∧in doubt∧ whether to try to go forward ∧or return∧, she saw a bush just above her, ∧of∧ which she tho't, if she could get hold ∧of∧ she could get up, & as she reached out her hand to the bush, she saw a little boy standing at the top, who reached out his hand; She grasped his thumb, & at this moment she was on the top and some one told her it was the Saviour—She then said she never had such happiness before.[64]

Both Cherokee and Christian worldviews place significance on the motif of the spiritual quest and the setting of the mountain as a site wherein sacred occurrences transpire. Additionally the Christ figure resembles one of the Cherokee "Little People," a being who acts to "facilitate her spiritual passage."[65] The missionary who recorded this dream in a letter noted that this moment was a turning point in Brown's conversion; in Martin's interpretation of the dream, "a traditional Cherokee spirit protector had convinced a young Cherokee woman that she could make a safe approach to Christ."[66]

Brown's eagerness for education and her simultaneous movement toward conversion illustrate the American Board's dual mission: "to instruct the natives in the Gospel, and to teach them the most necessary arts of civilized life. These ends are not pursued separately, but are carried on together."[67] Many Cherokees resisted the interweaving of education and conversion, however; the historian William G. McLoughlin, whose work on Cherokee history remains central to understanding contacts between Euro-Americans and Cherokees during this period, explains that "almost all Cherokees welcomed missionaries because they thought of them as teachers of the white man's skills rather than as proselytizers for the white man's religion."[68] Cherokees distinguished between education and conversion when they removed their children from schools as they neared conversion, much to the missionaries' irritation.[69] While some Cherokees rejected the American Board's conversion efforts and accepted its teachings, others perhaps saw conversion, in addition to whatever spiritual advantages the individual derived, as a means to accrue certain benefits and privileges, including advanced access to education. As Martin explains, "Conversion to Christianity often seemed an effective way to gain respectability, recognition from powerful whites, and a good education." Indeed "converts were able to use their enhanced access to the dominant culture to better promote the causes of their people. Conversion sometimes seemed a good way to expand career options as well as to find a circle of close, caring friends."[70]

Taking advantage of the opportunities for continued study that her conversion afforded her, Brown shared in the broader Cherokee tendency to value education in ways that were not fully sanctioned or controlled by the missionaries; she took pleasure in her academic work for its own sake and prized it for enabling her to share her knowledge with her fellow Cherokees. Her letters contain frequent references to her schoolwork, the books she was reading, and her immersion in her studies, until ill health brought about by tuberculosis eventually forced her to give them up. In a revealing moment in her diary, she writes, "If I had my education—but perhaps I ought not to think of it" (117). She seems to recognize in this statement that her desire for learning outstrips what is available and considered appropriate for her as a woman. Cherokees enrolled their daughters in the mission schools in large numbers and requested additional schools for girls, but American Board missionaries manifested their society's constraints on female education and did not make the opportunities for higher education available to young women like Brown. Brown's brother David left the Cherokee Nation to study at the Foreign Mission School in Cornwall, Connecticut, in 1820 and later furthered his education at the Andover Theological

Institute in Andover, Massachusetts. This would not be Brown's fate, and, as she neared the end of her life, she wrote long letters to David encouraging him to apply himself to his studies, perhaps projecting her own desires onto him as she began to sense that she would not be allowed to fulfill them herself.[71]

The pleasure Brown takes in her own learning is accompanied by a repeated emphasis on putting that education to work for her community in ways perhaps not fully recognized by the missionaries who educated her. In this she fits the definition proffered by Jace Weaver (Cherokee) of the "*communitist* (a combination of *community* and *activist*)," who is characterized by "an active commitment to native community. The community itself 'stands at the very center.'"[72] Weaver explains that "community is the highest value for Native peoples, and fidelity to it is a primary responsibility. . . . Traditions are not practiced for personal empowerment or fulfillment but rather to ensure the corporate good."[73] In her consistent linking of her pursuit of education with her community's welfare, Brown expresses her concern that unfamiliarity with Western ways could cause suffering for Cherokees, as when she comments that Cherokees "are perishing for lack of knowledge" (76). When she writes that she "long[s] to see Brainerd and receive more instruction, so that I may be useful to my people," she imagines her sphere of usefulness as existing in a broader arena than that of mere Christian conversion (73). On one occasion she tells her mother that she "did not wish to stay [in school at Brainerd] on account of my own pleasure; but that I wanted to get more instruction so that it might be for her good as well as ∧for∧ mine" (67). Brown explains that her mother had just lamented that "she wished she had never sent me to this school, & that I had never received riligious instruction" (67). Her mother thus particularly targets the teaching of Christianity in her critique of the school. Brown's response, however, effectively removes the term *religious* from the dialogue: her emphasis on her desire to receive "instruction" for her mother's and her own "good" indicates her efforts to help the women in her family, clan, and community to better accommodate to the changing roles thrust upon them by contact with Euro-Americans. As Brown demonstrates, education could be another path to retaining influence for Cherokee women; in Virginia Carney's words, "Education in [missionary] schools could indeed become a means of empowerment."[74] Cherokee women who were open to the teachings of missionaries (especially missionary women, with whom they sometimes crafted close emotional bonds) might have seen conversion as a means to gain several positive ends: to deepen women-centered relationships; to access power through Euro-American gender roles, which accorded women spiritual influence; and to extend "social and economic relationships across time and place, across boundaries of gender, race, and nation."[75]

Brown's parents generally seemed to support her educational achievements, though perhaps for reasons the missionaries were unable to recognize. *Memoir* reports that on one occasion while visiting her home, "irreligious white people" interrogated Brown about her beliefs: "They endeavored, though in vain, to perplex her mind, by objections against the Scriptures. But her parents were pleased, that she had learned so many good things" (179). This anecdote expresses her parents' pleasure in seeing her debate and defeat Euro-Americans on their own terms. It perhaps confirmed for them that their decision to have her educated was the right one, coming as it did during a difficult period in the family's history. Brown's enrollment at Brainerd coincided with what McLoughlin has characterized as the removal crisis of 1817–19,[76] and many Cherokees, including the Browns, found themselves making the high-stakes decision whether to remove to Arkansas. Missionaries sympathetically recorded harassment by Euro-Americans as the cause of the family's contemplated removal: "The old grey-headed man, with tears in his eyes, said he must go over the mississippi. The white people would not suffer him to live here. They had stolen his cattle, horses & hogs, untill he had very little left."[77] The situation was even more complicated than missionaries might have realized, however, since the decision to remove to Arkansas had weighty consequences, with financial implications as well as effects on one's status as a citizen of the Cherokee Nation.[78] Brown's parents briefly took her out of school in November 1818 because of a planned emigration to Arkansas but returned her only a few months later, in March 1819, when the family decided to postpone removal indefinitely. During the subsequent period, from 1819 to 1822, while Brown continued her education and thereby acquired a degree of social power and privilege, members of the family continued to debate the possibility of removal.[79] The question created internal division within the family, which Brown described in a letter to her brother: "You know mother is always very anxious to remove to that country, but father is not" (108). While missionaries interpreted the events in Brown's life—such as her brief removal from the school and her subsequent return—solely through the lens of the sacred drama they saw her enacting, she and her family were at the center of political dramas of lasting consequence to Cherokee interests.

"A means of great good to our people": Interpreter and Teacher

Brown's attainment of fluency in English and literacy, as her parents probably recognized, brought with it a form of power as a "cultural broker," to use Margaret Szasz's terminology. Szasz describes such intermediary figures as "emerg[ing] wherever cultures encounter each other" and "walk[ing] through a network of interconnections where they alone brought some understanding among disparate peoples."[80] Brown acquired benefits from such a role that proved quite useful to her parents and Cherokees more generally. As Perdue has demonstrated, in the emerging trade and political contexts of the early nineteenth century, men acted as intermediaries in contacts with Euro-Americans.[81] During a period of a general, though certainly not total loss of power for Cherokee women, Brown's active seeking of education and her efforts to continue it throughout every crucial juncture of subsequent years produced a cultural intermediary in whom a locus of power resided. Indeed Brown's status as the first American Board convert and the assistance she provided missionaries and Cherokees in their contacts might have been partially responsible for the relatively successful and mutually beneficial relationship that existed between the groups.[82]

In important ways, missionaries and Cherokees relied on Brown as a Cherokee-English interpreter. In 1818 missionaries had two lengthy conversations with her father for which Brown acted as interpreter, and on another occasion Brown translated a conversation that occurred between a Cherokee woman and the missionaries.[83] One can only assume that many more such acts of interpretation occurred than were recorded; a letter by the missionary Laura Potter noted that Brown "never seemed weary of interpreting for others."[84] When Brown journeyed to distant missions with missionaries, as when she accompanied William Chamberlain on a preaching circuit in August 1819, it is possible she was selected to go because she could execute the role of interpreter for the non-Cherokee-speaking missionary as they proceeded.[85]

In addition, her work as an oral interpreter might have extended to written translations. Cherokee leaders from Creek Path, near Brown's home, began negotiations for a school in their area with a letter. The missionary Ard Hoyt assigned a central role to Brown in the delivery of the letter: "This letter was brought by our sister Catharine and her brother David, who have been home to visit."[86] Could Brown, perhaps in collaboration, have written the letter she and David delivered? It is conceivable, given that the older generation of Creek Path leaders generally did not speak English and lacked literacy.

Brown's roles expanded when she became a teacher herself. When the Cherokee leaders at Creek Path learned that Brown would be the teacher at the newly organized girls' school that they had proposed, their enthusiasm led them to quickly erect a school building at their own expense and with their own labor, even before she arrived to begin her duties.[87] Her attainment of the role of teacher proceeded, at least to some degree, from her facility as a cultural intermediary; the missionary Daniel S. Butrick argued that Brown should be sent rather than a white missionary because "she can talk & there will be no good interpreter."[88] For her work, which she began in February 1820, Brown received the salary of a missionary and experienced the added benefit of living near her mother and father.[89]

In addition to interpreting and teaching in educational contexts, Brown also participated in the variety of religious exchanges happening at the missions. She interpreted sermons, translated Bible passages, offered religious instruction, provided literacy and religious teaching to African Americans, "gather[ed] little circles of her Cherokee friends for social prayer," and facilitated a female prayer society, taking "an active part in the devotional exercises" (251, 209). On one occasion she "held a religious conference, with prayer & praise, all in the Cherokee tongue."[90] She was known to "warn and exhort," thereby moving into spheres related to preaching (207). Cherokee traditions allowing women's participation in councils perhaps freed her from the prohibitions against public speech that Euro-American women faced and enabled Cherokees' acceptance of her public performances as interpreter, teacher, and exhorter.[91]

Homer Noley has considered the crucial work of the interpreter in mission contexts, claiming that "all through the history of European missions to the Native peoples of the Americas, a primary role player in the spread of the church has been the interpreter," a person whose "role was either downplayed or erased entirely in missionary reports."[92] Since most missionaries did not speak or understand Native languages, they necessarily had "to trust that the interpreter grasped the message in English and faithfully delivered it."[93] Because the Cherokee language had no words to express crucial Christian tenets, interpreters had an especially challenging task. One Cherokee interpreter explained that for particular words "not only the expression but the concept was wholly unknown to the Cherokees; for instance, the word forgiveness . . . is completely unknown among the Indians and . . . therefore there is no word to be found in their language by which this idea could be expressed."[94] Brown's interpretations must therefore have been creative acts, building on Cherokee understandings to create explications that would effectively transmit the ideas to her listeners. Indeed, like other interpreters, Brown in effect acted as "the preacher who was heard and understood by the Native listener."[95]

It is likely, then, that Cherokees perceived Brown as an active leader in her many roles—teacher, interpreter, exhorter—within the community. Brown gained a high degree of social status and respect from missionaries and Cherokees alike due to her educational attainments, exhibited in her work for the Cherokee and missionary communities. Relieved of her teaching duties in May 1821 by the arrival of a missionary couple, William and Laura Potter, at Creek Path, Brown resumed her studies while boarding with and assisting the Potters. In 1822 several events disrupted her studies: the extended illness and death of her brother John from tuberculosis; a period of ill health (a "bilious fever" [217]) and seeking treatment from a doctor, Alexander Campbell, in Huntsville; and the needs of her aging parents, who in the wake of John's death wanted her comfort and care at home. By February 1823 symptoms of tuberculosis began to present in Brown. (Her brother David would die from the disease in 1829.) She dictated her last letter on June 13, 1823, one month before her death on July 18, 1823. Her parents finally removed to Arkansas in November 1823, five months after her death.

Martin reports that, well into the twentieth century, Cherokees remembered Brown, calling her "the Priestess," emphasizing her "spiritual qualities" and status as the first female Cherokee schoolteacher, and memorializing her through Catharine Brown Sunday Schools and Catharine Brown Literary Societies.[96] Martin characterizes Brown as having "played a leading role in a Cherokee revitalization movement" of the early nineteenth century.[97] The historical record provides ample evidence to rebut views like the one voiced by Arnold Krupat when he wrote, "We will not learn of Cherokee lifeways in the early nineteenth century from Catharine Brown."[98] As Joshua B. Nelson (Cherokee) retorts, "What besides Cherokee lifeways do Brown's inexhaustible concern for community, especially women, her outdoor fasting, her interpretation of Christian precepts through Cherokee cultural symbols, and her worship in the Cherokee language teach us?"[99] Literacy and fluency in English allowed Brown to actively and directly contribute to the ongoing transformations in Cherokee life while balancing her individual gains in status with a communitarian focus on the Cherokees' well-being.

Brown's Writings

Recent scholarship on early Native literacy has prepared us to more justly appraise Brown's contributions to literary history. Scholars studying early Native writers have applied many of the insights coming from the field of Native studies to Native consumption and production of texts, broadly defined. Far from signifying an assimilative departure from an essentialized, ahistorical, and unchanging state of Indianness, reading and writing in English were skills put to many and varied uses by literate Indians in the service of Native communities and causes, these scholars have argued. As Kristina Bross and Hilary Wyss explain, "Indigenous leaders used their familiarity with English cultural practices (most notably alphabetic literacy) to forge what they saw as a stronger, 'better' Indian community that could balance various knowledge systems."[100] Cherokees were particularly strategic in their use of literacy to serve their own purposes; indeed Miles claims that "Cherokees employed the written word as their main weapon against Euro-American incursions."[101]

Yet the desire to locate resistance in writings by early Native authors—akin to the problematic desire to valorize resistant acts or identities over "assimilation" discussed earlier—continues to bedevil scholarship on Brown, who demonstrates little in the way of overt resistance in her writings. Justice, however, has offered a particularly nuanced reading of the Cherokee literary tradition that allows for a valuing of writing that is not obviously resistant. Building on the Cherokee values of "balance and complementarity," Justice argues that two general tendencies can be identified in many Cherokee writings: what he calls the "Chickamauga consciousness," characterized by "intellectual and artistic separatism, in a rhetorical rejection of literary, historical, or philosophical accommodation," and the "Beloved Path," which "places peace and cultural continuity above potentially self-destructive rebellion."[102] Both responses aim at the preservation of the Cherokees as a people and exist in "necessary tension" and "constant movement"; neither is superior to the other, neither seen as a betrayal nor a measure of authenticity. Indeed one individual might shift between positions at various moments in his or her life and in various contexts. In this way Justice avoids the polarizing tendency of binary oppositions and opens up the possibility of creating "a more nuanced understanding of the many ways that Cherokees have asserted nationhood, sovereignty, and self-determination," as when Justice reads a document like the Treaty of New Echota, which fraudulently signed away the Cherokee homeland in the Southeast, as a text engaged with "survival and endurance of the people."[103] Though Justice does not consider Brown, surely she fits into his generalization that "most of the Cherokee people have long fought to survive on the Beloved Path by shaping Eurowestern cultural, religious, and political structures to serve the interests of Cherokee nationhood."[104] The Beloved Path, he writes, "is a sometimes-treacherous balance of Cherokee autonomy and adaptation to White assimilative demands," a "delicate negotiation" walked by those who, in the case of Cherokees who studied at mission schools, were "deeply acculturated into Eurowestern values, even while they asserted their cultural distinctiveness as Cherokees."[105] Though Justice does not explicitly consider Brown, his analysis models a way of engaging with her writings outside of the restrictive resistant-assimilative binary.

Despite the compelling recovery and interpretive strategies afforded other early Native writers, the evaluation of Brown within a literary context has been slow to emerge. Her exclusion from the emerging canon of Native writers might have much to do with her writing of letters and a diary, which until recently have tended to be viewed more as historical documents than crafted literary texts, or because the full range of her writings has not been readily available to readers, a situation that *Cherokee Sister* remedies. Or her exclusion might result from the fact that until the publication of this volume, most of her writings could be accessed only from within the missionary-authored *Memoir* in which they are embedded, with the effect of rendering her authorship invisible. The few literary readings that do exist share a common limitation: they rely solely on *Memoir* for their analysis.[106] The result runs the danger of giving priority to Anderson's voice, therefore "ventriloquiz[ing] the words of missionaries and accept[ing] their judgments uncritically."[107] Brown's writings as presented in *Cherokee Sister* offer an antidote to this kind of reading.

Brown's written oeuvre comprises at least thirty-two letters written between 1818 and 1823 and a brief diary that she maintained from 1820 to 1822. Both genres in which she wrote are forms of life writing, a capacious category including many kinds of writing that represent a self or a life. As opposed to autobiography, which typically presents a narrative of a life from a position of recollection, letters and diaries capture aspects of a life or a self as they emerge in a particular moment in time. Letters and diaries are uniquely available to a large spectrum of writers, more than many other genres: they are flexible to the needs of individuals with varying literacy or education levels; both genres were taught within educational contexts and therefore were transmitted to broad swaths of the population; they require rather minimal resources in the form of pen, ink, paper, and time; and their address to audiences is not reliant upon print publication since they have tended to circulate through the mail or from hand to hand in manuscript form. In addition, both genres are uniquely associated with women. As Sidonie Smith and Julia Watson explain, marginalized Americans such as people of color, women, and the working classes did not have equal access to conventional narrative autobiography, the myths of Western, masculine selfhood it promulgated, or its publication venues in the nineteenth century, and as a result they turned to other autobiographical forms. Women, especially, "turned to diaries, journals, and letters as convenient modes of self-inscription. . . . Such genres were understood as properly feminine forms of the autobiographical for literate women during the nineteenth century."[108] Letter writing, as a mode of familial, class, and social relationship maintenance, came to be associated in the eighteenth and nineteenth centuries with women's performance of gendered social roles, while diary writing, with its connections to traditions of spiritual introspection, came to be seen as uniquely suited to women as well.

Although letters and diaries suffered critical neglect in the past, often seen either as purely private documents with little public significance or as historical documents primarily important for the information they reveal about the past or important figures, recent trends in literary scholarship have recuperated both genres. Scholars working within the field of epistolary studies have demonstrated that letters are key to understanding social relations and hierarchies of power, while scholarship on diaries suggests the possibilities for evaluating women's constructions of self in relation to available discourses of gendered identity. Critics working in Native American literature seized on autobiography as a central genre for exploration, but early work tended to prioritize narrative autobiographies rather than other autobiographical forms, thereby excluding a writer like Brown. More recent work focused on Native writers, however, has recognized the importance of these as well as other, nonalphabetic forms of cultural production.[109]

"WITH PLEASURE I SPEND A FEW MOMENTS IN WRITING TO YOU": BROWN'S LETTERS

The thirty-two letters making up part 1 of this volume constitute the only full edition of Brown's letters to date. Although claims to comprehensiveness must always be provisional given ongoing recovery efforts, the letters are presented here as a collected edition in order to enable readers to engage with her letters as texts employing particular generic conventions; to read each letter in relation to her other writings, outside of the framework of Anderson's interpretation in *Memoir*; and to encounter them with an awareness of the agency implied in her authorship. As William Merrill Decker notes, "The stories [letters] tell depend on the context in which they are read."[110]

The letters span the period from November 1, 1818, sixteen months after Brown began her education at the Brainerd Mission School, to June 13, 1823, only weeks before her death. Her letters have gone through various textual states, an important transformation akin to "distinct generic lives," in Decker's formulation.[111] All began as written holographs addressed to particular individuals and dispatched through the mail or other delivery modes. Some went on to be printed in missionary publications, sometimes framed by editorial comments, and many of these were reprinted in other periodicals, a common practice in newspaper publishing of the time. Many of the letters previously printed in periodicals were then reprinted in *Memoir*, alongside letters that had not seen previous publication.

When classified according to recipients, Brown's letters fall into three categories. The first category encompasses letters written to missionaries in the Cherokee Nation, some of whom had been her teachers and with whom she often had close, even quite intimate relationships, especially Matilda and Loring Williams, Flora and William Chamberlain, and Isabella and Moody Hall. The second category contains letters to donors and benefactors of the American Board, most of whom were women located in northern cities whom Brown had never met. Some of these recipients cannot be firmly identified. The third and final category includes letters to her brother David, who left home in 1820 to study at the Foreign Mission School in Cornwall, Connecticut, and later at the Andover Theological Seminary in Andover, Massachusetts. Two of Brown's correspondents do not fit tidily within these categories: Dr. Alexander and Sarah Campbell.[112] Both benefactors and friends, the Campbells, who lived in Huntsville, Alabama, were supporters of the American Board missions and knew Brown personally; she spent several months visiting at their house, returned during her last illness for Dr. Campbell's treatments, and died there.

All three categories of letters conform to the precondition of most letter writing in the nineteenth century: the desire to overcome the geographical distance separating the correspondents. In Decker's characterization, the letter is in its essence a "multivalent negotiation of human separation."[113] In all of Brown's recovered letters, she wrote to individuals who were separated from her by distance, a fact that informs the content of the letters. Much has been made by Anderson and recent critics alike of the extreme longing for the missionaries and school Brown articulates in her letters of November 1818 through March 1819, when her parents temporarily removed her from the school because of their plans to emigrate to Arkansas. Some scholars have read these letters, buttressed no doubt by Anderson's interpretation, as demonstrating Brown's alienation from her Cherokee family and community and her desire to identify fully with missionaries. But the only letters we have from Brown written to missionaries are those that are written under conditions of separation, and the longing for reunion that characterizes these letters should be read in relation to that fact. Her day-to-day proximate relationships with missionaries were probably complicated in ways this limited sample of letters can never represent, and should not be expected to represent, given the context of their production.

In a related vein, some of the letters one might expect are not contained in this collection. There are no letters written to her mother and father when she was separated from them while at school. Presumably she wrote them no letters because they were not literate in English or because the exchange of letters was not conventional in Cherokee society. Or perhaps she did write them letters, and they have not survived.[114] In addition, once Brown returned to Creek Path, she either lived with her parents or in close proximity to them and thus probably saw them frequently. Because we have no letters to her parents, we do not have documentation of the longing for home, family, and Cherokee practices she might have experienced as a homesick boarding school student, nor do we have direct expressions of affection for her parents, though quite certainly she felt that emotion for them since her letters and *Memoir* are full of testimonies to her dutiful and affectionate relationship with them. The record of letters is not balanced in terms of her epistolary audience, and therefore care must be taken in using them to construct any interpretation about her relationship to missionaries or Cherokees.

Categorizing Brown's letters according to recipient, as I have done, highlights the primacy of audience in letter writing. All commentators on letter writing have noted the importance of the recipient in the construction of the letter itself. Readers hold great power, according to Janet Altman, in their ability to elicit the content of the letter that the writer pens: "Awareness of a specific second-person addressee can alter the character and experience of the first-person writing itself."[115] All of Brown's letters are formulated within the conventions of evangelical Christian discourse, because all of them circulated to their recipients within missionary-constructed and -dominated contexts: they were either written to missionaries, mission supporters, or her brother David, who was educated in the same milieu. Brown masterfully fulfills the desires of each letter's recipient. To the missionaries from whom she was separated, she gives evidence of the success of their work with her, both educational and spiritual, and well as the strength of her emotional attachment to them. To donors to the missions, she provides evidence of the success of missionary labors while often making more general comments about the status of missions among the Cherokees. To David she offers some family news, but, more important, she buttresses his sense of purpose while studying so far away from home in a sometimes hostile context with her own expressions of faith and belief in him. Her

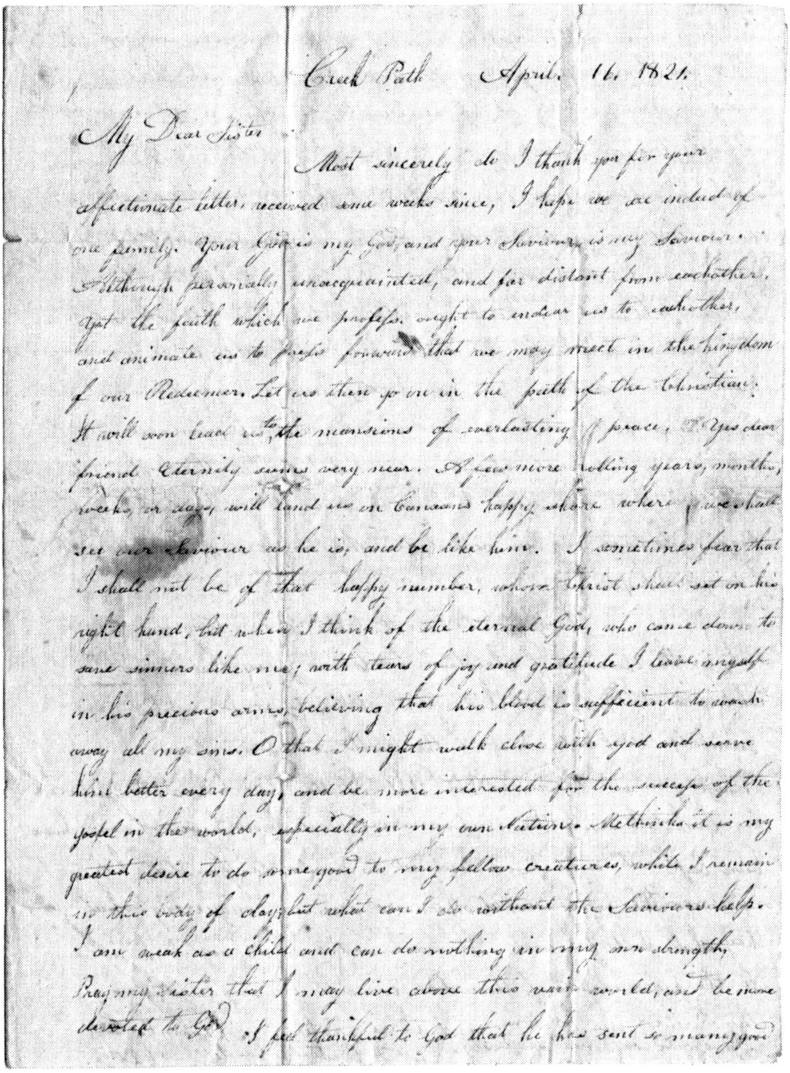
Creek Path April 16. 1821.

My Dear Sister

Most sincerely do I thank you for your affectionate letter, received some weeks since, I hope we are indeed of one family. Your God is my God, and your Saviour is my Saviour. Although personally unacquainted, and far distant from eachother, yet the faith which we profess ought to endear us to eachother, and animate us to press forward that we may meet in the kingdom of our Redeemer. Let us then go on in the path of the Christian. It will soon lead us to the mansions of everlasting peace. Yes dear friend Eternity seems very near. A few more rolling years, months, weeks, or days, will land us on Canaans happy shore where we shall see our Saviour as he is, and be like him. I sometimes fear that I shall not be of that happy number, whom Christ shall set on his right hand, but when I think of the eternal God, who came down to save sinners like me; with tears of joy and gratitude I leave myself in his precious arms, believing that his blood is sufficient to wash away all my sins. O that I might walk close with God and serve him better every day, and be more interested for the success of the gospel in the world, especially in my own Nation. Methinks it is my greatest desire to do some good to my fellow creatures, while I remain in this body of clay, but what can I do without the Saviours help. I am weak as a child and can do nothing in my own strength. Pray my sister that I may live above this vain world, and be more devoted to God. I feel thankful to God that he has sent so many good

Fig. 3. Catharine Brown's letter to Flora Gold, April 16, 1821. HLVC.

letters are more emotional and affectionate in tone to those individuals with whom she has personal relationships than to those she has never met. Thus her letters can be read as quite rhetorically sophisticated in construction, purpose, and tone.

Readers of Brown's letters, or indeed of any nineteenth-century letter, should guard against presuming that letters are the outpourings of interior thoughts or emotions. Scholars examining letters have repeatedly and insistently underlined the highly conventionalized form and function of letters in the early nineteenth century. Eve Tavor Bannet argues that conformity to convention should be an expectation of early letters;[116] originality or transgression of the expectations for writing letters would have been viewed as serious lapses in judgment and character. In Anglo-American contexts during the late eighteenth and early nineteenth centuries, letters were seen as an index to character, revealing not only simple letter-writing prowess but also judgment, refinement, and moral qualities.[117]

While the repetition of pietistic Christian sentiments in Brown's letters may become tedious for some modern readers—and has certainly contributed to the interpretation of Brown as a puppet who simply did missionaries' bidding—within nineteenth-century contexts the formulaic nature of her letters would have signified her facility as a letter writer and hence her status as an educated and moral person. Although no "letter-writer," or manual directing readers in the art of correct letter writing, is listed in the books contained in the Brainerd library in 1822, Brown did read several memoirs compiled from the letters of deceased women, which perhaps served as models for her letter writing.[118]

In addition, training in letter writing was quite formalized in the nineteenth century, functioning as part of the educational curriculum in many schools. Building on the long-standing view of letter writing as "a social behavior through which one's courtesy and civility were exhibited and measured,"[119] letter writing increasingly became an important part of curricula in schools. By writing letters, children learned "particular and circumscribed behaviours" that taught them to "behave according to the culture's dominant values."[120] The association of women with letter writing rendered it an especially important area of study and performance for girls. Merging "gender and genre," nineteenth-century letter writing manuals depicted "letter writing as an indispensable form of middle-class literacy and a performance of gendered decorum."[121] Brown's teachers would have felt that her letters, more than any other genre of her writing, showcased her adoption of Western values and her assumption of a properly gendered identity, according to a Euro-American viewpoint. By writing letters, Brown, like many other nineteenth-century girls and women, demonstrated her attainment of the values, behaviors, and attitudes of middle-class, white womanhood. The frequent publication of her letters is further evidence of her facility in the genre.

The inclusion of such letters in American Board records and religious periodical columns suggests that the kind of letter writing in which Brown engaged was common practice at the school and fulfilled an important purpose within the school's curriculum—not the least of which was securing additional benefactors for the mission by demonstrating the success of students being educated there. As David Murray reminds us, "We need always to ask about the *conditions of production and circulation* of any text.... In any situation where we have a text written by an Indian certain sets of conditions have to have been met.... It needs to have been in the interests, whether commercial, political, academic, or whatever, of those who controlled the publishing outlets."[122] There are no direct descriptions of Brown's act of letter writing, but a missionary account of another student producing a letter at Brainerd in 1821 remains. Ann Paine, a Brainerd missionary, records the following incident involving a student named Delilah Fields:

I had brought some presents from the children of Miss G.s school to the children of Brainard, and as Delilah frequently wrote letters, I requested her to write to Miss G. She declined said she should not have time. One evening however she came into my room and said she would now write. I immediately supplied her with pen and paper, but she said she did not know <u>what</u> to write. I dictated the first sentence and though perhaps I must tell her <u>all</u> but being much engaged forgot the subject. Perhaps in half an hour Delilah brought me the letter finished. I was surpized at her facility in writing and exclaimed, "Not one of Mss G's schollars could write as well." The spelling and one or two of the last sentences I corrected but the rest remained unaltered. It could hardly be believed in this vicinity that either the writing or composition was the performance of a child not yet twelve years old much less of a Cherokee girl, who had been in school but two years. An agent for the Religious Intelligencer requested a copy for publication and it was reprinted in the Herald.[123]

Complicated power dynamics mark this writing occasion. At first, the Cherokee girl resists the white teacher's request; she finally initiates the task at her own convenience, shaping the terms of the encounter by choosing the time and place when the writing of the letter occurs. An already experienced letter writer, Fields claims to be inadequate to the task; her statement that she did not know what to write suggests the uncomfortable fit between her experiences and the letter genre. Like Brown, Fields had no exact models for her letters, since letter-writing manuals did not include examples of letters written by Cherokee young people to white benefactors. Yet her education at Brainerd apparently introduced her to the mode of self-presentation most likely to please benevolent Euro-Americans such as Paine and "Miss. G." Fields's independence in the composition process seems to startle Paine. She assumes that she, as the teacher, will supply the content of the letter just as she supplied the materials for writing, but Paine's distraction with her domestic work allows Fields to claim the space of the letter as her own; Paine fulfills only the minimal editorial role of correcting spelling. The letter Fields writes in this context offers purely conventional Christian sentiments and shows a resemblance to many of Brown's letters.[124] It is not the content of the letter that is most important, this example demonstrates; it can be the context of its production that reveals its most crucial meanings.

"I JEST SIT DOWN TO ADDRESS YOU WITH MY PEN": THE RHETORICS OF BROWN'S LETTERS

Brown's very act of writing letters—however formulaic the contents may seem to readers today—thus takes on agential dimensions. In his investigation of the power dynamics inherent in correspondences, Konstantin Dierks argues that writing letters was a way to act in and on the world.[125] Those critics who tend to see Brown as a passive tool of the missionaries neglect to recognize the ways that her simple act of writing was an assertion of agency, a way to create certain effects or acts. Her letters are not merely some sort of demonstration (which situates her as a passive object of missionaries' agency); they are geared toward making arguments that will change minds on politicized issues surrounding Cherokees' status in the United States and lead to increased donations to missions, both of which would benefit the Cherokees in strategic ways. In addition, Dierks argues that letter writing demonstrated a "covert" form of power in nineteenth-century society, a privilege that marked an elevated social status and from which African Americans and Native Americans were generally excluded.[126] Brown's letters can therefore be seen as an intervention in racialized power structures. Her claiming the agency of letter writing disrupts the exclusionary trajectories of epistolarity and the racial and political power dynamics of the period.[127]

As Brown reiterates throughout her letters, her goal is to "be useful to my people," a strategy she enacts through her letter writing (73). While her purposes align with missionary goals in many, if not most ways, they also might exceed or move outside of them, as I demonstrated earlier in my analysis of her valuing of education for reasons different from those of the missionaries. As Martin has argued about David Brown's speaking tour of New England, it was perfectly plausible that educated Cherokees of the Browns' generation could pursue a distinct Cherokee agenda simultaneously with the mission agenda, carried out through the same mode though with different ends. Limited methodologies have led scholars to overlook the coexistence of such projects, according to Martin: "Another image, another project, always existed, interlaced, with the familiar one focused on missionaries' efforts to effect conversion. We need to recover that interlaced project, and we can do so, using the same archive, by shifting the angle of our approach to bring the Cherokee project into visibility."[128] Martin demonstrates that David gave speeches throughout New England to Euro-American audiences at the American Board's behest because doing so facilitated a Cherokee strategy to create a network of white supporters who believed in Cherokees' right to sovereignty. Similarly Catharine Brown's letters to white women in the North may be seen as a feminized corollary preceding David's lectures, deploying "writing skills and publicity channels derived from Christian missionary networks."[129] As Elizabeth Hewitt has demonstrated, letters were often a powerful tool to enact the union of disparate, politicized entities.[130] Recent scholarship reveals the ways that letters like Brown's played a much more central and significant role in the histories of reform movements and women's history than has traditionally been recognized. Miles, for example, argues that a Cherokee woman named Margaret Ann (Peggy) Scott Vann Crutchfield attempted through letter writing to enlist northern white women in the Cherokee antiremoval cause.[131] Brown needs to be inserted into the history Miles has begun to trace of how northern white women were influenced by and might have taken their lead from Cherokee women's activism surrounding the antiremoval movement. While Miles credits Crutchfield's letter with influencing Lydia Sigourney and through her Catharine Beecher, who then went on to write an antiremoval petition in 1829, Brown also corresponded with Sigourney; indeed Sigourney included Brown as a subject in her long poem, *Traits of the Aborigines* (1822).[132]

One strategy Brown uses to draw white northern women into a relationship with her is through usage of the word *sister*, one of the most frequently repeated words in her letters. A conventional form of address among Christian women, the term brings with it obvious connotations of familial relationships. Cynthia Cumfer has discussed how male "Cherokees reconstituted the foreign community as kin," using familial terms to emphasize "relationship and mutuality" in politics during the colonial period.[133] While Cumfer focuses particularly on the term *brother* as "a designation that assumed equivalent strength and resources,"[134] Brown's writings force the word *sister* into view, encouraging us to revise the masculinist narrative of Cherokee history that has privileged the rhetorical positionings of Cherokee men while suppressing Cherokee women's interventions into that history. Through matrilineal kinship ties, relationships among women were the primary structuring principle of Cherokee social formations. The Anglo-Christian moniker *sister* takes on a heightened meaning in Brown's frequent use of the word in her letters when read through Cherokee familial and clan structures. In claiming sisterhood with her female correspondents, all of whom were white women either raised or residing in the northern United States, Brown extends a particularly gendered form of an intimate and nonhierarchical relationship across the differences that rendered them "far distant from each other" (86)—differences of race and nation, none more crucial in this politically charged era.

Along with sisterhood, Brown's mechanisms for bridging those differences are her chosen genre and her religion. The act of writing letters, associated with women and imbued with class, gender, and racial privilege, inserts Brown into a preexisting community of (letter) writing women, providing her with an audience for her communications, a mode of circulation for her productions, and conventions for their formation. Her identity as a Christian woman heightens her affiliation with her correspondents, who similarly identify as Christian evangelicals, while simultaneously providing a common discourse, vocabulary, and set of stock images within which to deploy her ideas. For example, a recurring motif in Brown's letters that emphasizes her equal status— and indeed the equality of all Christian Cherokees—with Christian northerners is that of prayers simultaneously ascending to heaven. To Flora Gold, a pious young woman in Connecticut, Brown details exactly when the female society she has organized meets to pray. She instructs Gold, "May our Christian sisters in Cornwall meet at the same time that our united prayers may ascend together" (88). She gives the same instruction to an unnamed woman in Philadelphia and also claims that "our prayers have unitedly ascended together" (89). In her repeated use of this motif, Brown unites and equalizes Christian and Cherokee. Significantly she does not ask the northern women to pray for her or the Cherokees, a request that might suggest that their prayers had more efficacy. Instead she suggests that the northern women pray at the same time as the Cherokee women so their prayers mutually enact their goals. Her organization of a female benevolent society similarly signals her rejection of the view of Cherokees as supplicants dependent on northern benevolence, granting Cherokee women the agency to extend benevolence to others as well.[135]

So successful does Brown seem in using sisterhood, letters, and religion to bridge differences with her correspondents that her letters may begin to look indistinguishable from writings produced by Euro-American women who shared her faith. This is one of the challenges facing readers of this volume who may come with the expectation of encountering a resistant Indian voice on the page. Indeed Brown's most frequent closing address is "your sister in Christ," which seems to efface the Cherokee aspect of her identity altogether, as scholars have accused her of doing. This volume, by taking as its title *Cherokee Sister*, situates the Cherokee aspects of her writing project in relation to the Anglo-American contexts simultaneously—though not exclusively—informing her textual productions.

It is worth pausing to consider the expectations shaped by those broader Anglo-American cultural contexts, outside of missionary discourses, that Brown's readers might have brought to her letters. Did readers expect or hope for graphic descriptions of the "savagery" of her preconversion life? Terror-inspiring accounts of the Cherokees' brutal customs? Titillating references to the sexual promiscuity and polygamy of Cherokees? (After all, Brown's own father had three wives.) These are the sorts of accounts that published print sources on Native Americans would have prepared early nineteenth-century northerners to read. Yet Brown steadfastly refuses to satisfy any of those prurient expectations. She also rejects the stereotyped language, images, and cadences often attributed to Indians' speech.

Even within missionary discourses that filled the pages of religious periodicals, Brown refuses the more subtle stereotyping characteristic of much missionary writing. In her letters she attends to spiritual concerns rather than the cultural ones at the center of the missionaries' civilization agenda. She resists denigrating Cherokees' customs, traditions, or ways of life, only expressing regret at their lack of Christianity. Consider, for example, the description written by Laura Potter, Brown's teacher and friend, of the Creek Path mission, which was published in a periodical that also printed Brown's letters:

38

Two years since Creek Path was a place of the grossest ignorance. The Saviour's name had scarcely been heard among the people. They passed their time in idleness and dissipation; and most of those who were clad at all, were covered with rags. The Sabbath was known but by few, and these had been taught by the whites to consider it a holly day. But now, how changed the scene! many of them have become sober and industrious. They assemble regularly on the Sabbath for the worship of God, and manifest a tender solicitude for the welfare of their immortal souls. Their dress though coarse, is very neat and becoming. Seldom is a dirty garb seen in our little sanctuary. They frequently speak of their former ways of living, and express much gratitude that missionaries have been sent to teach them better things.[136]

In Potter's telling, lazy, dirty, naked, drunken Indians have become hardworking, neat, serious churchgoers who welcome the "better things" brought by the missionaries. Potter makes but passing mention of the "welfare of their immortal souls"; she instead attends to the exterior indications of cultural assimilation that garner her approval. In contrast, a letter Brown wrote, printed in the same periodical only two months after Potter's, emphasizes the spiritual state of the Cherokees.[137] Brown does not praise the missionaries for bringing civilization to the Cherokees, with its valuing of order, temperance, industriousness, or particular style of dress. She locates her discussion of the changes occurring among the Cherokees entirely on a spiritual plane. Because the missionaries' civilization program operates through worldly concerns, Brown seems unconcerned with it. In her view, Cherokees are simply people with "precious and immortal souls" (77).

Brown's letters, then, are most usefully approached as audience-aware, carefully crafted documents that sought to effect change in society. Her facility in writing letters to accord with missionary interests as well as Cherokee purposes does not mean that her relationship with literacy, letter writing, and publication was always a comfortable one, however. According to Potter, Brown's reaction to the publication of her letters was negative: "[Brown] was much distressed that so many of her letters had been published, and for a season, it was with difficulty, that we could persuade her to write to her correspondents. 'I suppose,' she said, the 'object at *first* was to show that an Indian could improve. But two or three letters would have answered this purpose as well as all I have ever written'" (247). Brown here reveals her understanding of her various audiences, readers' expectations, and the broader significance of her writings.[138] As I have argued throughout this introduction, resistance generally does not work as a framework for reading Brown's letters; if the reader approaches her letters looking solely for evidence of resistance, especially overt resistance, he or she will leave largely disappointed. But on this one occasion Brown seems to engage in explicit resistance, a resistance deployed through a refusal to write. In her protest over the publication of her letters, she refuses to perform in the public sphere of print culture to satisfy the purposes of the American Board. Her refusal to write can be read as a rejection of the objectification of her literacy and, paradoxically, a claim to agency. Signifying more than a simple acquiescence to missionary wishes, her writing deserves recognition as a complex act bearing religious, nationalist, and gendered meanings simultaneously.

"O PAINFUL IS IT TO RECORD": BROWN'S DIARY

Like letters, diaries find their origins in the telling of the events of a life but in a uniquely periodic manner, a kind of "serial autobiography."[139] Usually written in brief entries at particular moments over a span of time, diaries impart a sense of "immediacy, the sense of being involved in an actual life in process."[140] The dated entries, each of which offers interpretations of events that are "provisional at best," accrue meaning when read in relation to each other.[141] The diary form, according to Suzanne L. Bunkers and Cynthia A. Huff, is "simultaneously elastic and tight.... Its content is wide-ranging yet patterned, and what is excluded is as important as what is included."[142] Diaries offer particularly good opportunities for studying the writer's construction of a self in relation to the discourses surrounding her. Because Brown is attempting to construct and maintain a new kind of identity—simultaneously Christian and Cherokee in environments that do not necessarily facilitate the melding of the two—this act is particularly vexed, and her diary thus affords her "a literary space in which to negotiate versions of selfhood that both trouble and attract" her.[143]

A number of scholars have noted that diaries are often begun at moments of "tension, a disequilibrium in the life of its author, which needs to be resolved or held in check. A journey, a new role, a spiritual crisis—these are some of the sources of tension that can bring about and sustain a diary."[144] Brown began her diary when she left the mission school at Brainerd to begin teaching at Creek Path. This was a transitional moment in her life, as she moved from the role of student to that of teacher and took on an adult identity, leaving the community within which she was educated and nurtured in her emergent Christian identity. In individual entries, Brown recurs to particular topics such as her attendance at religious services and the desire to keep the Sabbath. Thematic arcs also pervade the diary as a whole: anxiety at leaving Brainerd and the missionaries there; worries about beginning her teaching; attempts to balance evangelizing with her sense of her own spiritual inadequacies; and preoccupation with her family members' spiritual states. Particular concerns preoccupied Brown as she left Brainerd: Would she be a successful teacher? Would she maintain her Christian beliefs once separated from the missionaries? How would her identity manifest itself in these new contexts? As Steven E. Kagle and Lorenza Gramegna argue, diary writing "offered an outlet" for the anxieties brought about by these transitions and additionally "provided an opportunity to alter or remove the source of that tension. By manipulating reality in a diary [writers] could sometimes create the illusion of control, lessen the sensation of risk, or make their restricted situation seem more satisfying."[145] Her diary seems to function in this way for Brown: it affirms her sense of identity as a Cherokee Christian in a context that threatens that fragile formulation. This is a different function from that of her letter writing, which attempts to create change in the broader world. Brown's diary seeks to solidify the self, which then mobilizes her to take action through her teaching, interpreting, exhorting, letter writing, and demonstration of her Christian identity in her actions on behalf of the Cherokee community. In this way, Brown's diary demonstrates the aptness of Kagle and Gramegna's point: "To the extent that a diary becomes a vehicle for the examination and direction of its author's life, it influences perceptions of and actions in the real world."[146]

Brown does not, however, construct this sense of self within the diary in a vacuum. Her writing there, like that of many women who write diaries, engages with the models and discourses available to her. The most obvious model for Brown's diary is the spiritual diary, characterized since the seventeenth century by a "common purpose and inspiration":

> the desire to record the punishments and favors of God in relation to the individual diarist's life and to chronicle the inner workings of her soul and behavior. Diarists are expected to analyze rigorously their inner spiritual state; to recount blessings and deliverances; to weigh sins and note the completion of daily spiritual duties; to quote Scripture and apply it to the vicissitudes of the day; and to use extreme language to convey the agonies and ecstasies of an existence dedicated to religion. . . . [Spiritual diaries are] comprised, more often than not, of standard, formulaic phrases and conventions, and marked by repetition of both content and style.[147]

As when reading nineteenth-century letters, modern readers should guard against the assumption that a diary will convey the outpouring of spontaneous emotions; like letters, spiritual diaries like the one Brown wrote followed rigid conventions. Since Brown began her diary upon leaving the missionaries at Brainerd, she may have been given the task as an assignment and intended to share the diary with her former teachers and spiritual guides on a future occasion. Diaries during this period were rarely conceived of as private documents; diary writers had imagined and real readers in educational, familial, and publication contexts.[148] As Lynn Z. Bloom notes, "It is the audience hovering at the edge of the page that for the sophisticated diarist facilitates the work's ultimate focus."[149] In this case, that audience seems to be made up of missionaries, which explains its lack of explicit references to the Cherokee world that Brown inhabits. Brown's consciousness of audience here, as in her letters, constrains the content of her diary; she writes, perhaps, to please her former teachers, convince them of her attention to her spiritual state, and affirm their own sense of mission through her success. But the emphasis on the self in diaries does not preclude an engagement with the outside world. In her diary, Brown positions herself in relation to a community of readers and writers, "enter[ing], however privately, into a discourse with a worldwide community of literate intellectuals."[150] She employed a religious vocabulary and method in order to write a self into being within the religious sphere of manuscript and print culture she was striving to inhabit. She did not attempt to render an individualistic, unique, distinct self but one that demonstrated her conformity to gendered definitions of Christian womanhood. She consolidated and practiced that self in her diary for a limited audience known to her and put it into action in her letters, which circulated by different means (the mail, print publication) and in different media (letters, periodicals, biography) to a broader audience.

Because the self she presents in the diary is constructed in relation to Anglo-American discourses, there is no explicit infusion of Cherokee identity into her use of the form. The diary as a genre facilitates and relies upon a Western notion of selfhood, thus Brown's Cherokee identity is not as obviously on display in the diary as her Christian identity.[151] The Western notion of self is antithetical to Cherokee notions of identity in many ways,[152] and the diary as a textual space within which to construct such a self has no analogue in Cherokee culture. But that doesn't mean Brown's Cherokee identity did not exist or persist or shape her Christian identity. As Phillip Round reminds us, print and manuscript literary forms "have provided essential 'opportunities' for many Native peoples. The 'acts of construction' that these texts have involved have never replaced cultural traditions but have merely supplemented them," ultimately "help[ing] them resist and regroup."[153] By consolidating her emergent identity in her diary before a narrow reading audience, she was able to deploy it in her letters as they circulated across national borders through the mail and in periodical publications.

Other Textual Representations

An array of other generic representations—poems, a drama, a biography—completes the contents of *Cherokee Sister*. These texts illustrate how Euro-American writers and readers engaged with Brown and the meanings of her life and writings through a variety of genres and perspectives. For example, the drama *Catharine Brown, the Converted Cherokee*, authored by an anonymous woman in Connecticut, is an example of the popular genre of the missionary drama. Often cited in scholarly examinations of Brown, Cherokee-missionary contacts, and American theater and drama (especially "Indian dramas"), *Catharine Brown, the Converted Cherokee* has never been reprinted in full since its initial publication in 1819. *Memoir of Catharine Brown* is given special discussion below because of its importance as an influential purveyor of Catharine Brown's historical legacy.

Memoir of Catharine Brown

Rufus Anderson began working on *Memoir* after Brown's death in 1823, registering the copyright in December 1824, with publication taking place in 1825. At this time, Anderson was the twenty-nine-year-old assistant secretary of the American Board; he went on to become foreign corresponding secretary in 1832 and maintained that post until 1866, "play[ing] a decisive role in shaping the policies of Protestant foreign missions" throughout the nineteenth century.[154] Anderson never appears to have met Brown, but he solicited materials by letter from those who did and gathered a selection of her correspondence for the volume.

Books like the one Anderson created are memoirs in an older sense of the term—biographies rather than autobiographies, as memoirs are often categorized today. Biography was an important and widely read genre in the nineteenth-century United States.[155] *Memoir's* construction follows a tradition established by Samuel Johnson's injunction to delve into individuals' characters behind public images and events as displayed in the "interior, private realm."[156] *Life of Johnson* (1791), James Boswell's biography of Johnson, exemplifies this "hybrid genre," with its inclusion of "autobiographical memoranda, rough notes . . . letters, diaries and conversations."[157] In the more immediate context provided by early American Christian evangelical and missionary organizations, biographies of prominent ministers took on this form.[158]

The involvement of women in the revivals, reforms, and missionary

movements of the first half of the nineteenth century generated readers interested in religious biographies that recorded the experiences of
"Christian women distinguished for piety but not for worldly accom-
plishments," a genre of "memoirs of pious women" that expanded dra-
matically after 1820.[159] While in the nineteenth century the title *Life*
or *Biography* pointed to the exploration of public personages and was
often attached to books about men, the term *memoir* was more often
applied to books about women and connoted a "more personal" tone
as well as "authorship or compilation by those who had known the
subject well."[160] Within this genre, memoirs that focused particularly on missionary endeavors provided readers with "a new archetype of
female evangelism that included sentiment, drama, pathos, heroism,
and an exotic setting, all in the name of God."[161] Indeed, Mary Kupiec Cayton argues, these memoirs created "a new kind of evangelical
sentimental literature that linked women permanently to benevolent
missionary activity."[162] The growth of evangelical publishing during
this period provided expanding publishing opportunities, venues, distribution networks, and readerships for such memoirs and a new open-
ness to women's participation: "The evangelical press invoked women,
courted them, printed their work, and relied on them for support."[163]
Despite this interest in women, the domestic nature of women's lives
could prove an obstacle to compilers assembling the autobiographies.
Compilers overcame a paucity of documentary materials by turning to
letters, journals, and the reminiscences of those who knew the women
best.[164] Anderson, like other male editors of pious women's memoirs,
"intervened to reshape women's experiences, choosing what to retain
and omit as well as reconfiguring texts through organizational strategies, prefaces, and footnotes."[165]

Anderson imposes a central narrative thread onto the material he
mines through his lengthy prose interpellations within the text. The
narrative he develops is most aptly summarized by the first sentences
of the concluding chapter: "Such was Catharine Brown, the converted Cherokee. Such too, were the changes wrought in her, through the
blessing of Almighty God on the labours of Missionaries" (253). Anderson insistently underlines Brown's transformation in identity, high-

lighted in the phrase "converted Cherokee," from "savage" or "heathen" to "civilized" and Christian woman. According to Anderson, "the labours of Missionaries" enacted the transformation of a vain, uneducated, heathen girl to a model of white Christian womanhood. The process of aligning Brown's identity with Euro-American norms is central to demonstrating his larger argument: Cherokees are susceptible to conversion; missionary societies such as the one he represents are the fittest vehicle with which to accomplish this work; and readers should therefore support their efforts both in monetary and ideological terms. Anderson sees Brown and wants the reader to see Brown as the ultimate evidence of the success of American Board missionaries.

Anderson worked with three primary forms of source material in presenting this interpretation: the *Brainerd Journal*, documents by missionaries and other Euro-Americans who knew Brown written expressly for the purpose of inclusion in the biography, and Brown's own letters and diary. The *Brainerd Journal* was the detailed record of events at the Brainerd Mission School from 1817 to 1823, compositely authored by a number of missionaries. Religious periodicals printed regular excerpts from the journal, and this is the source by which northern audiences first came to know about Brown and her experiences. For the original sources composed for incorporation in *Memoir*, Anderson seems to have approached no Cherokees to provide materials, whether oral or written, and no Cherokees contributed.[166] Anderson's strategy for gathering materials involved writing letters listing a number of questions to missionaries who taught and worked with Brown. Although the exact letter sent to correspondents has not been located, other letters that circulated between missionaries suggest that among the questions posed were these: "relating to the early life ∧of our dear sister∧ or to those scenes which passed while a pupil at Brainerd," "What did she know when she came to Brainerd?"; "What were prob∧ab∧ly her religious ∧views∧ at that time?"; and "Are there any interesting anecdotes of her while at Brainerd?"[167] Similar questions included in a letter Anderson sent to a missionary while gathering materials for a later biography of Brown's schoolmate John Arch suggest that Anderson's questions guided his correspondents toward producing a particular kind of biographical subject.

This subject was sundered from the Cherokee contexts from which the individual emerged, since most of the questions emphasized life after enrollment at the Mission School, and the subject was to be evaluated according to Christian and Western values, through questions ascertaining the subject's degree of industriousness, benevolence, and usefulness.

The third kind of source material Anderson incorporated into *Memoir* was Brown's writings. He included nineteen of her letters and the contents of a fragment of her diary, of which he had obtained a copy. Brown's writings constitute approximately sixty of the 180 pages of *Memoir*'s first edition, or 30 percent of the volume. Anderson edited her letters quite actively, although he claims to have used a light touch as he describes the letters and his editorial method: "The originals . . . are in a plain, intelligible running hand, and the orthography is very seldom incorrect. Alterations in the sense, are never made; and corrections in the grammar, but rarely" (186). In fact comparison of transcriptions prepared from manuscripts according to current editing practices presented here in part 1 to the versions Anderson presents in *Memoir* reveals that he consistently makes the following kinds of changes: inserts paragraph breaks; regularizes punctuation, capitalization, and spelling; omits entire sentences; rewrites the language; and inserts words. Some letters show lesser degrees of alteration than others, but most modern textual editors would consider Anderson's practices intrusive.

Anderson's editing obscures a number of important aspects of Brown's writings and writing practices, especially an accurate appraisal of her level of literacy and fluency in the English language, a measure of her growth and development as a writer over time, and a revelation of differences in the way she addresses various readers. Her letters to close intimates, for example, tend to have more errors than her letters to donors she does not know personally. This suggests a variety of writing practices, all of them potentially meaningful: that she wrote more hurriedly to personal friends; that while writing to them her mind was more preoccupied with what she was expressing than her manner of writing; that she was aware that her letters to donors might be judged for their correctness or that they might be published; or that she prepared rough drafts of letters to donors that she then recopied.

The reader of *Cherokee Sister* is encouraged to use the edition of *Memoir* presented here in various ways: to understand the rhetorical uses to which the missionary organization put its construction of Catharine Brown; to examine the dialogism of the text, constructed as it is by multiple voices; to consider how Anderson's framing of Brown's writings shapes their perceived meanings, especially when compared to the versions of the texts presented in part 1 of this volume; and to recognize *Memoir* as an important source in the preservation of a Native woman's writings and as a key historical document recording race, gender, religion, and politics in the era preceding Cherokee removal.

Notes

1. Brown's letters began appearing in periodicals in April 1819. During this period and preceding it, Native women's words rendered in print were mediated by editors or amanuenses who then published the accounts, as in the cases of "The Confession and Dying Warning of Katharine Garret" (1738) and Mary Jemison's captivity narrative (1824). The Cherokee women's petitions of 1817 and 1818 were not published at the time, although they are frequently reprinted in anthologies now (Perdue and Green, *The Cherokee Removal*, 122–23). Jane Johnston Schoolcraft, who has recently been called by her editor "the first known Indian woman writer," did not publish the writings she penned in the 1820s (Parker, *The Sound the Stars Make*, 2). Brown's closest competitor for the status seems to be Margaret (Peggy) Ann Scott Vann Crutchfield, a Cherokee woman whom Tiya Miles has identified as having a single letter appear in print in April 1819, the same month as Brown's first letter ("'Circular Reasoning,'" 239n36). Of course, as the process of recovery continues and the study of early Native writers deepens and expands, it is quite possible that earlier self-written publications by Native people will emerge.
2. Cayton, "Harriet Newell's Story," 409.
3. Hall, "Cherokee Mission," 20.
4. "Good Effected," 177.
5. "Good Effected," 177; "Miscellaneous Notices," 232.
6. "The Indian Cause," 74.
7. Rufus Anderson (1796–1880) began his affiliation with the ABCFM while still in seminary, became the Board's assistant secretary in 1823, served as its corresponding secretary from 1832 to 1866, and remained a member of

the Prudential Committee until 1875. See Harris, *Nothing but Christ*, for a full discussion of his career.

8. "Memoirs [*sic*] of Catharine Brown," 112.

9. On evangelical publishing in this period, see Brown, *Word in the World*; Cayton, "Harriet Newell's Story"; Nord, "Benevolent Books" and *Faith in Reading*.

10. Brown, *Word in the World*, 36.

11. O'Connell, "Literacy and Colonization," 509.

12. For scholarship on Brown, see Bellin, *Medicine Bundle*, chapter 2; Carney, *Eastern Band Cherokee Women*, 48–56; Gaul, "Cherokee Catharine Brown's Epistolary Performances"; Martin, "Almost White"; Martin, *The Land Looks After Us*, chapter 3; Martin, "Visions of Revitalization"; Moulder, "Cherokee Practice," 84–90; Perdue, "Catharine Brown"; Nelson, "Integrated Circuitry"; Schneider, "New England Tales"; Wyss, *English Letters and Indian Literacies*, 123–34.

13. See her omission, for example, from Kilcup's important anthology, *Native American Women's Writing, 1800–1924*.

14. I use the term *transnational* in this context to refer to the relations between the United States and the Cherokee Nation, a sovereign nation. For work on Native American literature and transnationalism, see Madsen, *Native Authenticity*; Huhndorf, *Mapping the Americas*. I share the perspective of the contributors to *Competing Kingdoms*, who see missionaries as crucial transnational actors, "not as a homogenous group of cultural imperialists but as people who reinvented the meanings of American nationalism and imperialism as they negotiated competing nationalisms and imperialisms in varying colonial settings" (Reeves-Ellington, Sklar, and Shemo, *Competing Kingdoms*, 2).

15. I have relied on McLoughlin's *Cherokees and Missionaries* (hereafter cited as *CM*), especially chapters 1–6, for my discussion of the political and religious backgrounds of the era in which Brown lived. My discussion of Brown's early years is also indebted to Martin's account in "Visions of Revitalization"; see also Perdue, "Catharine Brown."

16. Justice, *Our Fire Survives the Storm*, 6.

17. All told, between the 1780s and 1828, as many as five thousand Cherokees removed to Arkansas (*CM*, 240); this group came to be known as the "Old Settlers" to differentiate them from the Cherokees who were forcibly removed in 1838–39.

18. Miles, *The House on Diamond Hill*, 52–53.

19. Martin, "Visions of Revitalization," 65. Brown's family's slaveholding is mentioned in her diary (123), a passage expunged from Anderson's *Mem-*

oir. Anderson instead emphasizes her charity toward slaves, teaching them to read and instructing them in Christianity. The American Board held an official antislavery position (see McLoughlin, *The Cherokees and Christianity*, 44–47), creating some awkwardness for the missionaries as they worked with a people who held slaves and sometimes even hired slaves as laborers in their missions (Phillips and Phillips, *Brainerd Journal*, 432n4; hereafter cited as *BJ*).

20. Polygamy was a widespread practice among Cherokees. Scholars have explored the ways that polygamy "could strengthen communities by forging ties across clans and towns" (Miles, *The House on Diamond Hill*, 53) and might have contributed to Cherokee women's high degree of self-government (Perdue, *Cherokee Women*, 44). Missionaries excoriated the practice.

21. Brown, "Address of Dewi Brown," 33–34. Wyss discusses David Brown's life and work and this speech in *English Letters*, chapter 4.

22. *BJ*, 44. The editor has preserved the idiosyncrasies of nineteenth-century sources in this introduction. See "Statement of Editorial Method" for a description of the editing practices used for manuscript sources throughout the volume, including the introduction.

23. Gilbreath, "Biographical Sketch." Coody (b. 1787) was the sister of John Ross (1790–1866), who later became principal chief (1827–66), and wife of Joseph Coody (1779–1859), sometimes spelled Coodey (*BJ*, 435n11). Jane Coody was one of the first Cherokees to join the Brainerd Church, on February 1, 1818 (*BJ*, 406). McDonald (1746–1825), the grandmother of John Ross and Jane Coody, was admitted to the Brainerd church on June 13, 1819, at the approximate age of seventy-three. Missionaries characterized her as "perhaps as universally respected & beloved as any woman of the nation" (*BJ*, 476n8). Further description of McDonald is given in Gaul, "Ann Paine's 1820 Travel Narrative," 152.

24. Chamberlain to Potter.

25. Ellis to Potter.

26. Martin hypothesizes about Brown's relationship with John Ross and his family in "Visions of Revitalization," 72–73.

27. See McLoughlin, *Cherokee Renascence*, chapter 9, for discussions of Cherokee involvement in the Creek War.

28. McLoughlin, *Cherokee Renascence*, 266. Richard Brown's relationship with Jackson carried through Brown's signing of treaties in 1816 and 1817 ceding land to the United States (211, 230–31).

29. Martin, "Visions of Revitalization," 66. Martin discusses the attempted rape, but he does not seem to have had access to the source I quote below, which gives additional details of the event.

30. Numbers given parenthetically within the text direct readers to a page within this volume.
31. Campbell to unknown.
32. Block, *Rape and Sexual Power*, 82.
33. Shoemaker, introduction, 2.
34. Hill, "Weaving History," 133.
35. Johnston, *Cherokee Women in Crisis*, 2.
36. Johnston, *Cherokee Women in Crisis*, 3.
37. Johnston, *Cherokee Women in Crisis*, 13.
38. Perdue, *Cherokee Women*, 78.
39. Perdue, *Cherokee Women*, 115.
40. Yarbrough, "Legislating Women's Sexuality," 387.
41. Perdue, *Cherokee Women*, 7.
42. Johnston, *Cherokee Women in Crisis*, 50.
43. Miles, *The House on Diamond Hill*, 111.
44. Perdue, *Cherokee Women*, 9, 115.
45. Johnston, *Cherokee Women in Crisis*, 50.
46. Johnston, *Cherokee Women in Crisis*, 51.
47. Johnston, *Cherokee Women in Crisis*, 52.
48. Martin, "Almost White," 55. See Wyss, *English Letters*, 109–17, for a detailed discussion of the Brainerd Mission School and its curriculum.
49. Martin, *The Land Looks After Us*, 66.
50. Miles, *The House on Diamond Hill*, 69.
51. *BJ*, 161, 165.
52. Johnston, *Cherokee Women in Crisis*, 52–53.
53. *CM*, 129, 134.
54. Indeed missionaries' support of the Cherokee position in 1817–18 earned them a sharp rebuke from U.S. government officials *(CM*, 112–13), and some articulated strongly felt antiremoval positions during the 1820s and 1830s, eventually accompanying Cherokees on the Trail of Tears.
55. Hall to Evarts.
56. Arnold Krupat initiated this line of critique with his skeptical comment, "If there is a Cherokee dimension to Brown's text and to her sense of herself . . . [it] is not apparent to me" (*The Voice in the Margin*, 147), and this kind of evaluation has continued into twenty-first-century criticism. O'Connell, the editor of Apess's complete works, described Brown as "an Indian fully converted to the ways of civilization and Christianity" (introduction, xlvi). Bethany Schneider labeled Brown a "poster child" for the mission school who felt a "hatred" for Cherokee ways and a "loss of faith" in Cherokees' resilience and resistance ("New England Tales," 358, 362).

57. Martin's introduction to *Native Americans* offers a comprehensive consideration of the figure of the Christian Indian, upon which I have heavily relied in the discussion that follows. In "Integrated Circuitry," Nelson offers a useful discussion of the binaries undergirding scholarship on American Indians (18–19).

58. Martin, introduction, 14–15. A range of scholars have critiqued the colonialist dimensions of scholarship that displays a continuing desire for "authentic" Native voices; see Bernardin, "The Authenticity Game" for a synthesis of their arguments.

59. Martin, introduction, 3. For elucidation of these concepts, see Vizenor (Anishinaabe), *Survivance*; Warrior (Osage), *The People and the Word* and *Tribal Secrets*; Weaver, *That the People Might Live*.

60. Justice, *Our Fire Survives the Storm*, xvi.

61. Martin, "Visions of Revitalization," 85.

62. Perdue, "Catharine Brown," 86.

63. Nelson, "Integrated Circuitry," 23.

64. Hall to Evarts.

65. Martin, *The Land Looks After Us*, 71–72. For further discussion of this dream, see Martin, "Visions of Revitalization," 75–80; Nelson, "Integrated Circuitry," 22–23.

66. Martin, "Visions of Revitalization," 80.

67. Cornelius, *The Little Osage Captive*, 83–84.

68. McLoughlin, *Cherokee Renascence*, 357.

69. Perdue, *Cherokee Women*, 181.

70. Martin, *The Land Looks After Us*, 75.

71. In *English Letters*, Wyss discusses David's time in Cornwall and the ways Cherokee masculinity functioned in the mission schools (169–71). About Catharine's letters to David, Wyss provocatively speculates that "his salvation is very much dependent on his truly spiritual older sister; it is only her intercession that keeps her 'wild and bloody' younger brother on a properly spiritual path" (171).

72. Weaver, "From I-Hermeneutics to We-Hermeneutics," 22. See also Weaver's introduction of the idea of communitism in *That the People Might Live*, xiii. Martin makes a similar observation ("Visions of Revitalization," 84).

73. Weaver, "From I-Hermeneutics to We-Hermeneutics," 21.

74. Carney, *Eastern Band Cherokee Women*, 48.

75. Hill, "Weaving History," 135.

76. *CM*, 108.

77. *BJ*, 91.

78. Those who signed up and removed before 1820 received financial support from the U.S. government but lost their rights as citizens in the eastern Nation and faced uncertain circumstances in the West; those who signed up but did not actually go lost financial support for removal as well as citizenship rights in the East; those who remained had the option of signing up for a reserve, the possession of which could not be maintained, as subsequent events demonstrated (McLoughlin, *Cherokee Renascence*, 262, 265).

79. Sources conflict on John Brown's actions relating to removal during the period when Catharine attended Brainerd. McLoughlin identifies a John Brown as one of a group of Lower Town chiefs who, having signed up to remove in the wake of an 1817 treaty, failed to do so and subsequently engaged along with other Lower Town chiefs in a conspiracy to sign a fraudulent treaty ceding land to the U.S. government. They were assisted in this plot by Walter Webber, one of Catharine's half-brothers (the son of her mother from a previous marriage), who already lived in Arkansas. McLoughlin discusses this conspiracy in detail in *Cherokee Renascence*, 260–70. He names John Brown as a conspirator on 266. While there were two other men named John Brown living in the Creek Path area during this period (his son and grandson), John's age and leadership status make him seem the most likely candidate. Phillips and Phillips, however, assert that after the 1817 treaty, John Brown signed up for a 640-acre reserve in the eastern Cherokee Nation that was promised protection from future sale (*BJ*, 472).

80. Szasz, introduction, 3, 6.

81. Perdue, *Cherokee Women*, 131–32.

82. Coleman has written about female students enrolled at Brainerd in 1827–28 as cultural brokers ("American Indian School Pupils as Cultural Brokers"). Martin briefly and generally notes "Brown's rise to authority" without considering the broad range of ways that she gains status ("Visions of Revitalization," 82).

83. *BJ*, 44, 51.

84. Potter to Evarts, Nov. [?] 1824.

85. *BJ*, 128.

86. Hoyt to Worcester.

87. *BJ*, 176.

88. *BJ*, 176. Daniel Sabin Butrick (1791–1851), an ordained minister and Brainerd missionary from Massachusetts, was fascinated by Cherokee culture (*BJ*, 446n51). As the teacher at the Creek Path boys' school, Butrick resided with the Brown family in their home for a period of time and had

frequent contact with Catharine. Indeed his journal suggests that he conceived a sexual attraction for her, for which he viciously berated himself. For discussion of Butrick's crush, see Martin, "Visions of Revitalization," 82–83; Perdue, "Catharine Brown," 84,. Brown leaves no evidence in her writings of her response to, or indeed awareness of, his feelings.

89. *BJ*, 205.
90. *BJ*, 158.
91. McLoughlin, *Cherokee Renascence*, 10; Perdue, *Cherokee Women*, 55. The American Board did not license its first Native (male) exhorter, or lay minister, until the 1830s. Nonetheless evidence suggests that Cherokees converted by the American Board were exhorting informally at a much earlier date (*CM*, 339).
92. Noley, "The Interpreters," 58.
93. Noley, "The Interpreters," 58.
94. Qtd. in *CM*, 66.
95. Noley, "The Interpreters," 58. Cherokees seemed to have perceived interpreters as bearing authority. McLoughlin recounts an anecdote wherein an elderly Cherokee man protested the fact that a thirteen-year-old was interpreting for an American Board minister. The man's complaint did not have to do with her gender but her age: he "considered it inappropriate that a child should be given the role of instructing her elders" (*CM*, 200).
96. Martin, "Visions of Revitalization," 84.
97. Martin, "Visions of Revitalization," 62.
98. Krupat, *Native American Autobiography*, 115.
99. Nelson, "Integrated Circuitry," 26–27.
100. Bross and Wyss, introduction, 11. For influential work on early Native writers, see especially Joanna Brooks, *The Collected Writings of Samson Occom;* Lisa Brooks (Abenaki), *The Common Pot;* Justice (Cherokee), *Our Fire Survives the Storm;* Konkle, *Writing Indian Nations;* Round, *Removable Type;* Warrior, *The People and the Word* and *Tribal Secrets;* and Wyss, *English Letters and Indian Literacies* and *Writing Indians.*
101. Miles, "'Circular Reasoning,'" 234.
102. Justice, *Our Fire Survives the Storm*, 30.
103. Justice, *Our Fire Survives the Storm*, 31, 38. For Justice's reading of the Treaty of New Echota, see chapter 2.
104. Justice, *Our Fire Survives the Storm*, 41.
105. Justice, *Our Fire Survives the Storm*, 85, 65.
106. Bellin, *Medicine Bundle;* Moulder, "Cherokee Practice"; and Schneider, "New England Tales," all rely on *Memoir.* The exception to this rule is Gaul, "Cherokee Catharine Brown's Epistolary Performances," which fo-

cuses on Brown's letters published in periodicals. Perdue and Martin cite additional sources in their historical scholarship.

107. Martin, "Visions of Revitalization," 84.

108. Smith and Watson, *Before They Could Vote*, 8–9.

109. See the examples in Bross and Wyss, *Early Native Literacies*.

110. Decker, *Epistolary Practices*, 9.

111. Decker, *Epistolary Practices*, 6.

112. A Presbyterian minister and physician who sometimes treated the missionaries at Creek Path, Campbell (1789–1846) first met Brown soon after she enrolled at Brainerd, sent her books, and treated her during her final illness (Sprague, *Annals of the American Pulpit*, 651–55). He was an important source for Anderson in *Memoir*. Sarah Boyce Campbell (1792–1858) was his wife.

113. Decker, *Epistolary Practices*, 10.

114. I have discovered two letters from Brown's mother, Sarah, to David. These were probably translated into English and written out for her by someone else. Their existence, however, does demonstrate the engagement with letters by even non-English-speaking, nonliterate Cherokees during this historical period.

115. Altman, *Epistolarity*, 91.

116. Bannet, *Empire of Letters*, 56–59.

117. Schultz, "Letter-Writing Instruction," 121.

118. These include *Memoirs of Harriet Newell* and *Memoirs of the Life of Miss Caroline Smelt*. Ironically Brown's own letters were eventually incorporated into a similar kind of memoir by Rufus Anderson.

119. Schneider, *The Culture of Epistolarity*, 43.

120. Schultz, "Letter-Writing Instruction," 110–11.

121. Johnson, *Gender and Rhetorical Space*, 94, 84.

122. Murray, "Translation and Mediation," 74.

123. Gaul, "Ann Paine's 1820 Travel Narrative," 157.

124. Fields's letter was printed in the *Christian Repository*; see Field [*sic*] to Miss G.

125. Dierks, *In My Power*, xiv.

126. Dierks, *In My Power*, 7-8.

127. See Gaul, "Cherokee Catharine Brown's Epistolary Performances," 141–43, for further discussion of how racial issues informed Brown's letters in their composition and reception.

128. Martin, "Crisscrossing Projects," 68.

129. Miles, *The House on Diamond Hill*, 160.

130. Hewitt, *Correspondence and American Literature*, 2–3.

131. Miles, *The House on Diamond Hill*, 160.
132. See Miles's argument in "'Circular Reasoning.'" Although I have not been able to locate Brown and Sigourney's correspondence, a letter from David Brown to Sigourney in the collections of the Connecticut Historical Society confirms that his sister and the poet exchanged letters.
133. Cumfer, *Separate Peoples*, 27.
134. Cumfer, *Separate Peoples*, 28.
135. Ryan discusses examples of nineteenth-century African Americans similarly achieving "benevolent agency, which entailed both freedom from dependence and the capacity to aid others" (*The Grammar of Good Intentions*, 7).
136. Potter, "Creek Path." Laura Weld Potter (1800–1845) replaced Brown as the girls' teacher at Creek Path when she arrived with her husband in 1822 (*BJ*, 503n1). Approximately the same age as Brown, Potter became a close friend and, after Brown's death, an important source for Anderson's *Memoir*.
137. See Brown's letter of April 17, 1820 (76–77).
138. Murray explains that the consciousness of audience that Brown exhibits in this statement characterizes Native American writing more generally: "This awareness of being overheard by a white audience, or even of having them as primary audience is an important and continuing feature of Indian literature" ("Translation and Mediation," 75).
139. Kagle and Gramegna, "Rewriting Her Life," 38.
140. Blodgett, *Centuries of Female Days*, 156.
141. Blodgett, *Centuries of Female Days*, 156.
142. Bunkers and Huff, *Inscribing the Daily*, 1.
143. Simons, "Invented Lives," 262.
144. Kagle, *American Diary Literature*, 17.
145. Kagle and Gramegna, "Rewriting Her Life," 43.
146. Kagle and Gramegna, "Rewriting Her Life," 42.
147. Kouffman, "Women's Diaries of Late Stewart England," 75.
148. See, for example, Martinson, *In the Presence of Audience*, 6–7.
149. Bloom, "'I Write for Myself,'" 23.
150. Motz, "The Private Alibi," 190–91.
151. Despite this, Cherokee traces are present in the diary. As Perdue has argued, Brown's accompanying John to the mineral spring, detailed in the diary, shows a continued reliance on traditional Cherokee healing practices as well as the centrality of matrilineal relationships in her family ("Catharine Brown," 87). In addition, two moments in the diary have explicitly political stakes: John expresses his concern about the family's removal to Arkansas and refers to the Brown family's slaves, a part of the diary expunged from Anderson's version presented in *Memoir*.

152. See Smith and Watson, *Before They Could Vote*, 8 for a discussion of the normative "I" of autobiography and those it excludes.
153. Round, *Removable Type*, 224.
154. Harris, *Nothing but Christ*, 4.
155. See Casper, *Constructing American Lives*, for discussion of the genre.
156. Casper, *Constructing American Lives*, 4.
157. Nussbaum, *The Autobiographical Subject*, 118.
158. Casper, *Constructing American Lives*, 115.
159. Casper, *Constructing American Lives*, 115, 107.
160. Casper, *Constructing American Lives*, 116.
161. Cayton, "Canonizing Harriet Newell," 114.
162. Cayton, "Harriet Newell's Story," 415.
163. Cayton, "Harriet Newell's Story," 414.
164. Casper, *Constructing American Lives*, 116.
165. Brown, *The Word in the World*, 94.
166. The exceptions to this rule are one letter by David that Anderson includes in *Memoir* and a scrap of paper with comments attributed to Brown's sister Polly Gilbreath that is part of the Congregational Library archive of Anderson's source texts. Yet even David does not appear to have been given the opportunity to respond to Anderson's questions; his sole letter included in *Memoir* is one written to missionaries about his reunion with his family after he left New England and does not even mention Catharine, who had been dead for a year.
167. Hall to Evarts.

I
COLLECTED WRITINGS, 1818–1823

Letters

To Matilda Loomis Williams (Eliot Mission)

Manuscript, CBP Item 21;[1] *Panoplist*, July 1819; *Guardian, or Youth's Religious Instructor*, Nov. 1819; *Memoir*, chapter 2

Brainerd, Nov. 1, 1818

My Dearly beloved Sister

I have been wishing to write to you ever since you left us.[2] you can hardly tell how my heart ached when I parted with you, expecting never to see you again in this world, but when I remembered that you were in the hands of the Lord, and that he would dispose of you as he pleased, it gave me joy equal to my sorow. O how I rejoiced to think that you were going to carry the glad tidings of sal∧v∧ation to a people ho who had neve∧r∧ heard about the dear Saviour. I ∧do∧ hope and pray that the Lord will bless your labors among them as he has here, We were very lonesome when you left us, especialy at our prayer meeting, but I hope our hearts were united in love. I was very sorry to hear that you was sick, but it rejoiced me to hear that you were [illegible] recovering.[3] O my dear Sister I will join with you in praising the Lord for his goodness in restoring you to health; I shall never forget you, and your kind endeavors to bring me to a knowledge of the Saviour. Sometimes I feel the love of God shed abroad in my heart, and feel as if I would be willing to give up every thing in this world to Christ. O how good it is to enjoy the presence of God. O that I might always enjoy it; but my heart is so bad and so prone to leave the God I love, that I am afraid he will leave me, O my dear Sister do pray for me.

all the cherokee brothers and sisters are well Three of the schollars

viz Lydia lowrey[4] Alice, ∧and∧ Peggy Wilsion we ∧hope∧ have obtained
an interest in the Saviour; ~~Alice there father~~ ∧Mr. Wilson∧ came here
and wishes to take his daugters on a visit to Mr. B∧r∧owns; nearly a
week after he sent back word that he was not going to send them back
to school again, we felt very much grieved to hear it.[5] I expect my
father here every day. I do not know whether I shall go to the
Arkansaw or not.[6] ∧I∧ feel grieved when I think of leaving all my
Christian friends, and of going far from all religious people, into a wild
howling wilderness where[7] no star shines to guide my wandering feet,
to the babe of Bethlehem, wher no warning voice is heard to keep me
in the straight path that leads to heaven. When I look to that dark
region I start back, but when I think of my [~~illegible~~] ∧two∧ brothers
there and my dear parents who expect soon to go, I feel reluctant to
stay behingd, and leave them to perish alone. Brother and Sister Hall
and Sister Sarah are on a visit to Knoxville;[8] they have been gone
nearly three weeks; we look for them every day. Sister Hall has been
sick and thought it would do her good to ride out.[9] Sister Matilda kiss
Lowisa for me; I long to see her and hear her talk.[10] Mr. Canhouse left
us last thursday and James Fields has gone with him ∧to∧ the North.[11]
Tell brother Williams and Kingsbury that I remember them, most
affactionate and all so all the dear Brothers and Sisters at yellobusha.[12]

from your Loveing sister Katharine Brown

MATILDA WILLIAMS

My dearly beloved ∧friend∧

I just sit down to write a few lines to you which I know will
pl∧e∧ase you I have now found a graciou∧s∧ saviour which I would
not depart f∧r∧om ~~it~~ for a thousand worlds O may we ever pray for
each other that we may at last meet in heaven never to part once. I
was wandering in the darkness But god was pleased to turn my heart
near him ask Mr. ~~w~~∧W∧illiams to pray for me all the family are well
hoping you the same state of health. Give my love to all your dear
friends—your most affectionate frien∧d∧

Lydia Lowrey

MRS. WILLIAMS

O My Dear beloved freand

I will write you a few lins ∧[illegible]∧ which I hope you will be very glad when you recive it I am going to school I have been here five weeks and I [~~whan~~] ∧want∧ to stay three year's. but I dont know whether my people will let me s∧t∧ay that long. My sister betsy[13] is gone to school to knoxville. I would be very glad to see you, but I do not know whether we shall see each other in this world, but I hope to meet you in heaven. The Missionar[ious?] tell us a great many things about the dear savior; and I will try to go as they tell me. Give my love to Mr. Williams and all the the Missionaries there. from your friend

    Polly Burns[14]

MRS. WILLIAMS

My dear sister

I should have written more to you, but I thought you would be pleased to have some of the other girls write. I know you would be glad to hear from Grana McDonald[15] O how it would rejoice your heart to hear her talk she told me that she felt lost when you went away. Sister Lydia and myself went to see her and stayed with her all night, she wished us to sing and pray with her. She told Sister Lydia she wished to join the Church with her; she also told her that she felt very hapy when she prayed, I hope we shall pray for each other while in this world and at last meet in our heaven fathers kingdom never more to part. farewell my dear sister, from your sister

    Katharine Brown

MRS. WILLIAMS

  This ribin is a present from sister Lydia to her Dear Louisa

    Lydia

  [Left margin, page 3] The ribin which I mention I omit to put in on the count of pastage

To William and Flora Hoyt Chamberlain (Brainerd Mission)

Manuscript, CBC; *Religious Intelligencer*, May 8, 1819; *Religious Remembrancer*, May 8 1819; *Guardian*, Nov. 1819; *Panoplist and Missionary Herald*, Apr. 1819;[16] *Memoir*, chapter 2

Fort Deposit December the 12th [1818]

to My Dearly beloved Brother and Sister Chamberlin

I jest sit down to address you with my pen but is this all am I so soon called to bid you a dieu, and see your faces no more in this world[17] O my beloved friends, you k∧no∧w not the love I bear to that blessed spot where I have spent so many happy hours with you but it is past never to return.

dear friends I weep my heart is full, tears [illegible][18] flow from, my eyes while I write, and why is it so, do I murmur? God forbid Ought I not to praise the Lord for what I have received, and trust him for every thing O yes, His ways are best and He has graciously promised, that all things shall work together for good to those that love him; But do I love him have I that love to him, which will enable me to keep all his [illegible] commandments do I love him with all my heart, O that the Lord would search me and lead me in the way of eternal life.

since I left you leading a very lonesome life and not hearing the gospel preached but once that is when father Hoyt was here, and Myl∧o∧[19] they came [illegible] here on Tuesdy evening I was sitting in my room I heard a knocking at the door. I bid them come ~~ing~~ in and [~~illegible~~] who but brother Mylo appeared, ∧I∧ inquired if any body was with him he said his father was at the door that rejoiced me very much. ~~I have taken~~ and I injoyed very much while they was here blessed be God for sending them here to instruct us. I am here amongs a wicked set of people and never hear prayers nor any Godly conversation, O my dear friends pray for me I hope you do there is not a day passes but I think of ∧you∧, and the kindness I received during the time I staid with you. it ∧is∧ not my wish to go to the Arkansaw but God only knows what is best for me. I shall not attempt to tell you what I have felt since I left you and the tears I have shed when I called to mind the happy moments we passed in singing the praises of God however I bear it as well as I possibly can trusting in our dear Saviour who will never leave nor forsake them that puts their trust in him it may be possible that I may see you once more it would be a great hap∧P∧iness to me if I dont go to the Arkansaw perhaps I may but if I ~~shall~~ should go it is not likely we shall meet in this world again, but you will excuse me for my heart feels that which I cannot express with my pen. When I think and see the poor thoughtless Cherokees going on in sin I can not help blessing God ~~tha~~ that he has led me in the right path to serve him Father will start to the Arkansaw about some time after Christmas but I am not certain that I shall go.

I thank you for your kind let∧t∧ers do write to me every opportunity, I shall conclude w[ith] my love to all my brothers and sisters at Brainerd Sister flora, do kiss all the children for me. I shall expect letter from all the little girls O may we all meet at last in the kingdom of our blessed Saviour never more to ~~to~~ part

Farewell, my dear brother and sister Farewell
from your affectionate
Sister in Christ Catharine Brown

~~MRS.~~ FLORA CHAMBERLIN

To Moody and Isabella Hall (Knoxville, Tennessee)
Memoir, chapter 3

Brainerd, May 30, 1819.[20]

My dear Brother and Sister,

With pleasure I spend a few moments in writing to you this evening, to tell you of my safe arrival on the 23d of this month. O how great was the joy that I felt, when meeting the dear family at Brainerd, with whom I have long desired to be. Yes, dear brother and sister, God has returned me back once more, where I can be with Christian friends, and get more instruction. If it is the Lord's will, I hope to stay here two years longer. O that I might improve the great privileges, which I now enjoy.

It appears strange to me, that I am not more interested in the cause of Christ, when he has done so much for me. But I will now give myself up entirely to Him. I should be willing to leave every thing for God, and to undergo any sufferings, if it would but make me humble, and would be for his glory.

My heart bleeds for my people, who are on the brink of destruction. O pray for me, my dear brother and sister. I long to see you and your little one. I am your affectionate sister,

    Catharine Brown.

To Loring S. Williams and Maltilda Loomis Williams (Eliot Mission)

Manuscript, CBP Item 16; *Memoir*, chapter 3

Brainard July 5 1819

My dear brother & sister Williams

Altho I have long omitted answering your affectionate letters my heart has been often with you. yes dear brother & sister I do not forget you & all the pleasant meetings we have had together when you was here—But pain is mixed with the pleasure when I think they are gone no more to return. & when I think of the kind instruction I received from you before you left this place my heart swells with gratitude I feel much indebted to you for them—But more particularly to that god who sent you here to instruct the poor ignorant Indianss in the way that leads to everlasting life. Oh my dear friends may the Lord ever bless you & make you the ~~honored~~ instrument of doing great good where he has called you to go. ₐthough you may be called to go—ₐ through many trials & troubles— But remember, my ~~dear~~ ₐbeloved ₐ brother & sister all our trials & troubles here [~~illegible~~]²¹ will only make us richer there when we arrive at home—A few more day I hope our weary souls will be at rest in our Saviours kingdom where we shall enjoy the presence of the blessed Saviour forever—When I wrote you before I expected to go to the Arkansaw & never to see this place again; but the Lord has in mercy ordered it otherwise—He has permitted me to live with the dear missionaries here again though my parents were very much against my staying & could not bear to think of leaving me behind. My mother[22] said if I staid here she did not expect to see me again in this world—Indeed she wished she had never sent me to this school, & that I had never received riligious instruction—I told her if she was a christian she would not feel so—she would be willing to give me up to Christ & all she had. I told her I did not wish to stay on account of my own pleasure; but that I wanted to get more instruction so that it might be for her good as well as ∧for∧ mine I filt very sorry for my parents I thought it was my duty to go in obedience to their commands & commit myself to the will of God—I know ~~that~~ the Lord could change the hearts of my parents—so they were perfectly willing for me to stay here two years longer I left them in March They expected to set out in that month for the Arkansaw—They had already prepared for the journey But the Lord has ordered so that that they concluded not to go until next fall—I don't know whether they will ∧go∧ then or not—I cannot tell you now what they have calculated to do—I hope you will pray for them & also pray, for me, that I may become useful to my dear people—My heart bleeds for their immortal souls. oh that I might be made the means of turning many souls from darkness unto marvelous light.

Oh ~~my~~ dear brother & sister I love you much & feel the time is short when we shall sit down with our Saviour & feel that love that no words can describe Oh how I long to see little Louisa & her little brother—Brother Wms give them a sweet kiss for me—I hope you will excuse me for not writing more this time I shall write you again soon / Give my love to my dear br & sister [~~illegible~~][23] Kingsbury & also all the dear missionaries there—From your affectionate

Sister in Christ

C. Brown

P. S please to accept this little present for my little darlings—learn them to say Aunt Catharine

To Moody Hall (Taloney Mission)

Memoir, chapter 3

Brainerd, Oct. 25, 1819.

A few moments of this day shall be spent in writing to my dear brother. It seems a long time, since you left us.[24] I long to see you. I long to hear from you. I hope the Lord is with you this day, that you enjoy the presence of our dear Redeemer. My sincere desire and earnest prayer to the throne of grace, is, that your labours may be blessed, and that God would make you the instrument of saving many souls from eternal destruction.

O how I feel for my poor Cherokee brethren and sisters, who do not know the blessed Jesus, that died for us, and do not enjoy the blessings that I do. How thankful I ought to be to God, that I have ever been brought to the light of the Gospel, and was not left to wander in darkness. O I hope the time is at hand, when all the heathen shall know God, whom to know is life everlasting.

My dear brother, may we be faithful to our Master, knowing that in due season we shall reap, if we faint not. Our pilgrimage will shortly be ended, and all our trials will be over. Do not forget me in your daily prayers, for I need very much the prayers of God's children. My heart is prone to leave my God, whom I love. From your unworthy sister in Christ,

Catharine Brown.

To Moody and Isabella Hall (Taloney Mission)

Manuscript, CBP Item 15; *Memoir*, chapter 3

Brainerd Nov 1819

How solemn my Dear brother and sister is the idea that we must soon part[25] Perhaps the next time we meet will be in eternity Befor the bar of God there we shall either enjoy eternal hapiness or endure the rath of God forever O my dear brother and sister if we are prepared to meet our God in peace we shall surely be happy But my

beloved brother and sister how can I be permited to meet you in
heaven my heart is so prone to sin a gainst God that I am sometimes
a fraid he will leave me O do remember me in you prayers do not
forget me that all these doubts may be removed from me and that my
soul [illegible]²⁶ may be washed in the blood of Jesus Christ may we
all be washed in that blood which was shed on Calvary for the
remission of our sins, and may we be faithful to our God while we
live in this world.

And at last be permited ∧to∧ inter in to the Glory of our God Yes
dear brother and sister time is short there is no resting place here
b∧e∧low we are journeying to eternity we ∧will rest and∧ get home. all
ways remember your sister C who needs you prayes for she is a great
sinner

I love you much an feel that the time is short when we shall set
down with our Saviour and feel that love which no [illegible]²⁷ words
can discribe Farewell my [dearest?] brother and sister may the Lord
go with you and be with you forever²⁸

From your sister C

M. & I. HALL[illegible]²⁹

To a member of the Brainerd Society

Religious Remembrancer, Mar. 11, 1820; *Boston Recorder*, Mar. 18, 1820³⁰

Brainerd, Jan. 1, 1820.

My beloved friend and sister in Christ,

I am happy to answer your affectionate letter which I received
sometime ago, and read with much joy. I will assure you, my sister, it
gives me pleasure to hear of you, and that you feel so much interested
for the Mission at Brainerd and the poor benighted heathen. O how
great, how rich is the name of our Lord and Redeemer! My heart
flows with gratitude and joy upon every remembrance of the
goodness and mercy of God. Yes, I may well be thankful to him who
was willing to come down into [illegible] and shed his blood on
Calvary for the remission of our sins. O, when I look away to Calvary

there I see the blessed Jesus hanging upon the accursed tree and groaning away his precious life for us. Was this for our sins, "was it for crimes that I had done, he groaned upon the tree!" O, yes,—it was for my sins, my cruel sins, that he bowed his head and gave up the ghost. O that my tears might flow continually for my sins. But I know, not by tears, that we shall obtain heaven; no, not through any worth of worthiness of our own; but alone through the crucified Saviour, who is now a glorious and exalted Saviour. Then how it becomes us to follow the example of him who hath done so much for me while I was yet a sinner. I often think of the dreadful situation I was in a few years ago, and bless God that he has ever put it into the hearts of his dear people to come out here, and to bring us the glad news of salvation, and not only sent them, but has caused some of us to embrace the Saviour which is freely offered to us in the gospel. With pity I look upon my fellow [heathen] who are yet in darkness, living without God and without hope in the world. But I hope and pray that if the Lord has begun his good work among us, he will carry it on until all become acquainted with our blessed Redeemer.

Accept my sincere thanks for the good books you sent me. I have not yet read much in them, but think I shall receive much benefit from them. Dear sister, let us pray for each other, that we may be faithful to God; and if we shall never have the opportunity of seeing each other in this world, may we meet on Canaan's happy shore, where we shall never part again.

From your affectionate friend and sister in Christ,
Catherine Brown.

To A Lady in Connecticut
The Little Osage Captive, 148–50;[31] *Memoir*, chapter 3

Brainerd, Jan. 12, 1820.

Dear Sister in Christ,

I thank you much for your affectionate letter, which I received on the 23*rd* of December. O! how great, how rich is the mercy of our dear Redeemer, who has made us the subjects of His kingdom, and led us, as we trust from death unto life! My dear sister, I can never express my gratitude to God, for his goodness towards me, and my dear people. Surely it is of *his own glorious mercy*, that he is sending to us the Gospel of the Lord Jesus, in this distant land, where the people had long set in darkness, and were perishing for lack of the knowledge of God. Blessed be his holy name! O my sister! let us rejoice continually in our Lord and Saviour, and as we have put on Christ, not only by outward profession, but by inward and spiritual union, let us walk worthy of our high and holy vocation, and shew the world, that there is something in true religion. And may the Lord give us strength to do his will, and to follow continually the example of our meek and lowly Jesus. I thank you for the present you sent me, which I received as a token of love. The Mission family are all well, and also the dear children. Many of them are serious, and we hope they love and pray to God daily. O that I were more engaged for God, to promote his cause, among these dear children, and my people! I am going soon to visit my parents, which is an hundred miles from here, and expect to stay two months. I hope you will pray for me, that the Lord would bless my visit, and renew the hearts of my dear parents.

    Your sincere friend
    and sister in Christ,
    Catharine Brown.

To a Young Lady in Philadelphia
Religious Remembrancer, July 1, 1820; *Christian Watchman*, July 8, 1820[32]

Fort Deposit, Jan. 28, 1820.

Very dear Friend,

    I received your kind letter last week, by brother David.[33] It gave me much pleasure in reading it and other letters from Brainerd. It is now about three weeks since I have been here with my dear parents. Although I am here in this wilderness where I can see no Christian friend to converse with, or hear any thing of the humble religion of the gospel; but blessed be God he is always with us wherever we are. At home or abroad; on the land, or the sea. O how sweet, how excellent is the promise of God to his children. And therefore I have no reason to complain for friends in this world, or desire any of my own comfort in this life. I hope to meet the children of God in a better world, where the Christians are collected to spend eternity in singing the song of Moses and the Lamb. How thankful did I feel when I saw brother David, as I hope he has embraced the blessed Saviour. He is now rejoicing in the service of our God. How shall we ever thank and praise God enough that he has answered our prayers for him. O, dear friend, should we not bow before the King of kings, and say with our whole heart, not unto us, but to Thee shall be all the glory. My friend may we not cease to pray for the heathen. I know you often think and pray for them. What a happy time it will be when we meet all our dear friends in heaven.—Shall not the heathen join with us, especially the dear Cherokees. What will God say to those who have been faithful, and have been made the instruments of bringing many souls home to God. A short time since, when my nation was in darkness, and all was blind. I hope God has opened the eyes of many sinners like me. He has now begun his glorious work in our land, and I hope He will prosper his missionaries, and carry on his work until all the nation shall become acquainted with our blessed Redeemer. My dear parents seem very serious, and I hope they will soon be devoted to God. I would ask your prayers for them. O how many poor heathen do I see around me; even the Creek Indians often pass by this place, ignorant, and do not know that God who made them, or what world they are in. Jesus, the Lamb of God, who died for us, only is able to save and make them know that they have immortal souls. I have spent this last week with my sister K., which is about 10 miles from this place. She seemed very much affected that she was a sinner. She says she wants to be where she can hear preaching often. O how much do I thank God for bringing my people into the knowledge of himself; may this encourage us to be more engaged at the Throne of Grace for sinners. We know that our

God is a God hearing prayers; he will, in his own time, send his gracious answers. I have received letters from Brainerd. They are all well, the school prospering. It will be, I expect, a month before we return. I long to see Brainerd and receive more instruction, so that I may be useful to my people.

Sabbath evening. I have been this day reading the good book, the life of Mrs. Harriet Newell; you have probably read it.[34] O what a good missionary she was. After reading this invaluable book, I cannot help feeling a deep concern for the salvation of the heathen.—She was indeed a professor of the meek and lowly Jesus. But now I must leave you, my dear friend, after requesting your prayers for me that I may be faithful to my Saviour. And wishing you the light of God's countenance, I bid you adieu.

  Catharine Brown.

             Brainerd, March 8, 1820.

Dear Friend,

 I am happy to speak to you from Brainerd. I wrote the foregoing when I was at home; but had no oportunity to send it. I returned to school on Saturday, and was truly happy to see the mission family once more in this world. And to be permitted by my heavenly Father once more to hear the Gospel's joyful sound. I have, indeed, enjoyed greater happiness than tongue can describe. The mission family are all well. And also the school children. There are now upwards of 30 girls in the school. You would be delighted to see how much they are engaged in singing the praises of the Redeemer, who loved and gave himself for them. Many of the children are serious, especially Lucy Field; we have some hope she is a Christian.[35]

 I expect brother David will join the church before a great while. He expects to go to the north, & enter the school at Cornwall.[36] He feels a great desire to do good among our people; and I hope the Lord will make him a good missionary. I hope you will write to me soon, and let me know what you are doing for God.

  From your affectionate sister in the Lord.
  Catharine Brown.

To Isabella Hall (Taloney Mission)

Manuscript, CBP Item 13;[37] *Memoir*, chapter 3

Brainerd March 8the 1820.

very dear Sister

with pleasure I take my time [tis] this morning to address you with my pen And[38] tell you my ardent love to you is still much as ever. That is Christian affection which the world knows nothing of Though the Lord has seperated us a while in this world that we can no more behold each other in our flesh and participate our feelings together as we use to

But why should we murmer for a short sepration. Is it not for the sake of our Crucified Saviour. Do we not feel willing to part with all our earthly friends and suffer most any thing in this world for the sake of doing good to the poor perrishing souls who are are yet ignorant about the Saviour. O dear sister have you not al ready exper[inanced] the trials of this world. you can not tell how painful it was to me when I heard that you have been sick and that you had no one to help you but my poor brother Hall[39] O my dear brother and sister do you not rejoice that you are counted worthy to suffer for Christ sake. We know the Lord is good and all things will work together for good to those that love him and put there whole trust in him. And O now dear ever dear sister what shall I say to you. How can I possibly express my feelings—could we see each other we would talk and feel[40] weep and sing and pray together almost without ceasing. But our Heavenly Father has separated us Perhaps we loved each other more than we loved him that we did not pray to him and praise and thank him as we ought to. And now is it not so dear sister—did we not neglect our duty and grow cold and careless when we were together—Now we feel sorry; but the Lord will forgive us. Still dear sister we can pray for each other. Dont you think our prayers often meet at the same [illegible][41] time at the Throne of grace our Heavenly Father will grant all our request Yes he will [do it] for [the] Jesus his dear sons sake O then let us pray on and never cease to pray for each other while he lends us breath and when in heaven we meet shall see him whom our soul loveth. It not be long sister f[42] before we shall meet in our Fathers—House. to go no more out. Dear brother and sister do not forget me—pray ∧for∧ your poor unworthy sister C she will never forget you. O Let us rejoice continuly and praise the Lord for what He is doing among this people. Lord has given us another dear brother in Christ. My Dear brother David is now rejoiceing in his blessed Redeemer he has a gr∧e∧at desire to do good among our people. I expect he will leave us in a 2 or 3 weeks for Conwell to study divenity and prepar to preach the Gospel of Jesus Christ. I do hope and pray that the Lord will go with him and enable him to do much good in the world. Brother David and myself spent 7 week with our dear parents returned back to school last week.[43] I hope to continue in school sometime longer but know not how long My Dear Mother feels that she cannot splare me much longer in school I dont know but my parents will come after me [illegible][44] next Fall Therefore I wish to learn as I can befor I return.

And now dear sister may we both be faithful to our Lord and do much in the world And when time shall be no more with us in this world my we be permited to meet in yonder world where Christians are collected to sing the praises of Moses and the Lamb through all eternity.

From your Sincer Sister in Christ C B

MRS. HALL

P S O how much I want to see my little Ginnett[45] and here[46] her talk dear sis[t][47] g[i]ve her a sweet kiss for her aunt C I hope the Lord will make her a good Missionary.

MISS HALL

To Mrs. A.H. (Philadelphia)[48]

Religious Remembrancer, June 17, 1820; *Religious Intelligencer*, June 24, 1820

Brainerd, April 17th, 1820.

My beloved friend and sister in Christ,

With much pleasure I spend a few moments to answer your kind and interesting letter, which I received some time since I trust you will pardon my not writing sooner. I assure you I shall never forget my kind sisters in Philadelphia. The box of clothing which was sent to the dear children, was very thankfully received by the Missionaries. I fear I do not feel thankful enough to our Heavenly Father, and to the friends of Missionaries, who are giving their property to promote the Saviour's kingdom in this heathen land. But I hope and pray that the Lord will reward them for their labour of love, to the perishing souls of their fellow creatures. Surely I have great cause for gratitude to God that he has been so good as to send missionaries here in this distant land, to tell us about God and the way to happiness. In great mercy has the Lord remembered us; O that I might love him more and serve him better. It is not long since the joyful sounds of the Gospel of Christ was never heard in this place, and the Bible was unknown to us; we knew not Christ Jesus who died for us, and all such sinners as we are. Surely the Lord hath been our helper; blessed be the name of the Lord, for his mercy endureth forever. I think every day of the love of God, in giving his Son to die for us, while we were yet sinners; and praise God for sending Missionaries out from a distant land, to shew us the way to heaven, and to preach the gospel to us, poor ignorant people. We have long been in darkness, and were perishing for lack of knowledge. But now we see a little light. The missionaries have directed us to the shining Star of Bethlehem, which will guide us to a seat of glory. Remember me, your unworthy sister C., that I may ever be faithful to my trust, and not go astray as a lost sheep. Pray that I may find Jesus Christ as my Chief Shepherd, to the saving of my soul. The Lord has been truly gracious to me and to my beloved people, in sending us the glad news of salvation, and in sending his

Spirit with his word to enlighten our minds, and move us to embrace the blessed Saviour. But O my dear sister, how many or our brethren and sisters are yet in darkness, living without God and without hope in the world. They have precious and immortal souls to be lost or saved. O, may I then be willing to sacrifice any thing for the sake of bringing the heathen, especially those of my own Nation, to a knowledge of God and the Saviour, whom I have found to be so precious in my heart. I have been some time on a visit to my parents. My brother David, who has been in school sometime at Brainerd, was with me. We had a very agreeable time with our dear parents, in telling them about the Saviour. I hope the Lord will soon bring them from darkness into the light of the Gospel. We talked also to some of our neighbours, who appeared willing and attentive to receive instruction.

Brother Butrick, one of the Missionaries, has gone since to preach the gospel to them; and set up a school in that neighbourhood.[49] I hope the Lord will make him the instrument of doing much good among that people. Respecting the school—There are now upwards of 80 scholars in school. Sister Sarah has the charge of the girls' school, a number of them are serious, and we hope they do love God. Brother David, who I mentioned before, was received as a candidate for baptism the first of this month.[50] He appears much engaged in the cause of the Redeemer. He expects soon to go to Cornwall to study divinity. He says it is his greatest desire to do something for the Saviour while he lives in the world.

The Mission Family wish to be remembered in love to you, and also your Cherokee sisters in the Church present their Christian love to you.

> From your heathen sister in Christ,
> Catharine Brown

MRS. A_H_.

77

To David Brown

Manuscript, CBP Item 14; *Memoir*, chapter 3

Brainerd, May 16, 1820

My very Dear Brother,

I cannot express my feelings this evening, ~~especially~~ when I read your kind letter. My heart is full; but we know, dear brother, ₐthatₐ our ~~dear~~ Saviour will order all things right. I am very sorry to hear that you have lost your [~~illegible~~] ₐhorseₐ, and cannot go on any farther.[51] What will you do now? you can't go with out a horse: but let us not be troubled about these trifling things the Saviour will direct all things for our good and for his own glory. If it is best that you should go on, he will provide for you in some way.[52] Let us only my dear brother put our whole trust in God and be humble at the feet of Jesus. We can do nothing in our own selves; we are like little children if we look to our own strength, we would fall and destroy our own souls. It is impossible for me express how I felt the morning you left us. My heart was full; but I thought if I should never see you again in this [~~illegible~~][53] world, I would meet you in a better world where we shall never again be separated from each other Had not Christ died for us, to redeem our souls from everlasting pain, the Saviour had compassion on us to renew our hearts.

O how thankful we ought to be to God who has brought us from darkness into the light of the Gospel. But many of our dear people are yet deprived of this great privilege.

They know not the Saviour which we have found so precious[54] Yes our own dear parents are yet living without God and without any hope in the world.

O my dear brother David let us pray for them without ceasing. let us weep continually and ask God to give them a new heart for the sake of his son Jesus Christ. He will surely hear us if we ask in faith.

Now dear brother what I say I would talk with you all night[55]I could not tell you all I want to. I hope you will not forget me in your prayers, and you must remember your sister C will never forget you.

When you are far from this place your poor sister C will be praying for you. Good night Dear Brother till we meet again

Catherine Brown

To Jane Murray (Lansingburgh, New York)
Religious Intelligencer, Sept. 30, 1820

Talony, May 26, 1820.

Dear Sister in Christ,

It is not because I have forgotten you that I have not written before. I assure you, dear sister, your kind letter was very refreshing to my cold heart, and I hope was thankfully received. I trust my kind sister will pardon my not writing sooner. I have been so engaged in my studies that I hardly had time to write letters.

I am now with our beloved brother and sister Hall on a visit from Brainerd. If God willing I shall return in 2 or 3 weeks.

Surely, there must be something in that religion which causes us to love Christians—even those whom we have never seen. Well, if we are the disciples of Christ, let us be united in spirit, and be one in the Lord our Saviour. Dear friend, I am writing this to you just as I would talk to your dear sister Hall,[56] whom I hope is a dear sister in Christ. I love you, though I have never seen you. Sister Hall has often spoken of you, and told me that you love the Saviour Jesus Christ: therefore I rejoice to tell you that we are sisters in Christ. Yes, I hope God has received me and adopted me for his child. O, how great is the loving kindness of the Lord our God, who has brought me from darkness into the light of the gospel. I often think what my situation was a few years since; when I was ignorant about the Saviour, and knew nothing of his holy character; but was blind in sin. O, how kind the Lord has been to me, that I was not left to wander in darkness, and slight the world of God, as many others do. It was sovereign grace alone, that I was made to hear the voice of God, while many of my people are yet living without God, and without hope in the world. O that I may love God more and serve him better. O, how I love the dear Missionaries who have left their native country, and come so distant to bring the glad tidings of salvation to my perishing heathen land. I know you would rejoice to see the glorious and happy day, when this land and all the Nations shall know and praise our dear Redeemer. We have truly long been neglected by the Christian world; but why should I complain, our Lord sent his glorious word in due season. The harvest is great and the labourers but few; let us pray therefore that the Lord would send more labourers into this wilderness to reap the harvest.

Dear Sister, pray much for us, and do not forget to pray for me, that I may be entirely devoted to God, and not forget the profession that I have made. Sister Hall is quite feeble; though she is much better than she has been for some time past. She wishes to be remembered affectionately to you and to all her dear friends in the north. Brother Hall commenced a School here last week: he has now 25 scholars, and expecting some more soon. The people in this neighbourhood are very much engaged about learning, and many we hope are serious.

Dear Sister, let us pray without ceasing, especially for this School, that the Lord would bless them, and bring home many dear chosen ones. I would be glad to write you a long letter, if I had time, but I must conclude. Remember me at the throne of grace.

Catharine Brown.

To David Brown (Cornwall)

The Little Osage Captive, 151–53;[57] *Memoir*, chapter 4

Creek-Path, Aug. 12, 1820.

My dear Brother,

Your dear lines I received this evening, for which I thank you. I hope they will not be the last you will write me. O dear brother, how much it would rejoice my heart to see you this evening, and converse with you face to face! But our good Lord has separated us, perhaps never to see each other again in this world. I often think of the morning you left Brainerd. It was a solemn hour, and I trust it was a sweet season to our souls. We wept, and prayed, and sung together before our dear Saviour; and longed for that blessed day, when we should meet, to part no more. What is a short separation in this world? Nothing compared to an eternal separation! How thankful we ought to be then, my dear brother, that we have a hope to be saved through the blessed Lamb of God. Yes, I trust when our bodies shall die, our souls shall be raised above the sky, where we shall dwell together, in singing the praises of Him who bought us with his precious blood. I hope we shall meet our parents, and brothers, and sisters there. Since you left, the Lord has reached down his arm, to take sinners from darkness, into the marvellous light of the Gospel. Dear brother, let us praise and rejoice continually in the Lord, for his goodness to our dear people, in giving them hearts to love and praise his holy name. Surely the Lord is with us here. We feel his presence. Our dear father and mother are inquiring what they shall do to be saved. Mother says she is grieved to think her children are going to leave her behind. But she says she will pray as long as she lives, and that the Saviour will pardon her sins, that she may go with her children to heaven.

I hope you will write to our parents as often as you can. I sometimes think the Saviour has given them new hearts, especially our dear father. He appears quite changed.

Soon after you left Brainerd, I was called here to take charge of a school of females, about two miles from home.[58] I take great delight in teaching. The number of girls in school is twenty-eight. They are very good children, and learn fast. Sister Anna is assisting me in the school.[59] She rejoices with us to hear from you in this distant land.

O dear brother, I hope you will pray for me. Pray that I may do good to the immortal souls of my pupils. Sometimes the work appears too great for me, and I am almost discouraged. But I know, He that has called me to work in his vineyard, is able to keep me.

I could tell you a great many good things, if I had time. But I must stop, after asking your prayers for all your Creek-Path friends. I hope

when you return to your nation, you will find many Christians. Farewell, dear brother; may the Lord be with you, and prepare you for great usefulness in the world. This is the prayer of your sister
Catharine Brown.

To Moody and Isabella Hall
Manuscript, CBP Item 12; *Memoir*, chapter 4

Creekpath. Nov.—19—1820

My Dear brother & sister

This is the first opportunity I have taken to answer your kind letter which you wrote some time since. I thank you much for it and hope you will forgive me for not writing to you sooner. I [illegible] think of you every ∧day∧ and long to see you once more in this world, I often think of the happy moments we used to spend together while I was with you at Brainerd but those happy hours are past past never to return I hope we shall be prepared to meet in heaven if not in this world where we shall neve[r aga]in[60] be seperated. O my dear friends dont you sometimes long to see that glorious day when Christains shall be collected from all parts of the world to sing the praises of our dear redeemer. O what a happy day it will be for Christains and shall we be there too, some times I am afraid I shall never get to that happy place which God has prepared for the rightous my wicked heart is so prone to sin and grive the holy spirit of God. but I know the blood of Christ which was shed on calvary is sufficient to wash a way all my sins and prepare me for his eternal glory. I will therefore commit myself to him God and say here I give myself to the it is all that[61] I can do. O how good it is to lie low at the feet of Jesus and feel ourselves washed in his precious blood. we then have no reason to fear what the world can do to us but if the saviour had not dyed for us what hope could we have had for the world to come we should have been meserble forever. I think I have great reason to ∧be∧ thankful to God that I was permited to hear the joyful sound of the gospil while many of my dear people are yet ignorent and have never heard of the Saviour. My dear friends I cannot tell you how much I love you because you were willing to leave your native Land and your dear people to come in to this heathen world to instruct me and my people in the way of salvation, O may the Lord bless and reward you for your labor of love to the perishing souls. You must pe‸r‸haps have some triles and trubble to go through in this world as other Missionaries do but we ought to rejoice that we are worthy to labor for God. Our days will soon be past and if we are the children of God we shall soon be at rest in the bosom of our dear saviour.

I hope that God will bless you continuly especially that he will be with sister Hall, I have thought much of her lately and do long to see hear from her, I shall never forget how I felt when I was going to leave her she took hold of my hand in praytime and we wept together with our dear Saviour. I then thought if I should never [see her][62] in this world I shall meet her in heaven never more to part. I hope that you will but remember me at the throne of grace and when ever I pray for myself I shall all ways try to pray for you—

My [F][63] Father and Mother brothers and sisters, wish to be remembered affectionately to you. Do write often, I am all ways happy to hear from you.

I have not any pertecular news to tell you about this place, our brothers and sisters in the church are all well and sends [illegible][64] much love to you.

A few days since we received a long letter from brother David he was well when he wrote.

Also we received a few lines from his teacher he sais David makes good progress in learning.[65] H[66] he sais the agents of that school had agreed to receive cousion John Brown [will be received?][67] if he should be sent on.[68]

I hope you will write to cousin John.

I would be very glad to write you a long letter but I have not time now Tell sister Mary I will write to her soon.[69]

From your sister C Brown

MR. & MRS. HALL

To David Brown (Cornwall)

Religious Intelligencer, July 7, 1821; *Missionary Herald,* Aug. 1821; *Boston Recorder,* July 14, 1821; *Religious Remembrancer,* July 21, 1821; *Christian Repository,* July 28, 1821; *Memoir,* chapter 4

Creek Path, February 21, 1821.

My dear Brother,

I received your kind letter some time since, and it gave me great satisfaction to hear from you. I should have written to you before this time, but did not know how to send to Brainerd. I am truly happy to hear that you feel so well contented with your situation in school, and that you are well pleased with your dear instructor. Our dear parents are in good health. They have removed from the place where they lived before, and are now living with brother John.[70] I think they have truly passed from death unto life; they seem to be growing in grace and in the knowledge of Him who has redeemed their souls from hell. Indeed you cannot imagine how different they seem from what they did when you left us. All they desire now is to do the will of our dear Saviour. This work is the Lord's, and no doubt he will keep them and carry them safe through this sinful world, until he receives them to his heavenly kingdom. O, dear brother, truly the Lord has heard our prayers for the souls of our parents. We have great reason to rejoice. May we not say, not unto us, but to thy name be all the praise. You have doubtless heard that brother J. has joined the church.[71] Dear brother D. my heart is full while I am writing. How shall I express my gratitude to God for bringing him to a knowledge of the Saviour. He says sometimes he feels happy in praying to God, and feels willing that he should do with him as seemeth good in his sight.

My brother David, when we look back and see what the Lord has done for our family in the course of a few years, O let us call upon our souls and all that is within us to praise our God for his great blessings to us.

I sometimes long to see your face once more in this world, to converse and pray with you before our Saviour. I often think of the happy hours which we spent when we were at Brainerd, when we first tasted the sweetness of religion, and when we used to take each other's hand to walk and sing our favourite hymn,

"Come we that love the Lord."[72]

We then knew the happiness of saints, and felt that religion was not designed to make our pleasures less. But now our heavenly Father has separated us for a time in this world; I hope for his glory and for the good of perishing souls around us. We have much to do for our Saviour. As we hope we are children of the most high God, let us be good soldiers, and not be weary in well doing, for in due season we shall reap if we faint not.

Father and mother send love to you, and to the scholars in Cornwall. I hope you will write to us soon, and let us know how you do.

Adieu, dear Brother, till we meet again.

Catharine Brown.

To David Brown (Cornwall)
The Little Osage Captive, 154–56;[73] *Memoir*, chapter 4

Creek-Path, 1821.

My dear Brother,

Although we may be separated many hundreds of miles, the God of the Universe, whom we serve, will often give us the enjoyment Himself, which you know is of far greater value than all this world can afford. Last Sabbath was a very solemn and interesting day to us. Rev. Mr. W. from the state of New York was here—a very pious and engaged Christian. We were much refreshed by his kind instructions. I think it was truly a pleasant day to my soul. The sacrament was administered, and we were permitted once more to sit at the table of the Lord, and commemorate his dying love. Mr. S.[74] was baptised. Also an infant of Mrs. F, named Samuel Worcester. The congregation were attentive and some of them were affected to tears. I hope the time is not far distant, when all the heathen shall be brought to the knowledge of the Redeemer. We have recently formed a Female Society in this place.[75] The members pay fifty cents a year. I trust you will pray that we may be blessed, and that we may be instrumental in the great work of building up the cause of the Redeemer. I can never be sufficiently thankful to God for sending us Missionaries, to teach us the way we should go. We love them as our own brothers and sisters. That you may enjoy the light of our Saviour's countenance, while in this short journey of life, and finally be received to mansions of eternal glory, is the prayer of

   Your Sister,
   Catharine Brown.

To Flora Gold (Cornwall, Connecticut)

Manuscript, HLVC;[76] *Connecticut Journal*, date unknown; *Religious Intelligencer*, Sept. 22, 1821[77]

            Creek Path April 16, 1821
My Dear Sister

Most sincerely do I thank you for your affectionate letter, received some weeks since, I hope we are indeed of one family.[78] Your God is my God, and your Saviour is my Saviour. Although personally unacquainted, and far distant from each other, yet the faith which we profess ought to endear us to each other, and animate us to press forward that we may meet in the kingdom of our Redeemer. Let us then go on in the path of the Christian. It will soon lead us ∧to∧ the mansions of everlasting peace. Yes dear friend Eternity seems very near. A few more rolling years, months, weeks, or days, will land us on Cannans happy shore where we shall see our Saviour as he is, and be like him. I sometimes fear that I shall not be of that happy number, whom Christ shall sit on his right hand, but when I think of the eternal God, who came down to save sinners like me; with tears of joy and gratitude I leave myself in his precious arms, believing that his blood is sufficient to wash away all of my sins. O that I might walk close with God and serve him better every day, and be more interested for the success of the gospel in the world, especially in my own Nation. Methinks it is my greatest desire to do some good to my fellow creatures, while I remain in this body of clay; but what can I do without the Saviour help. I am weak as a child and can do nothing in my own strength. Pray my Sister that I may live above this vain world, and be more devoted to God. I feel thankful to God that he has sent so many good missionaries to this Heathen country to teach us the way of life. But what are these few missionaries, in this dark land a mong so many hundreds of immortals, who are yet unconverted My dear friend though you are at a great distance, you will surely remember these poor heathen at the throne of grace. You say that you sometimes think, ~~that~~ you should be willing to leave your native land to carry the glad tidings of salvation to the heathen. Should you ever be directed by the Providence of God to this western wilderness, you should be truly welcome to your red brethren and sisters. You can hardly imagine how ignorant we are, and how much we need more good missionaries to instruct us. I can not express how much I love and thank those who have come from a far distant land to labour for the welfare of my people, who have long been neglected. May they be made instruments of doing much good.

I rejoice to hear that the Lord is doing a great work in the churches of Christian lands and pray that he will continue to Pour out his Spirit till all are brought to the knowledge and experience of the truth as it is in Jesus. Perhaps you will rejoice to hear that a little church has gathered in Creek Path since the missionaries have been h[ere]. Seven have been baptized and four received as candidates for that holy ordinance. We hope several others are seriously inquiring what they shall do to be saved. The wo[rk] is the Lords, and to him be all the praise. Most of these dear converts are my relatives. My Parents, one brother, and [three?] sisters, I think, [~~illegible~~] give good evidence of piety. Mr. Butrick has left Creek Path, and Mr. and Mrs. Potter have taken his place.[79] I very much esteem them. Methinks they are devoted Christians. Mrs. P. has the care of the girls school. I expect to attend.[80] Our little number of females, have agreed to meet on the third monday of every month for prayer and religious conversation. Mrs. P. reads, and explains the bible. O how precious is the word of God. These meetings are very refreshing. May our Christian sisters in Cornwall meet at the same time that our united prayers may ascend together.

Please to inform brother David that our brother John, health is improving. The rest of the family are [well] [illegible] send our warmest love to him Tell him I re[ceived] his [letter][81] a few days since, which made us all ve[ry] happy. I intend writing to him soon. I hope he is making great progress in his studies, and will soon be prepared for usefulness in the world.

Do my sister write again soon, and often. Let us converse with each other by letters. May we at last meet in the kingdom of our blessed Saviour, and sing his praises throughout Eternity.

    Yours, in the bonds of the Gospel,

    Catharine Brown

MISS FLORA GOLD

To Mrs. A.H. (Philadelphia)

Religious Remembrancer, July 7, 1821; *Weekly Recorder,* July 25, 1821

Creek Path, June 2, 1821.

My dear Sister,

Though I have long delayed writing, I have not forgotten the kind letter with which you favoured me last fall. Having been engaged in my studies since I came here, I have not written as much as formerly. But what can be more improving than a correspondence with a disciple of Jesus. Surely I ought to consider it my greatest privilege, to converse with those whom I hope to meet in Heaven, and spend an eternity in their society.

How happy, my dear friend, are all those who walk in the fear of our Lord Jesus Christ. The ways of holiness are peace, and pleasantness. I think I never received such enjoyment as since I have hoped my heart is renewed by divine grace. I am sure that true happiness in this world can be found only in religion Numerous have been the tender mercies of God toward me poor sinful worm of the dust.

"Why was I made to hear his voice,
    And enter while there's room,
While thousands make a wretched choice
    And rather starve than come."[82]

O how thankful ought I to be, that I have not been cut off in the midst of my sins. When I reflect on my past life, before I was brought to see my sinful character, and the vanities of the world, my heart is full with gratitude, to God, that he has opened my eyes to see the corruption of my heart.

When I first entered the school at Brainerd, and saw Christians, I was not pleased with them: I thought they were entirely deprived of pleasure, and did not like to hear their converse on religious subjects, through fear I should lose my enjoyments, and that others would ridicule me. Now I feel quite different. I do not care for the scoffs of the wicked, if I can enjoy the presence of my Saviour and live to his glory. The Lord has been merciful in sending his Gospel to this heathen land, and I hope the time is not far distant when the Sun of Righteousness will shine on all those who are now sitting in darkness and in the shadow of death. It is now about one year since the glad news of salvation reached this place, and 7 souls have already been brought, as we hope, from nature's darkness into the light and liberty of the gospel. Many others appear to be earnestly enquiring the way to Heaven. A church consisting of 6 members has been established. One brother, and three sisters of mine, are communicants. My parents and another sister, I think give evidence of piety. Let us pray much, my sister, for the continuance of the Holy Spirit among this people. The Lord has promised that "if two of you shall agree on earth touching any thing, it shall be done for you of my Father who is in Heaven."[83] I have attended to your request, and hope our prayers have unitedly ascended together. I will now state to you that our little number of females meet on the third Monday of every month, for prayer and religious conversation. This is very refreshing to our souls. Pray with us at the same time, that the Lord would bless us for the sake of his Son Jesus Christ. Mr. Butrick, who had the care of this school for a time, has returned to Brainerd, and Mr. and Mrs. Potter have taken charge of it. They have lately come from the North, and expect to spend their days among the heathen. Mrs. P. has charge of the girls. I think the children here improve as fast as those at Brainerd. Some of them who have been in the school only one year, can now read in the Testament. I shall probably attend the school until I complete my education.

Dear Sister, I hope you will write again soon. Pardon me for not answering your letter before, and I will in future try to be more punctual. Mr. and Mrs. P. join with me in respects and christian love.

Your affectionate sister in Christ,
C. Brown.

MRS. A_H_.

To David Brown (Cornwall)

Guardian, or Youth's Religious Instructor, Oct. 1821[84]

Creek Path, Cherokee Nation, June 4, 1821.

Dear Brother David,

With pleasure I spend a few moments in answering your kind letter, which came to hand April 30. I assure you it gave me much pleasure to hear from you. It seemed almost like seeing you. I frequently read your letter, and think of you, and try to ask God to be with you, and bless you. How much more would it rejoice my heart to see and converse with you, face to face. I hope to see you again in this sinful world; but God only knows, whether we shall ever meet here again or not. Methinks I can say from the heart, the will of the Lord be done; though I have spent many solitary hours thinking of you since you left home. Though our bodies of clay are separated for a season, still our hearts must be forever united. And oh! may the love

that God has given us, which is stronger than death, continue to
dwell in us, till it is perfected in glory. Then, dear brother, let us dry
up our tears, and be resigned to the will of God; knowing that all
things shall work together for good to those that love Him. O! how
inexpressibly kind has our Heavenly Father been to you and me, in
permitting us to taste the joys of true religion! When we look back to
the time, when we were strangers to the commands of the living
God, with how much astonishment should our minds be filled, that
God has had compassion on us! Had not his sovereign mercy
snatched us as brands from the burning, we might have been now
lifting up our eyes in torment, and with the rich man pleading for
one drop of water to cool our parched tongues. O! let us call upon
our souls and all that is within us, to bless the Lord for his
distinguishing mercies. Let us be faithful unto death, and soon we
shall receive a crown of life. Yes, my brother, I hope we shall at length
arrive at the right hand of God, our distant home; where we shall
drink full draughts of those pleasures that ever flow. Then all our
works will be over. O! when we consider that our lives will soon be
closed by death, and that our bodies will then moulder in the dust,
we ought surely to be humble, and improve our precious time in the
service of God. I hope you live near the Saviour, and enjoy the light
of his countenance. Have you not often felt, while pouring out your
soul before God, a desire to go to any part of the Heathen world, to
teach those who are yet destitute of the Gospel, the way of life? And
do you, my dear brother, pray and weep for those Heathen, your
distant friends, who have no one to tell them of their awful situation,
and lead them to our blessed Saviour, who is able to save them from
eternal death?

I look forward, with pleasure, to the time when you will be
prepared to return to this nation, and preach Christ to those who are
still ignorant of his great salvation. Be faithful, my dear brother, and
pray without ceasing for our dear people, and for christians who are
labouring for the welfare of our nation, and especially for the
Missionaries among us, that they may be the means of bringing
many souls to God. I hope the time is not far distant, when the glad

news of salvation will be spread through the world, and when stately churches will be every where erected, for the only living and true God. Then let us be engaged, in some corner of the world, to instruct the ignorant, and plead with them to turn to God. Let us work while the day lasts, for the time will come, when we cannot plead with sinners, to flee from the wrath to come. Yes, now is the time to do good, and now is our salvation nearer than when we first believed.

I would write you more frequently, my dear brother, had I time; and also write to your companions in school. Tell them their friend and sister Catharine thinks of, and prays for them. Ask them to pray for the Mission, and church at this place, that we may not faint.

You will expect to hear the particulars concerning Creek Path. Dear Father and Mother are well as usual, and, in a religious view, appear as well as ever. Sometimes I can have no doubt, that they are the Lord's sincere friends. I expect they will be baptized soon. Brother John appears to grow brighter in religion. His health is much better than when I wrote last. He has thought some of visiting you, as he finds riding beneficial; but I think it doubtful whether he will ev take so long a journey. Our sisters, Susannah, and Susan,[85] are well, and appear to be growing in grace, and in the knowledge of God. All the members of the church seem now more engaged, than for some months past. I hope the Lord is about to pour out his Spirit upon us. Mr. S———, and a man by the name of Sa-wa-kee, with his wife, we think are earnestly enquiring the way to eternal life, and hope they will at last be found among the followers of Jesus. Mrs. B. is very thoughtful. You had heard that Mr. R. F. was serious. I am sorry to say, that I fear he has been led astray by some wicked people. He does not attend meeting much, and sometimes goes to the landing, on the Sabbath, to transact business. Our Saviour has said, "by their fruits shall ye know them."[86] But we must pray that he may be brought to a true repentance of his sins, and may choose God for his friend and portion. To-day, being the first monday in the month, the people met in the school-house for prayer. The assembly was small, but serious, and solemn. I thought much of you, and wished you were present; but I know you recollected us at the throne of grace.

I am now boarding with Mr. and Mrs. Potter, and spend my time very pleasantly. They are agreeable, and I think devoted Missionaries. I love them dearly, and hope they will be a means of great good to our people. My leisure hours I spend in reading. Have lately been much interested in reading the "Guardian for youth." of which I have received ten numbers, as a present, from Mr. Dodge of New-Haven. I intend to read, next, the Memoirs of Mrs. Issabella Graham.[87]

I am glad to learn that you have meetings on Sabbath evenings, and especially that you pray and converse in your own language Our Father's family have, for some time past, held prayer meetings, on the same evening. Thus you see, (though we know it not) our prayers have ascended, at the same time, and in the same language.

Do, my brother, write often, and let us know how you proceed in your studies, and in the service of Christ. We are always happy to hear from you. When I read your last kind letter, our parents wept for joy.

Father, mother, brother, sisters, uncle P———, and brother and sister Potter, send love. May the Lord bless you, and grant you the consolation of his Spirit, is the earnest prayer of your affectionate sister,

Catharine Brown.

MR. DAVID BROWN

To Unknown

Religious Remembrancer, Oct. 13, 1821; *Religious Intelligencer*, Oct. 20, 1821; *Boston Recorder*, Oct. 20, 1821

Creek Path, Cherokee Nation, August 10th, 1821.

Dear Brother,

Your kind letter of May 4th gave me much pleasure. And I thank you for it. You have also my thanks for reminding brother David to write. [That of May-fourth was a joint letter.][88] I think since he has been at Cornwall he has made considerable progress in his studies. I trust God will give him wisdom and prepare him to preach Christ to the heathen. I am now with my parents, a short distance from the local school in this place. I usually reside in the family of Mr. Potter, (now teacher of the school) and having been recently engaged in my studies, have neglected some of my correspondents. I am very happy at home since my friends have embraced religion. It is truly pleasant for brothers and sisters to live in the fear of God. When their hearts are united in the love of Christ, it is like a little heaven below. O that such streams of pleasure may continue with us while on earth, and may we be finally admitted to the mansions above, where is peace forever. One of my brothers is in a very low state of health.[89] His disorder is apparently a consumption. I fear he will not recover. It would indeed be a trial to lose this dear brother: but why should I complain? I ought rather to say, "The Lord's will be done. His ways are not as our ways, nor his thoughts as our thoughts."[90] Methinks I can truly rejoice that the Lord of Zion reigneth, and will dispose of mortals as seemeth good in his sight. This summer has been remarkably warm in this country, and very unhealthy, especially to those who live near the Tennessee river. Several of our neighbours have died this season, but I cannot say they leave the world with joy and peace. The religion of Christ, which is the most important thing, is yet needed in this heathen country. There are but few who can say, "By grace are we saved."[91] Most of the people are ignorant and unwilling to come and acknowledge him who came to seek and to save that which was lost. O that sinners may come to the foot of the cross, and make their peace with God, before death overtakes them. I think sometimes, if Christians here were more faithful to God, they would see his work prospering, and many enquiring what they must do to be saved. But the work is the Lord's and he will carry it on in his own way and time. I hope you pray that we may have a revival in this place. The present number of pupils in this school is forty, though only about twenty-five constantly attend. Mr. P. has ten in his family:[92] one of these is a Creek girl, an orphan. Her parents were killed in the Creek war,[93] and she was taken prisoner. She has since resided in the family of a Mr. T. of Huntsville, Alabama, where she has been treated with great kindness. Mr. T. has lately met with some temporal misfortunes, but still engages to aid in her support, as far as his circumstances will permit. The name of the child is Mary Stewart; she is about 12 years old, a very amiable girl. I do hope this dear child has been sent to the Missionaries, by a kind providence, for the good of her own soul, and the souls of others. I have this day returned to the habitation of the dear Missionaries, and rejoice once more to be in their society. Mrs. P. is an excellent woman. I hope to receive many useful instructions, while I live in the family. I can write no more at present, as I must get a lesson in my geography. Remember me, dear sir, at the Throne of Grace. Pray that I may abide daily at the feet of Jesus.

    Your's respectfully,
    Catharine Brown.

To Isabella Hall (Taloney Mission)
Manuscript, CBP Item 10[94]

Brainerd Oct. 16 1821

My Dear beloved sister.

    [illegible][95] You have been much in my mind of late and do sincerely thank our Heavenly Father in permiting me to behold my Christian friends once more on this Earth it is ∧seems∧ good to see brother H. my instructer whom I have long been wishing to see but how much more it would rejoice my heart ∧to∧ see you once more in this world When I left home I thought I should ∧perhaps∧ have the peasure of seeing you at Brainerd but since it is not the will ∧of∧ our Saviour to see ∧you∧ at this time I hope I shall yet some day be permitted to make you a long visit at Taloney Last Sabbath was very solemn and interesting day to us in meeting round the table ∧of∧ our bless Saviour. I wish you could have been with us, but I hope your heart with us if not in [d][96] body. How astonishing to my heart when I condid∧sid∧er what God has done for me us creatures in the lowest ranks of his rational beings a poor worms of the dust should should be permitted to approach at his table and pertake of the dying love of the son of God O that we may [become?] feel more sesible of our great previleges and d[97]lie low at the feet of Jesus. dear sister, may you ever be clothed with humility in every situation of life and rejoice in Christ Jesus our Lord I persume dear Sister you have had many trying and painful hours[98] since you have been at taloney of which I sometimes ∧weep∧ for you before our Saviour and ∧at∧ the same time rejoice the Saviour makes me rejoice that you ∧are∧ counted worthy to [illegible][99] suffer for his sake perhaps you may do more good by your daily prays for the heath[en] round you than any other way may you have the Satisfaction [of][100] seeing many sinners coming to the knowledg of Christ by your instrumentality Let us remember that all our sufferings here below will only make us richer there when we get home arive at home to our Heavenly Fathers house. I hope to meet ∧you∧ there if not in this world where tears shall be wiped from our eyes and where we shall see our Saviour as he is and be like him I ∧hope we∧ shall pray ∧be∧ constantly in pray for each other till ∧we∧ meet again that we may e∧n∧joy the light of our Saviours countenance and be happy the short time we live in this world. He is our friend who will never forsake us one smile[s?][101] from Heaven is [bett][102] worth far more better than all the pleasures of this vain and sinful world. I hope you will allways remember I am your sister and will never forget ∧you∧ as long as I love the Saviour though we are seperated for a time in our bodies of clay I believe the tie which bind our hearts in Christian love shall never be broken. I would gladly write more if I had time but I hope you will jest look [of][103] over these few lines from your unworthy sister who love you and pray for you every day. I hope to write to ∧you∧ again soon. I expect to return home next week with my dear Mother brother and sister Potter. I reside in the family of brother P. a short distant from my parents and attends their school they our dear brother and sister I love them dearly Sister ∧P.∧, will write to you. I wish you could see her I think you would love her for she is jest like you. and that makes me love her. my tenderest love to dear little Jennet[104] and a kiss from her aunt Catharine. Please to write to me when it is convient convenient.

    Yours affectionately C. Brown

To David Brown (Cornwall)

Religious Intelligencer, Apr. 20, 1822; *Christian Secretary,* Apr. 27, 1822; *Boston Recorder,* Apr. 27, 1822[105]

Creek Path, Cherokee Nation, Feb. 16, 1882.[106]

My dear brother,

As Mr. Ross[107] has lately arrived from Brainerd, and will probably return in a few days, I improve this favourable opportunity of writing a few lines to you. Are you still living as a stranger and pilgrim in the earth?[108] Is the Saviour near your heart, and the object of your chief delight and conversation? I trust that you will continually possess and imitate that meek and lowly spirit, which Jesus possessed in the days of his flesh. I should like to converse with you all day. When I consider the distance we are separated, my ever dear brother, I weep. But the Lord is a present help in every time of trouble. I think I never have desired so much to see you, as I have these several days past. Happy should I be, could I but see you this moment, and relate to you our late trials and affliction, which we have received from our kind heavenly Father. I hope you will lean on the Saviour, who is able to give the consolation which you need, and recollect we are in the hands of an infinitely wise and good Being, who will order ever thing for his glory, and the best good of his children. Since we are the children of a glorious and holy God, may we be submissive to all the dispensations of his Providence, not only in prosperity, but also in adversity, and say, The will of the Lord be done.

I can scarcely compose my mind to write; but you will easily imagine our situation at present, and what I would say, if you were now here. You have recently received the account of brother John's affliction with a consumption. And, no doubt, you have often thought of him, and hoped to see him again, when you return. But the Lord has ordered otherwise. He has taken him to Himself. Yes, our beloved brother is no more! He is dead! Distressing news to you, I know, my brother, and to us. Come, then, let us weep together; and while we mourn for our absent brother, let us remember Jesus Christ, who, we trust, has sanctified his heart, and brought him to love God in sincerity. O! let us bless God, that we do not weep for him who lived and died without hope. It is now two weeks since he departed this life to eternity.[109] It is indeed the most painful event that ever has taken place in this family. I think, I feel for our dear father and mother. They mourn much for him. I do not wonder; for he was their only son who was here, and on whom they depended for every comfort of life, and support in their declining days. Do not forget to pray for them, particularly that the Spirit of God may dwell richly in their hearts, and support them in this short journey of life. They appear more like Christians than before. Father said, brother John was not ours, but the Lord's, and he had a right to take him whenever he pleased. He appears to pray more fervently, and takes a greater delight in attending family duties, morning and evening. But I must hasten to give you a more particular account of our departed brother. . . .[110]

Though he suffered great pain, not one word of complaint was heard from him, during the whole of his sickness. He appeared reconciled to the will of God, and said the Saviour suffered more than he did. He said he was perfectly willing to be in the hands of God, and to be disposed of in such a way as seemed Him good. He said he was not afraid to die. About one week before his death, he tried to talk to the family, but being very weak, was not able to say much. Though he spoke but few words, it was truly affecting, and I trust will never be forgotten by us. May we remember his words, and imitate his holy walk. He said—It is now more than a year since we began to follow Christ, and what have we done for him since that time? Do we live like Christians? I fear we are too much engaged about worldly things. When the people come to see you, I do not hear you tell them about the Saviour: and ask them their feelings with respect to another world. We are professors of religion, and why do we not show it to others? He added particularly, you should remember to keep the Lord's day. You are too much engaged in the kitchen on the Sabbath day. You should keep the blacks from work, and take them with you to meeting: when you return, keep them still in the house, and not let them play any on this day.[111] He looked earnestly toward me, and asked if the missionaries cooked on the Sabbath? I told him, they generally made preparations on Saturday. He said, that is what you ought to do. He used frequently to ask me to pray with him, and read and explain the Bible, which I did with great pleasure. For three or four days before he died, he was deranged. When he had his reason, he appeared very pleasant, would smile, &c. The night before he died, he spoke your name frequently.

Sabbath morning, the day that he died, being told it was Sabbath, he requested us to sing and pray with him, which we did. Immediately after this he fell into a state of insensibility, in which he continued till about 5 o'clock, when his spirit ascended to his heavenly home. On Monday, P. M. February 4th, we followed his remains to the cold and silent grave, and bid him a long farewell. It was hard to part with him; but a great consolation, that we shall soon meet in the kingdom of Christ, never more to part. His Christian life was short; but long enough to prove, that Christ's religion was not in vain. I often remember, he was always ready to instruct and guide the dear heathen to the cross of Christ. I remember those affectionate eyes so often bathed in tears for his poor countrymen. But he has gone before us, and will no longer weep for us, and the dear Cherokees in darkness. His lips are silent in the grave. His prayers are not heard on earth. Here I stop—my heart bleeds. O! may we follow his example, as far as he followed Christ, and live devoted to God; be in constant readiness for our own departure, that we may at last meet our brother around the throne of that blessed Redeemer, who has brought us from death unto life eternal. I hope you will not think we are unhappy, or that we wish you to return. Father and mother are willing you should stay as long as you think best. Write to them often. May God bless you, and make you an instrument of great good to your countrymen, is the prayer of your truly affectionate sister,

Catharine Brown.

To Alexander Campbell (Huntsville, Alabama)

Manuscript, CBP Item 9, in Alexander Campbell's hand[112]

Creek path March 16th. 1822

Respected Sir

Your kind letter was handed me day before yesterday by Mr. Little. I have only time to write a few lines as he expects to leave us in the morning. I thank the Lord for his goodness in sending his dear children here to visit the school, and encourage our hearts. My heart ought to glow with gratitude to my Heavenly Father for the many mercies that I have received from him, but oh how unthankful am I to him, that even since I have professed to love the Lord Jesus Christ often have I been led away into the world and grieved the Spirit of a holy God. But oh may I put my trust in him who is able & willing to pardon all my sins and make a true child of his. How vain this world appears in my eyes. It is nothing but vanity sin & gloom. Sweet is the thought of soon beholding the face of our Redeemer who once groan∧e∧d upon the cross for sinners like me. How happy shall we feel, my dear Friend, when we arrive at the shores of immortal felicity to reign with Christ through never ending eternity.

I rejoice to inform you that little Nelly is much better, indeed she is most well. her mother wishes me to thank you for your visit and said she hope to have the pleasure of seeing you again in Creek path with Mrs. Campbell I thank you for your kind invitation to visit you. I fear it would give you too much trouble to send for me, and the time for staying with you would be short. Should you however send I shall be happy to go and spend a few days with you, and return with Mr. P. from B.

Please sir accept my thanks for the Geography and Atlas: I received them as a token of love and hope they will be of great benefit to me

In haste I remain very respectfully
Yours
C. Brown

DR. A. CAMPBELL

To Matilda Williams (Eliot Mission)
Pittsburgh Recorder, Mar. 27, 1827[113]

Creek Path, May, [1822].

My Dear Sister W—Most sincerely do I thank you for your kind
epistle handed me a few days since by our beloved brother Mr.
Kingsbury, whom I rejoice to behold once more in the flesh, and
converse with him on the love of our precious Redeemer. He is now
gone to Brainerd—expects to return this way shortly—will probably
spend a few days with us.[114] I did not expect ever to see him in this
lower world.

The Providence of God is truly kind to those who serve him. May
his visit to Brainerd and Creek Path be a great benefit to his brothers,
and sisters. I love him most dearly, because he has been the means of
doing much good in my Nation. O may the Lord go with him
through this short journey of life, to bless his labours to many
immortal souls[!][115] O my dear sister, should I be permitted to see
you and brother W. once more in this world, I should be almost too
happy.

Your letter was truly refreshing to my cold spirit. What a great
privilege that we are permitted to converse with one another by
writing, when we cannot see each other's faces. You have doubtless
heard what the Lord has done for the people in Creek Path. In the
course of a few years many wandering souls have been brought to the
knowledge of the truth as it is in Jesus. The Lord has remembered my
poor people; blessed be his holy name. What shall I render to him for
his unspeakable mercies to me and my people, in granting us the
hope of everlasting salvation through a Redeemer. Most of my
father's family, I trust, have [tr]uly chosen that good part which shall
never be taken from them. They are now rejoicing in the hope of
eternal glory.

The number of those who belong to this church is about nine, who,
I hope, have passed from death unto life; some of them appear to be
growing brighter every day in the God of love which they have
found. O how thankful ought I to be to God that the news of

Salvation has ever reached this dark land. May we pray more and more earnestly that the Lord might carry on the glorious work which he has commenced, until all the nations of the earth shall become acquainted with the only living and true God. May you, dear sister, persevere in the good work of your Lord and Master in, which you are called. Though you may have many painful trials to go thro' in a Missionary life, you will receive a crown of reward for your labours[;] yes, an unfading crown of immortal glory.

After a life of toil and sufferings, it will be enough to [hear] those sweet words, *Come, thou good and faithful servant, enter thou into the joy of thy Lord.*[116] Sometimes I feel willing to suffer almost anything, to give up any earthly pleasure, if I could be the means of saving one immortal soul from everlasting death. I weep when I consider how many of my fellow creatures are yet perishing for lack of knowledge, while I am enjoying the light of my Heavenly Father's countenance. And yet how little do I feel for their wretched state, while they are running into eternal burning before my eyes[!] I know not how others feel, but O my wretched heart[!] how stubborn, how unfeeling; and stupid it is[!] Remember me, dear sister, at the throne of grace. Pray that I may be awakened, and be more engaged in the cause of my blessed Redeemer. I am unworthy of your prayers.

The local school here is but a short distance from my father's where I usually reside when I am attending school. I have not attended constantly since last fall, being, most of the time, confined at home with my dear brother, who has died with the consumption. He had been sick a great while, and suffered much. But the Saviour was with him to comfort & bless him, even in the hour of death. I weep for the loss of my brother. We know that this is a painful providence, but the Saviour says, *"Be of good cheer." "All things shall work together for good to those who love God."*[117] I shall see my brother's face no more in this world. His soul is gone to God. It is a great consolation to think that he is now happy in Heaven with his dear Saviour, on whom he depended for salvation. O may this teach me to know that I too must soon die[;] and may I be in constant preparation for my own departure, that I may meet him in the kingdom of Heaven.

We received a letter from Brother David a few days since, stating that some of the students in Cornwall expect to go on a mission next Fall to Owyhee, to carry the glad news of salvation to the [heathen?].[118] David has a great desire to devote his service [in the great] cause of his Creator. I hope God will prepare him for usefulness in the world.

I think the school in Cornwall must be very interesting, where are so many [illegible] from different parts of the globe to learn about Christ, and receive instruction. We have reason [to hope that many] will return home to be a great blessing to their nations. We ought to rejoice that the latter day of Millennial glory is just approaching, when a nation shall be born in a day, and when all shall know the Lord from the least to the greatest. We know that it is not for *our* [sakes] that he is doing this; [but for] his name's sake—and that he should be [glorified] [illegible], in all his works and ways.

I am very glad to hear that you have commenced another school in the Choctaw nation[119]—hope you enjoy much of your Saviour's presence, while you proclaim his name to others.

Be not discouraged; but persevere in well doing. The God, for whom you labour, I hope, will set up his banners at Bethel, and many of our [dear] Choctaw brothers and sisters will become the followers of our Saviour Jesus Christ.

It is possible I may visit you, next vacation, with brother and sister Potter. But I dare not promise. Perhaps it will not be convenient for us to go so far. The Lord [knows] best. Give my warmest love to brother [illegible] [thank him] for the present he sent me—have not [forgotten] him and his kind advice so soon. O how can [illegible] my former Instructor, and one who has [been] the means of bringing me to a knowledge of Christ? How is my [little] favourite S. and her little brother? I should like to see them very much. Do kiss them, for their aunt Caty. Remember me to all the Choctaw children in your school. I hope they will soon become Christians.

I must say farewell, dear sister: may our prayers ever mingle together for each other, and, O may we never forget the perishing souls around us[!]

Do write often as you can consistently; and may the God of all grace be with you forever[!]

> From your affectionate sister
> in Christ Jesus,
> Catharine Brown.

To Moody and Isabella Hall (Taloney Mission)
Manuscript, CBP Item 8;[120] *Memoir*, chapter 4

Creek Path June 1. 1822.

My dear Brother and Sister Hall.

I know not what you think of me for not writing to you before this time. It is not because I have forgotten you that I have not written before. You are still in my rememborence, and will ever be; while I live. Though separated from each other, I [illegible] trust the tie that binds us in Christian love, will grow stronger, and stronger, until we shall be completely perfect in Heavenly glory.

How sweet, and reviving is the thought, that we are not to continue long in this vain, and wicked world; that this is not our a biding place but we are traveling to a never-ending Eternity, where we hope soon to rest in the city of our God, and join in the holy throng in praising him who was slain for us.[121] But oh! the dreadful thought for those who have not an interest in the Lord Jesus. No hope for the world to come! They travel on as though they were blind, and asleep until their souls are forever lost in Hell!

My dear brother and sister may you do much for the cause of Christ, and be instrumental of bringing many souls to happiness. Be patient in all your trials and hardships, remembering that you are labouring for God, and not for man a lone. The Saviour will give you an unfading crown of glory in due season. I often think of the glorious day, when I shall meet you and all the good Missionaries, in the Kingdom of our Saviour, never more to part. I shall then be always with those dear friends who have told me so much about a Heaven, and taught me to love and serve Christ. I hope you will not forget to pray for me that I may possess more of the spirit of Christ. I try ∧to∧ pray for you every day.—

The ∧school∧ here is very small; only about 15. scholars attend constantly and 10. of these beside myself, board in Brother Pothers family. The pupils in general make good improvement. The prospect of religion is encouraging. Meetings of the Sabbath, and weekly conferences are well attended. The church appears well. Last Sabbath I for the first time met my Parents at the table of our Lord.[122]

I have many things to tell you, but my health, will not allow me to write much at one time, from what little I have now written, I begin to feel a pain in my side, My health has been feeble for some weeks past, but my complaints are not very alarming.

I shall try to visit you next vacation, if life is spared. Will my dear brother and sister write soon,

   To their affectionate—
   Catharine

MR. AND MRS. MOODY HALL

[Upper margin of the reverse side of the page] P.S. Brother and sister Potter desire to be affactionately remembered to you, and Mr. and Mrs. Parker.[123]

To David Brown (Cornwall)

Memoir, chapter 4

Huntsville, Aug. 30, 1822.

My dear Brother,

I am sorry to tell you, that I have but a few moments of time to write this evening. I came here the 13th inst.[124] and expect to return in a few weeks.

I left our friends all very well, and walking in the fear of God. I should have written long before this, had I not been sick; but my health is now much better than it was when I left home. Brother David, remember that your sister Catharine loves you much, and prays for you every day. I trust you will not return before you are prepared to preach the Gospel. Let me know your feelings in this respect when you write again, and I shall know how to pray for you. I do not expect you to go through all the studies, that ministers generally do in New England, but wish you to be qualified enough to withstand the enemies of God, and teach the truths of Christianity.[125] If your health does not permit you to study, and your hesitation of speech still continues, I should not think it was your duty to pursue your studies.

However, I know the Lord will make every path of duty plain before you. Do not think we are unhappy. It is true we were greatly tried, last winter, in losing our dear brother. But, blessed be God, it was not more than we are able to bear.

We feel it was good for us to be afflicted, knowing that the Lord is good, and will always do what is right. I have not time to write all I wish to send you. When I return home, you shall have a long letter from your affectionate sister

    Catharine.

To David Brown (Andover, Massachusetts)

Memoir, chapter 4

Creek-Path, Jan. 18, 1823.

My dear Brother,

Yours of Nov. 2, 1822, was received a few days since. I am much gratified to hear, that you are to continue in New England another year. I hope you will be the better qualified for usefulness to our countrymen, when you return. I pray for you daily, that God may be with you and bless you in your undertaking.

I feel anxious to see you, yet I am willing to have you stay until you have received further education. How has your mind been exercised since you entered the interesting Seminary at Andover?[126] Are you living in the enjoyment of the religion of Christ? We must, dear brother, live near to God, and be engaged in his cause, if we would be his followers. Let us, then, not calculate to live in idleness and ease, unconcerned for the salvation of souls.

We are under great obligations to honour God before the world, and to be active in his service. Let us not hide our talents in the earth, for the Lord will require them of us. There is a crown of glory laid up for those who are faithful unto the end.

It is now eleven months, since our dear brother John departed from this lower world, and entered the unseen regions of eternity, where I hope he is now walking in the streets of the New Jerusalem, filled with holy love. Oh boundless love, and matchless grace, of our Lord and Saviour Jesus Christ! How happy shall we feel when we land on the shores of eternal felicity. There we shall meet our dear brother, and all who have gone before us, and shall reign in the paradise of God forever and ever.

I often think of our relations in the Arkansas. I long to hear of their conversion. Let us not neglect to pray for them daily; particularly, for brother W.[127] The Lord, I hope, will renew his heart, and make him abundantly useful to the cause of missions.

We rejoice to see brother A.[128] once more in our dwellings. After a long journey from the Arkansas country, he arrived here, much fatigued, in the latter part of November. He intends to spend a few months with us, and then return with sister Susan. I do not feel very well about her going into the wilderness, and far from Christian society, where she will perhaps have no religious instruction.

Her mother has removed thirty or forty miles from the missionary station [at Dwight.][129] But we commend her into the hands of the Almighty, who is able to keep her from evil, and from all the temptations of this delusive world. I am glad to hear from our relations in that country. Brother Walter was expecting to set out in a few days for the city of Washington, and had thoughts of visiting some of the northern States before he returned. It is likely you may see him in New England. He has placed brother Edmund[130] in the missionary school at Dwight, to continue three or four years. He has become very steady and attentive to his books. I hope the Lord will give him a new heart, and prepare him for usefulness.

Brother W. has given up trading, and has commenced farming. He has purchased land in the Osage country, at the Salt Springs. Whether he intends removing his family to that place, I know not. It is my prayer, that he may be brought to bow to the sceptre of King Jesus, in whom is life everlasting. As for our going to the Arkansas, it is not decided. Perhaps we shall know better, when you return. You know mother is always very anxious to remove to that country, but father is not. For my own part, I feel willing to do whatever is duty, and the will of our parents. I feel willing to go, or stay. The Lord will direct all things right, and in him may we put all our trust.

We had the pleasure of seeing your schoolmates McKee and Israel Folsom.[131] They called on us on their way to the Choctaw nation. They said there were many good people at the north. They had rather live among the Yankees, than any other people. I hope they will be very useful to their nation.

Mr. Potter has gone to Brainerd on some business, and I shall stay with Mrs. P. until he returns. We expect him home this week. I hope he will bring a large packet of letters from our Brainerd friends. Mrs. P. is engaged in teaching school while her husband is absent. Several of the scholars are very attentive, and make good progress in their studies. Sarah is in the first class. She is a good girl to learn, and is much beloved by her teacher. She has begun to read the Bible in course, and has read partly through the Memoirs of Miss Caroline Smelt.[132] When I wrote to you last, I was in a declining state of health, and for that reason I left my studies to have more exercise. The Lord has been pleased to restore me to my usual health, and I now feel pretty well.

I spent two months in Huntsville, last spring, in the family of Dr. Campbell. Mrs.————is a very pious and engaged Christian. I became acquainted with several pious families in Huntsville, who, I believe, feel interested in the cause of missions. The pious ladies made up clothing for the children in Creek-Path. We hope this is only the beginning of a missionary spirit in that place.

I am glad to tell you, that our female Society is growing in its numbers. We have collected nearly double the sum this year that we did last. The Society has concluded to send our money for this year to the Arkansas mission.

I am glad the people are so willing to assist in advancing the Redeemer's kingdom in our heathen land. May the glorious period soon arrive, when all the nations of the earth shall be brought to the knowledge of the truth as it is in Jesus. Oh, dear brother, though we are widely separated in person, yet we are near in spirit, and can unite our prayers for the approach of this happy day.

O let us do with our might what our hands find to do. I am now in my little study. I have spent in this room many happy hours in prayer to my Heavenly Father. But Oh, how cold and stupid my heart is! How little I feel for the salvation of souls!

Oh, for a closer walk with God,
A calm and heavenly frame;
And light to shine upon the road,
That leads me to the Lamb.[133]

Please to write soon, and tell me every thing respecting your present situation.
Catharine Brown.

To Flora Gold (Cornwall)
Manuscript, HLVC[134]

Creek Path Jan. 26. 1823

I hope my dear Sister, you will pardon my negligence in not answering your most affectionate letters, received some weeks since. It is not through forgetfulness, or want of affection that I have not written to you of late. Let me assure you, my dear Sister, that I take a deep interest in reading your letters, and nothing but want of time has prevented my writing to you oftener. I was very interested with an interview of our Christian friends, Mr. Bascoine and Mr. Gibbs called on us on their way to the Choctaw Nation.[135] They left us early this morning to pursue their journey. It is plesent to meet with Christians in this world, even those, whom we have never before seen—what will it be when ~~Christia~~ Christians, from different parts of the globe, shall meet in Heaven, where sin and sorrow is unknown. Oh what a happy day will that be to those who are the true friends of Christ. I have thought a great deal of the Missionaries, who have left their native land and all their dear friends, for the sake of Christ and his cause, they will undoubtedly be fully rewarded at that day, when they shall see many heathens who have been brought, by their instrumentally to the knowledge of Christ, on the right hand of God. Oh there is a crown of immortal glory laid up for those who are faithful unto death. Let us then be faithful in whatever place we are to glorify, love, and put our constant dependence upon him, who has given us eternal life. We have much to do, or ought to do for our Saviour. I have had many precious seasons with my Christian Sisters of late, praising and adoring that dear Saviour who has transported us, as we hope, from the power of darkness into the glorious liberty of the children of God, Last monday I had the satisfaction of meeting with our female society at Mr. Ross. I think we had a pleasant time; a larg number were present; and all seemed to be of one mind, and appeared very anxious to come on the Lords side, to contribute some thing for the spread of the glorious gospel a mong the heathen. Our contributions amounted only 12. dollars. The society agreed to send the money to the Arkansaw Mission. I hop and pray that our mite may be accepted of God who has put it in to the [illegible] a few females to give their mite to the support of his good cause, I feel it a great privilege to be allowed to assist in building up the Redeemers kingdom, in our heathen part of the world. When I consider how many millions of our fellow mortals are yet without the light of the Gospel, and are perishing every day for want of knowledge; my heart burns with in me, and I am ready to cry out, Lord why is it that Christians are no more engaged to promote thy caus I know not how it is with others, but I am astonished at myself how [so] unfaithfully I live, while I see every day, those around me standing on the brink of everlasting despair. The souls of men are worth incomparably more than such a world as this, Let us my dear Sister, remember that our days will soon be ended. Our road in which we ar journeying towards eternity, will soon come to a close, oh that we might love[136] [illegible] Christ, and that all our time and talents might be spent to his glory. I have just received a letter from brother David, I am glad he has gone to Andover. I hope will be better prepared to to do good when he returns home.

I should be very h[appy] to receive another letter from you. [illegible] the Lord Jesus Christ dwell in your [illegible] continually, and make you useful a[s] long as you live in the world,[137]

From your affectionate sister

Catharine Brown

MISS FLORA GOLD.

P.S. Brother and Sister Potter send their respects to you.[138]

To David Brown (Andover)

Memoir, chapter 4

Brainerd, Feb. 10, 1823.

My dear brother David,

I am at Brainerd, on a visit from Creek-Path. My heart is filled with gratitude to God, in being permitted to see these dear missionaries once more, and unite with them in praise to our Lord and Saviour. I feel truly attached to Brainerd, where I first found the Saviour; and O how I love the dear sisters, with whom I have spent many happy hours, both in school, and in walking to the house of worship. But those happy hours are past. We must be contented, and look forward to that day when we shall meet to part no more.

I left home last week, in company with Mr. Boudinot,[139] and sister Susan. Hope my journey will be beneficial to my health. If our dear father and mother are willing, I intend to pursue study again, as soon as I return home.

There is some seriousness among the people in our neighbourhood.

Several are very anxious to receive religious instruction. When I return, I think I shall make it my business to go round, once in two weeks, to read and explain the Scriptures to the females.

I cannot but hope the Lord will continue to have mercy on our people, and will bring many to the knowledge of the truth as it is in Jesus.

I hope you will write to our dear parents soon. They are always happy to hear from you.

From your affectionate sister
Catharine Brown.

To Sarah Boyce Campbell (Huntsville)

Manuscript, CBP Item 9, copied in Alexander Campbell's hand;[140] *Memoir*, chapter 5

Creek Path April 17. 1823

My dear Mrs. Campbell

My heart was made truly glad this morning by the arrival of Dr. C. I have long been very anctious to see him on account of the low state of my health. For two months past my health has been declining, and I am now reduced to extreme debility. This affliction I view as coming from the hand of ~~God~~ my heavenly Father; I deserve correction, and hope to bear the chastening rod with humble submission.—I have a wish to recover that I may be useful to my poor countrymen; but know that all human means will be ineffectual without the blessing of God. I pray that Dr. C. may be the instrument in his hands of restoring me to health. If the weather were pleasant, I should be disposed to return with him. If I do not take a journey this spring shall probably pay you a visit

I thank you for your present & wish I had something valuable to send in return. Dr. C. will hand you a little ribbon which may answer to tie your caps when you wear it remember Catherine

Mrs. Potter sends love, and hopes to receive a visit from you ere long—Much love to the children.

Farewell my friend, my sister—May heaven grant you its choicest blessings, and reward you an hundred fold for all your kindness to me. Again I say farewell. May we meet in Heaven

> Yours affectionately
>
> C. Brown

To David Brown (Andover)

Manuscript, CBP Item 3, written in Laura Potter's hand from dictation by Brown; *Memoir*, chapter 5

Limestone, June 13, 1823.

My Dear Brother,

~~Sister~~ ∧Mrs.∧ Potter has told you the particulars of my illness, and I will only tell you what I have experienced on my sick bed. I have found that it is good for me to be afflicted. The Saviour is very precious to me. I often enjoy his presence, and I long to be ~~with him~~ where I can enjoy his presence without any sin. I have indeed been brought very low, and did not expect to live untill this time, but I have had joy, ~~that~~ ∧such as∧ I never experienced before. I longed to be ~~I longed to be~~ gone; ~~Was~~ was ready to die at any moment.[141] I love you very much, and it would be a great happiness to me to see you again in this world. Yet I dont ~~yet I dont~~ know that I shall. God only knows. We must submit to his will. We know, that if we never meet again in this world, the Lord has prepared [~~furnished?~~] a place in his heavenly kingdom where, ∧I trust∧ we shall meet, never to part. ~~through Eternity~~ We ought to be thankful for what he has done for us. If he had not sent us the Gospel, we should have died without any knowledge of the Saviour. You must not be grieved when you hear of my illness. You must remember; that this world is not our home, that we must all die soon.

~~I do not know what the Lord designs to do. He has brought me here by his kind providence~~

I am here under the care of Dr. Campbell, [illegible] ∧and his∧ very kind family. My ~~M~~∧m∧other and sister Susan are with me. Since I have been here, I have been a great deal better, and the ~~Dr~~ ^Doctor^ sometimes gives [good?] encouragement of my getting well. But we cannot tell. I am willing to submit myself to the ~~hands~~ ^will^ of God. I am willing to die, or live, as He sees best.

I know I am his. He has bought me with his blood, and I do not wish to have any will but his. He [illegible] is good, and can do nothing wrong. I trust if he spares my life, he will enable me to be faithful to his cause. I have no desire to live in this world, but to be engaged in his [illegible] service.

It was my intention to instruct the people more than I had done, when I returned from Brainard; but when I got home, I was not able to do it.

It was a great trial to me not to be able to visit our neighbors, and instruct them. But I feel that it is all right. It is my prayer that you may be useful, and I hope the Lord <u>will</u> [still] make you useful to our poor people. We were all glad to see brother ~~Webber~~ ^W.^, and felt almost as if you were both here. He is a ~~He is a~~ precious brother. But I am sorry that he needs one thing—that is religion But there is yet hope for him if we are faithful to pray for hi[m.]

I talked with him a great deal: he was willing to hear, and seemed anxious to know abo[ut] it He went to meeting with us every sabbath.

I was surprised to hear him say he never kep[t][142] the sabbath. that he always worked as much as on any other day. I told him it was wrong and he promised he would quit it and go to meeting

I hope you will come this way when you come from the North. Dr. C says It will not do for me to go to the Arkansas; even if I get able this summer. if I go there I shall not live through next winter. I shall write again soon if I am able.

> From your affectionate Sister
> <u>Catharine</u>.[143]

P.S. I felt this evening as though I could ride if I had a little more strength.

The above was written down verbatim from your sister's lips L.W.P.

Diary

Manuscript, CBP Item 11;[144] *Memoir*, chapter 4

PRIVATE DIARY OF CATHARINE BROWN.

Brainerd, 1820.

May 30. Tomorrow morning I shall leave this School, perhaps never to return. Three years since I entered the school at Brainerd. I was baptised in the name of the holy Trinity, on the 25. day of Jan. 1818 and admitted to the holy Communion at the Lords table on the 29 of March of the same year.[145]——————It is truly painful to me to part with my dear christian friends; Those with whom I have spent many happy hours in the house of worship. I must bid them farewell. This is the place where I first became acquainted with the dear Savior. He now calls me to work in his vine yard,[146] and shall I refuse to go in this great work of the Lord, for the sake of my christian friends, and my own pleasure, while many of my poor red brothers and sisters, are perishing for lack of knowledge? O no—I <u>will</u> <u>not</u> refuse to go. I will go where-ever the Savior calls me. I know he will be on my right hand, to grant me all the blessings that I shall need; and he will direct me how to instruct those ∧dear∧ children who will be under my care.

31. This morning I set out from Brainerd with my dear Father. Travelled about 20 miles. Thought much of my dear christian friends. Whether I shall ever see them again is uncertain; the Lord only knows.

2. Have been very sick to day—Blessed be God, I am now a little better. Hope I shall be able to travel on tomorrow. The Lord is very kind and

merciful to all those who put their trust in him. Last night I slept on the floor without any bed. Felt quite happy in my situation. Though very sick in body, yet I trust my heart was well.

5. Have arrived at my Fathers—but am yet very unwell.—Have a very bad cold. Am sometimes afraid I shall not be able to teach school at Creek-Path. We slept two nights on the ground with our wet blankets, before we got home.

20. Blessed be God he has again restored me to health. This day two weeks since, I commenced <u>teaching</u> the girls school.[147] O how much I need wisdom from God. I am a child, I can do nothing—but in God will I trust, for I know there is none else to whom I can look for help.

Sept 5. This day I received a letter from brother David. I rejoice much to hear that he has arrived safely at Cornwall, where he intends to finish his education, and prepare to preach Christ to ~~his~~ our pereshing Countrymen. May the Lord be with him, and [~~prepare~~] ∧make∧ him useful as long as he lives in the world; and at death may he be received at the right hand of God—is the prayer of his affectionate Sister Catharine.

May 1. 1821. Commenced boarding with Mr. and Mrs. Potter.[148] My Parents live two miles from this place. I think I shall visit them almost every week, and they will come [~~illegible~~] see me, often.

May 2. ~~1~~. I love to live here very much. It is a very retired, and good place to study. Every thing looks pleasant round the school-house. The trees are covered with green leaves, and the birds sing very sweetly. How pleasant it is to be in the ∧woods∧ and hear the birds, and [~~illegible~~] all living Creatures praising their Maker. They remind me of those words in the bible—Remember thy Creator in the days of thy youth.[149] O may I never again be so stupid, and careless, but may I remember my Creator to love and serve him, the few days I have to live in this world; for the time will soon come, when my body shall be laid in the ground, and my immortal soul appear before God, to give an account of all the ∧deeds∧ of the body. Help me O God to live to thy glory even unto the end of my life.

May 3, ~~1821~~. I think I feel more anxious to learn than I ever did before, and to understand the bible perfectly. Although I am now so ignorant, the Savior is able to teach me to understand all the good books that I read and prepare me for usefulness among my people.

5. [18 I think I feel more anxious.] Saturday evening. Again I am brought to the close of another week. How have I spent my time through the past week? Have I done any good for God, and to my fellow creatures? I fear I have done nothing to glorify his holy name. Oh! how prone I am to sin, and grieve the spirit of a holy God, who is so ∧kind∧ to me in permitting me to live in this land of the living, where I may have time to prepare for Heaven. O may I improve these precious moments to the glory of my God.

6. Sabbath evening. How thankful I ought to be to God that he has permitted me once more to commemorate the dying love of a crucified Savior, who has shed his precious blood on Calvary for the remission of sins. It was indeed a solemn season to me and I hope refreshing to each of our souls. While sitting at the table,[150] I thought of my many ∧sins∧ which I had committed against God through my life, and how much I deserved to be cast out from his presence forever. But the son of God who was pleased to come down from the bosom of his Father, to die on the Cross for sinners like me, will I hope, save me from death, and at last raise me to mansions of eternal rest, where I shall sit down with my blessed Jesus.

8. This evening I have nothing to complain of, but my unfaithfulness, both to God and my own soul. Have not improved my precious moments as I ought. Have learned but little in school, though my privileges are far greater than many others. While they are ignorant of God and have no opportunity to hear or learn about him I am permitted to live with the children of God, where I am ~~permitted~~ ∧instructed∧ to read the bible, and understand the character of Jesus. O may I be enabled to follow the example of my teachers, to live near the Savior, and do much good for my fellow creatures, while I live in this world. I wish very much to be a missionary among my people. If I had my education—but perhaps I ought not to think of it. I am not worthy to be a Missionary.

May 14. Mr. Hoyt called on us this week on his return from [Elliott] ∧Mayhew∧. He gave us much interesting intelligence respecting the

Choctaw Mission. Mr. H. expected to have brought Dr. Worcester with him but he was too sick to travel, and was obliged to stay behind.[151] He hopes to be able to come on soon. I long to see him. He has done a great deal towards spreading the Gospel, not only in this Nation, but in other Heathen Nations of the Earth. May the Lord restore his health, that he may see some fruits among the Heathen for whom he has been so long laboring.

29. This day I spend my time very pleasantly at home with my dear friends. Find that brother Ɉ John is the same humble believer in Jesus, walking in the path of the christian. I am truly happy to meet my dear Parents and Sisters in health and rejoicing in the hope of eternal glory. O may God ever delight to bless them, and pour his spirit richly into their hearts. I am much pleased to see them making preparations for the Sabbath. They have been engaged nearly all day in in preparing such food, &c as they thought would be wanting tomorrow. I think brother, and sister _ have done much good here respecting the Sabbath.

30. Sabbath evening. This day attended another solemn meeting in the house of God. Mr. P. preached by an Interpreter. I think more people than usual attended. All ∧seemed∧ attentive to hear the word of God. Mr. P. spoke of the importance of keeping the sabbath holy. I hope it will not be in vain to all those who were present. May the precious word of God reach their heart and cause them to forsake all their sins, and follow his commands.

June 13. This day being the first Monday in the month, the people met to pray and receive religious instruction.[152] It was truly an interesting time. The Congregation though small was serious, and solemn. One man and his wife, who have been for some time serious, staid after the meeting; and Mr. and Mrs. _ entreated them earnestly to seek the Lord while he was near unto them. They appeared very solemn—said they wished to know more about God that they might serve him the rest of thier days. We hope and pray that they may be truly converted ~~to God~~, and become our dear brother, and sister in the Lord.

July 1. This day I think I have enjoyed much in my mind. Was permitted once more to sit down at the table of the Lord and commemo-rate the dying love of a crucified Savior. O how good the Savior is in permitting me to partake of his grace, while many others are ignorant of it. O may it not be in vain that I enjoy these great privileges. May I improve them in such a manner as I shall wish I had done when I come to leave the world. P.M. we went to Mr. G's, where Mr. P. had appointed to preach once in two weeks. Most of the people present were whites from the other side of the River. It was pleasant to hear a sermon preached without an interpreter.

Sept 2. O that God would keep me from sin, and make me worship him in spirit and in truth. Think I have had a very good time, to day in praying to my Heavenly Father. I see nothing to trouble me but my own wicked heart. It appears to me the more I wish to serve God the more I sin. I have never done any thing good in the sight of a holy God. But this warfare I must expect if I would be a ~~child of of God~~ follower of Christ. The time is short when I shall be delivered from this body of sin, and enter the kingdom of Heaven.

3. The first Monday in the month. No doubt many christians have been this day praying for my poor Nation, as well as for other Heathen Nations of the Earth. O! why do I live so stupid and so little con-cerned about my own soul, and the souls of others? Why is it that I pray no more to God? Is it because he is not merciful? O! no. he is good, kind, and merciful, and always ready to answer the prayers of his true children. O! that I might pray more, to my Savior, and have more love to him, than I ₍now₎ have.

4. I am now with my sister. Expect to spend a few days with her. Hope the Lord will be with us, and make our communion sweet.

Visited at Mr._s but had no opportunity of conversing with Mrs._ as we intended to do, on religious subjects. Mr._ said he had seen so many different ways of professing christians that it was hard to tell who were right. I felt too ignorant to instruct such a well edu-cated man. Though I knew that there was but one way under Heav-en whereby we can be saved, that is if they would come to him who came to seek and to save that which was lost.

7. Mrs. R. dined with us, and we spent the time very pleasantly con-

versing on religious subjects. She appeared very serious, and wished to be instructed. Expect to return home tomorrow if the Lord will.

9. Returned yesterday from Sister G's. Found the Mission family in good health. I cannot express how much I love the Missionaries with whom I now live. I do not feel my privileges until I am away from them and mingle with worldly people. Then I long to get back to be with christians. I rejoice and bless my Heavenly Father that he has kept my dear brother John, and permitted me to see him once more in the land of the living. I am sorry to see him so unwell, and feel afraid that he will not recover. But the Lords will be done and not mine. I know that he will do all things for the good of those that love him. Brother P. returned from Huntsville last week. Said he saw many good people who were willing to do something for the Mission.

20. Left home, in company with brother J. and sister S. for the purpose of visiting the Sulphur Springs in Blount County Alabama.[153]

21. About 12-o clock we came to a place where there was a Spring which was said to be of the same quality of those we had intended to visit, and we concluded to make it the place of our abode for a few days. We spread our tent a few yards from the water; and at night spread our blankets on the ground and slept very well.

22. Feel very uneasy about my brother. He appears more unwell. O! may the Lord be with us in this lonesome place.

23. Brother J. drinks the water, and bathes in it, but has yet received no benefit. I do not feel as well as I did before I came here, and almost wish to return immediately. Perhaps it is lying out that makes me feel sick. But if brother J. had a comfortable place to sleep, I should not care for myself. The Lord knows what is best for us; he has brought us here.

24. We expect a boy with our horses to day, and ∧[we]∧ hope to get home tomorrow. Saw Mr. J. R. to day in a very low state of health. Conversed with him a little on the subject of religion. This I really felt was my duty, as I thought likely I should never have another opportunity, to see him again in this world. He said he was very wicked, and afraid to die. I told him we were all wicked—but the Savior who

was willing to die for us, would pardon our sins if we would only give ourselves to him. He said when he was in health he did not do his duty towards God, and if he recovered he would try to do better. As he was not able to converse much, I ~~left~~ commended him to God, and left him. He is able to make him his dear child, and prepare him for Heaven.

Jan. 13. 1822. This was truly a solemn and interesting day to me; and one which will never be forgotten. My dear Father, and Mother were baptised in the name of the Holy Trinity, and Mr. S. for the first ˄time˄ admitted to the holy Communion. How kind is our Creator in his willingness to take notice of us sinful worms of the dust, and allowing us to become acquainted with Jesus Christ. O may we walk close with God, and be enabled to set such an example to others that they also may be led to glorify our Father who is in Heaven.

Jan. 14. I have not attended School since last vacation, being at home constantly to take care of my sick brother. He has failed very fast the past week. I fear he will not live many days. The will of the Lord be done.

16. My dear brother is very low. Perhaps he will soon depart from this sinful world, and fly to the arms of his blessed Redeemer. I had some conversation with him this evening, on the subject of religion. His mind seemed to be in a happy state. He asked me whether I thought we should stay here; or go to the Arkansas after his decease. I told him I hoped he would be restored to health. He said he thought that was very doubtful, and added—I think brother W. will soon come for you after my departure. My heart was full—I could not answer another word.

18. Brother Butrick, and John Arch who have been visiting us for a few days past—left this morning with the intention of going round the Nation to preach Christ to those who are yet in darkness. Probably this will take t[hree] months. May the Lord go with his dear servants, on their long journ[ey] through the wilderness, and bless their labors to many immortal sou[ls].[154] I cannot sufficiently express my gratitude ˄to God˄ in sending out Missionaries to this distant land to teach us about Jesus Christ the way of salvation; that we who were

wanderers in the wild woods might find the road to Heaven and live. How kindly are they inviting us to come and partake the rich feast, which is pro has been provided for all those who will accept it. Yet how few are willing to come. Frequently do I weep for my brothers and sisters when when I consider their awful situation while out of Christ, and willingly would I offer myself for their assistance were I qualified for a religious teacher. I hope God will prepare me to do some good among the Heathen. O! that it may be my greatest desire to obey, and do the will of my Heavenly Father. I am determined to pray for my people while God lends me breath; and when my voice is lost in death may Jesus take me home to Heaven, to join with millions of saints in singing the praises of R∧e∧deeming love through a never ending Eternity.

20. The people met in the Schoolhouse for the worship of God, as usual. Many appeared serious and attentive to hear the word of God truth. Four children of Mr. S were baptized. May God take them in his arms and bless them and train them up for usefulness in the world. Brother S. is a lovely man. He is truly a follower of the meek and lowly Jesus. O may he be faithful unto death.

21. Attended a female meeting in Sister P.'s room. Had a very happy season I hope the Savior was with us.

22. Received a letter from Miss A. H.[155] The dear Sisters at Brainerd are still dear to me, and I shall always remember their kindness to me while I lived in the family.

29. Eternity seems very near. A few days more if I am indeed a child of God, I shall walk the golden streets of the new Jerusalem. O! happy day when I shall see all the christians who have ever lived—and God himself will be my happiness.

30. Brother John is very low. Is senseless most of the time. I fear his time is very short in this world. He must soon depart and go to be with our Father who is in heaven. May we be submissive, and thankful to our Heavenly Father for every event of his Providence knowing that he has brought us into the world, and has a right to take us from it whenever he sees best. One great consolation is that our brother will soon be freed from pain, and rest in the bosom of his dear Jesus.

31. Had the pleasure of seeing brother and sister P. at this place.—I love them, as my <u>own</u> brother, and sister.

Feb. 2. Brother J. is very sick. O thou blessed Jesus take him not away by this sickness. Restore him to health that he may live long and be a great blessing to our Nation. But O may I be submissive to thy holy will.

Sab. Morn. 3. O painful is it to record that my dear brother J. appears this day to be on the border of Eternity. Lord come near to us at this time. Help us to give up our dear brother to thine hand.

Evening. Brother John is no more. O distressing thought; he has gone to [re]turn[156] no more. But we shall soon go to him. I trust indeed we have much reason to believe he has gone to Christ his Savior. Through his sickness he seemed reconciled to the will of God, and said he was not afraid to die. He said though his sufferings were great; they were nothing in comparison with Christs sufferings. About one week before he died he spoke to the family as follows. "It is now more than one year since we began to follow Christ and what have we done for him? Do we live like christians? I fear we do not. I do not hear you talk to the people about our Savior when they come to visit you. We are professors of religion, and why is it that we do not show it to others. You should allways remember to keep the sabbath holy. You are too much engaged in cooking on the sabbath, so that you cannot get time to converse about God. You should keep the blacks from work, and ~~not suffer them~~ take them with you to meeting, and when you return keep them still in the house, and not let them work any in the kitchen." He asked me if the Missionaries cooked on the sabbath? I told ‸him‸ they made preparations before sabbath. He said "that is what we ought to do." He frequently requested me to read and explain the Bible to him which was my greatest delight.

PERSONS REPRESENTED.

MR. HOYT, a Missionary.

MR. CHAMBERLAIN, Instructor and Agriculturalist.

MR. ELLIOTT, a visitor at Brainard.

MR. THORNTON, a benevolent gentleman residing
in New-England.

MR. OLMSTEAD, a farmer.

The Father of Catharine Brown.

MR. HICKS, an Indian Chief of piety and intelligence.

MRS. HOYT.

MRS. CHAMBERLAIN.

SUSAN, daughter of Mr. Hoyt.

CATHARINE BROWN, a converted Cherokee.

The mother of Catharine Brown.

Chiefs, Women and Children.

Catharine Brown, the Converted Cherokee:
A Missionary Drama, Founded on Fact

....

A Lady of Connecticut

New-Haven

S. Converse Printer

1819

2

NINETEENTH-CENTURY
REPRESENTATIONS
OF CATHARINE BROWN

Scene—partly in New-England;—mostly at the Missionary station at Brainard.

SCENE FIRST.

In New-England.[1]
[Mr. Thornton is discovered reading a religious newspaper.]
[Enter Mr. Olmstead.]

MR. OLM. Good morning friend Thornton.

MR. THO. Good morning neighbor Olmstead.

MR. OLM. I don't see what you find so very entertaining in those religious newspapers. I seldom come in, without finding you reading a magazine, or a report of some charitable society, or some publication of that kind. It is as much as I can do, to read the political news; and learn what is going on in the political world.

MR. THO. I confess it is my greatest joy to witness the wonderful improvements, which are making in the moral state of the world.

MR. OLM. Well, I have no time for discussing those subjects now. What say you to a removal to the south.

MR. THO. I am not uneasy with my present situation.

MR. OLM. Well, then you may live amongst these rocks and hills. For my part, I am tired of plowing and doffing, where I cannot find dirt enough to cover a hill of corn, without turning my hoe sideways. The winters are milder in the south, and the land is more feasible. My farm is advertised for sale, and in a few weeks I intend to be in the state of Mississippi.

MR. THO. Have you never feared, the health of your family, would be less secure, in a southern climate?

MR. OLM. I am not one of that sort of people who are always borrowing trouble. Other families live there, and why cannot mine?

MR. THO. Are you not afraid of the Indians, who reside in that country? They are sometimes accused of being troublesome.

MR. OLM. Fie.—Do you think I am afraid of Indians? They'll soon have to make their escape, I warrant you, and take up their residence on the other side of the Mississippi. There was a whole township of them destroyed last year, by a Capt. Wright, I think it was; and others will have to share the same fate, if they don't go farther back into the woods.

MR. THO. Then the plan is to cut off the savages, and take possession of their lands by violence. I had much rather hear you say you intend to *civilize* the wild licentious savage; to tame his ferocious nature, and teach him the principles of Christianity.

MR. OLM. Teach the birds Christianity. It is impracticable. What does it signify, to spend time and money for nothing?

MR. THO. Let us not pronounce the civilization of the Indians impracticable. Why are not the natives of this country, as capable of improvement, as those of Africa and the western Islands?

MR. OLM. Well, what if they are?

MR. THO. Then we have encouragement to make exertions, in their behalf. On one of the Islands in the Pacific Ocean, there has been erected in the course of a few years eighty-four houses for Christian worship, and the Sabbath is better observed than it is in most Christian nations. In South-Africa, there are hundreds now laboring in the field, and in the work-shop, who, a few years ago, were sunk lower, in vice and ignorance, than the savages on our borders.

MR. OLM. Whether they are capable of improvement or not, I have no notion of sparing such monsters of cruelty, to go forth with tomahawk and scalping knife, against the defenseless inhabitants of our new settlements. This would be a new sort of benevolence.

MR. THO. I am far enough from wishing to encourage the savages, in the horrid work of human butchery. But have they not been provoked by the whites? Have not their lands been taken from them without their consent, and their cattle driven off? No wonder that while smarting under injuries, they have sought revenge. What else can you expect of a people who have never been taught to forgive injuries? I hope if you go to the state of Mississippi, you will have occular demonstration of the practicability of civilizing the Savages. For there is in that vicinity, a missionary station at a place called Brainard, where the work has been most auspiciously commenced.

MR. OLM. I don't know anything about that. Perhaps if it is so, I may be convinced of the wisdom and expediency of the undertaking; but I have no time to lose,—the hour has arrived when I am to wait on a gentleman, who has it in contemplation to buy my farm. *(Bows and goes out.)*

SCENE SECOND.

At the Mission-House at Brainard.
[Mr. and Mrs. Chamberlain, are discovered sitting; Mr. C. reading and Mrs. C. sewing.]
(Some one knocks.)
[Enter Brown, his wife and daughter Catharine. The daughter is dressed in all her finery: Jewels, wampum, &c.]

MR. C. Walk in my friends, you are welcome at Brainard.

FATHER. We come to get our daughter instructed.

MR. C. We will receive her into the family, and do our best to have her fitted for usefulness in the world.

MOTHER. She may stay a year; and if she likes you, and you like her, she may stay longer, and learn and know all she can, so as to be smart, and I should like to have her made good; only she most good enough now; she our only daughter.

FATHER. We going to see our cousins and we will leave her here. If we come back this way, we will call and see you, and talk more about it. Good bye.—Good bye.

[Exeunt Brown and wife.]

MRS. C. Then you are willing to reside with us a while, and learn the manners, customs, and principles of christian people.

CATH. Yes ma'am—*(mincingly.)*

MRS. C. We will walk in the other room, and I will introduce you to the rest of the family.

CATH. Well ma'am—*(haughtily.)*

[Exeunt Mrs. C. and Catharine.]

131

MR. C. *(alone.)* How vain that young creature appears. If I did not believe there was a Supreme ruler of the universe, who has the hearts of all men in his hands, and who can turn them as the rivers of waters are turned; I should have no hope, that she would ever love anything but Indian finery. But who knows what may take place. If the Almighty should see fit to snatch her as a brand, from the burning; she may even in the course of a few weeks, become so altered, that one would hardly take her to be the same person. Thanks be to Jehovah, there is such a consolation, as the throne of grace. I shall remember this vain creature, and plead most earnestly in her behalf.—*(someone knocks.)* Walk in.

[*Enter two Indian women, named Loory and Mammoo.*]

LOORY. Are you the school-master? We come to take home our boys.
MR. C. They will not be willing to go.
MAMMOO. We the best right to them, they must mind us.
MR. C. They are learning finely, they must not go.
LOORY. They must go, we say so. They must do as we tell 'em.
MAMMOO. I wish you would call them, we in a hurry.

[*Exit Mr. C.*]

LOORY. I spose they love to live here, it looks so nice, and that man looked good natured.
MAMMOO. When the boys come, we must look a sharp eye at them, and they will not dare say a word. *(They look round and view the curtains, &c.)*
LOORY. What a fine blanket. *(Looks at the carpet.)*
MAMMOO. *(Points to the curtains.)* How fine that blanket would look on our shoulders.

[*Enter Mr. C. and two boys—boys look sober.*]

LOORY. *(Looks sharp.)* Boys you must go home; your fathers took you away, before we fixed you fine. You come here without clothes. They give you them clothes, the missionaries did; but there is no wampum on them. Come skip off. [*Boys hang their heads and go out very sober. The women drop a courtesy and Exeunt.*]

MR. C. sits down. [*Enter Susan and hands him a letter.*]

SUSAN. Have the boys gone? I intended to have given them some little books.

MR. C. Yes they have gone; it is a pity, but we must be submissive.

[*Re-enter boys—very joyfully.*]

BOTH. We have come back again, they have gone and left us.

SUSAN. *(Looks surprised and pleased.)* How happened it?

JOHN. We cried, and cried, and cried, and made as much ado as we could, and they became willing finally, and went and left us.

SUSAN. I am very glad. Step and get your lessons,—I shall be in school soon. [*Exeunt boys.*]

[*Enter Sarah—highly delighted.*]
(Mr. C. begins to read the letter.)

SARAH. Miss Susan, Miss Susan, will you step and help your mother unpack the bundles. Oh! I am so pleased, I can hardly talk.

SUSAN. Why, what's the matter Sarah?

SARAH. Oh the ladies in Philadelphia, have sent our little ragged Indian children, a parcel of new clothes. They have sent the boys jackets and trowsers, and the girls frocks, stockings and shoes; and some calico bonnets.

SUSAN. Do the children know it?

SARAH. Yes madam. And you can't think how they act; some are jumping for joy—some are laughing, and some are almost crying, they are so pleased.

SUSAN. Well you may step out, and I'll come in a few moments, when I have read the letter.

(Mr. C. hands her the letter.)

MR. C. It is from the ladies in Philadelphia.

[*Curtain drops.*]

SCENE THIRD.

The following members of the Missionary family, are assembled.
MR. *and* MRS. HOYT, MR. *and* MRS. CHAMBERLAIN, *and* SU-
SAN.
The gentlemen reading, the ladies knitting or sewing.

MR. HOYT. How gratified our christian friends will be, when they are informed of the bright prospects of the Missionary station.

MR. C. Little did we expect such prosperity, when we entered this wilderness.

MRS. C. It is delightful to believe, that Catharine Brown, is numbered among the hopeful converts. She appears earnestly engaged in the cause of religion. It is not long since she came here, all covered with finery. Now she dresses in a becoming manner, and is modest and humble in her deportment.

SUSAN. *(Looks out of the window.)* A gentleman is riding this way. He appears to have come from a distance. It is a friend I hope. Perhaps he is from New-England. He has alighted. *(He knocks.)*

MR. HOYT. Walk in. *(Walks towards the gentleman with an extended hand, and receives the hand of the gentleman.)* Is it possible! That Mr. Elliott has come to visit us? Our friend that takes such an interest in the mission? Welcome, sir, thrice welcome, to our dwelling. *(Presents him to the family.)* This, sir, is Mrs. Hoyt, and those are Mr. and Mrs. Chamberlain, and that is Susan our daughter.

MRS. HOYT. We are happy to receive you, sir. How is your health, and how have you been prospered, on your journey?

MR. E. My health is much improved, and I have abundant reason, to be grateful to that Being, whose goodness, and mercy, hath followed me; and by whose permission, I have at length arrived at this desired spot.

MRS. C. *(After taking his hat and whip.)* Sir, you are very welcome here, and most cordially will we entertain you; *(hands a chair,)* sit down sir, and it will not be long, before we shall have some refreshment ready for you.

[*Exit Mrs. C.*]

MR. E. *(Sits down.)* How is the health of the family; and how does the mission prosper?

MR. HOYT. We are in general, well; in excellent health, except some slight indispositions, of which we hope soon to recover. Jehovah is to be praised, for his goodness to us; but especially for his gracious visitations, to this nation of Indians.

MR. E. Do you begin so seasonably, to see the fruits of your labours?

MR. HOYT. Already are we rewarded for leaving our country, and friends; and taking up our residence, with these children of the forest. Already has God owned our labours, and crowned them, with unexpected success. We have a charming school; our little girls, improve in their work, and in knowledge, beyond our expectations; and our boys, are diligent, both in their labours and in their studies. And we have reason to believe that some here, have passed from death unto life, and are now enjoying, that peace of conscience, which the world can neither give nor take away.

MR. E. Who are those concerning whom, you give such joyful intelligence?

MRS. HOYT. One of our own daughters, like Mary, hath chosen the better part. Two coloured people, and some natives; one of whom is Catharine Brown, a Cherokee.—She is interesting in her manners, and we think she gives unfeigned evidence, of having experienced religion.

MR. E. I should like to see her.

MRS. HOYT. Susan, step and call her.   [*Exit Susan.*]

MR. E. What is the age of this young Cherokee?

MRS. HOYT. Seventeen. When she came here, she was gay, ignorant and vain. She can now knit, sew, and spin; can read well, and writes a decent hand—and her deportment, is such as I think, will highly interest you. She is coming.

[*Enter Susan and Catharine, dressed neat and plain.*]

SUSAN. *(To Mr. Elliott.)* This sir, is Catharine Brown, a scholar of ours. Catharine, this is Mr. Elliott, a gentleman from New-England.

MR. E. How do you do, Miss Catharine?

CATH. I thank you, sir; by the blessing of Providence, I enjoy excellent health.

MR. E. How do you enjoy yourself in this mission family, who are not fond of levity, or vain behavior?

CATH. I can hardly describe the enjoyment I take; this last year has been the happiest of my life.

MR. E. Why so happy? You was brought up, I suppose, to be fond of dress, and show, and to love frolicking and dancing.

CATH. Very true, sir. But since I entered this worthy family, I have had my views of things quite altered. I have realized that my whole life has been sinful—that my affections were placed on things, of little value. I now hope, sir, the remainder of my life will be devoted to him, who is worthy of our greatest regard. I hope to be enabled to glorify my father, who is in heaven.

MR. E. But are you willing to give up your ornaments, and to relinquish the society of your merry companions, for the sake of enjoying that religion, which cometh down from above?

CATH. I have done it already, sir, with the utmost freedom. All my costly jewels and trinkets; my gay ribbons and plumes; I have most willingly given to the charity-box, and keep only these single drops, which I wear in honour to a friend I have lost.

MR. E. I hope my dear friend, you will be enabled to persevere in your Christian course.

[*Enter Mrs. Chamberlain*]

MRS. C. *(To Mr. E.)* Mr. Elliott, will you walk in the next room, and partake of some refreshment, I have prepared?

MR. E. *(Rising.)* If you please madam.

MRS. C. Catharine, will you sit to the table and wait on the gentleman?

CATH. With pleasure, madam. [*Exeunt Mr. E. & Cath.*]

MRS. C. Susan do you stay here, there is company coming. They appear to be chiefs or head men.

MR. H. Whilst our friend is refreshing himself, I think I will take a short ride.

[*Exit Mr. Hoyt*]
[*Enter two Chiefs, each leading a boy, with their women, each leading a girl.*]

MR. C. Walk in my brethren, you are very welcome here.

FIRST CHIEF. My good sir, we belong to the nation of Choctaws.[2] That's my lady and these my children.—That's a brother Chief, and those his lady and children.—We wish you to instruct our children.

MR. C. We are willing to receive them into the school. Sit down my friends—come here my children; are you willing to live with us a while, and learn our ways? *(They all advance and make obeisance.)*

MRS. C. You wish your daughters to be instructed in knitting, sewing, and in such things as we judge most proper.

FIRST WOMAN. Yes Ma'am—we wish you to instruct them, like white folks' children, and we want to have them learn about the great God, that made that sun and moon.

MR. C. *(Takes the boys by the hand.)* My boys, are you willing to leave off hunting, and wandering, for the sake of being industrious, and to learn your book?

FIRST BOY. Yes sir. *(Bowing.)*

SECOND BOY. Yes sir. *(Bowing.)*

MRS. HOYT. Come here my little girls, are you willing to have me for your mother, and you be my girls for a time?

FIRST GIRL. Yes ma'am. *(Courtesying.)*

SECOND GIRL. Yes ma'am. *(Courtesying.)*

MRS. C. We will take charge of the children—it is our business—we delight in it; and the more of these red children we can obtain the better.

SECOND WOMAN. Folks tell us, you be missionaries, and can make bad folks good: We want our children made good—we 'spose we be too old.

MRS. HOYT. No my friend, you are not too old, to be sorry for your sins, and the mercy of God, is very great, to all those who repent of their sins, and forsake them.

SECOND CHIEF. Well, if that's being good, we are good already—for we all sorry we sin—when we was coming down here—we all talked about it, and we said we was.

(The Indians wipe their eyes.)

FIRST CHIEF. We pray the good Spirit take away our sins—we don't know much about Christian's God.

MR. C. My friends, if you will tarry awhile with us, we will endeavour to enlighten you in the christian religion; we feel for you, and greatly desire your salvation.

FIRST CHIEF. We want missionaries to live with us—we can't stay here—we can't leave our little ones—we can't leave our cattle—we fraid the white people take away all our cattle, whilst we come here— we must go back.

SECOND CHIEF. What makes christian people like Cherokees better than Choctaws; we want missionaries and schools as well as they do.

FIRST WOMAN. We want you to tell good people, that Choctaws wants missionaries.

SECOND WOMAN. You please tell our children all about your God— when they get learning—they come home—they tell us—we shall hearken and hear what they say—we shall believe all you tell them.

FIRST CHIEF. Well my children, we must leave you with these good missionaries—you mind all they say to you.

FIRST BOY. Well father, we will.

SECOND CHIEF. You must be manardly, and make a bow when they say so; when they tell you to hoe and work, do you do it, and do you be good natured.

SECOND BOY. Well sir.

FIRST WOMAN. Now girls, do you act like women, and see every thing the white women do, and try to act just like them.

GIRLS. Yes ma'am, we will.

MR. C. I am sorry to part with you my friends.

FIRST CHIEF. I thank you sir; we would stay one day more, but we want to be present at a Talk to-morrow; a council is called to consult on the affairs of the nation.

MR. C. How great a council is called?

SECOND CHIEF. Twelve Chiefs, are to have a talk about missionaries and schools. They meet at brother Hicks'—our brother that is so good, and that has so much education.

MR. C. Mr. Hoyt, I think will meet you there.

SECOND CHIEF. My good sir, we hope he will.

FIRST CHIEF. It is time to go.

ALL. Good bye.

MR. C. Good morning my friends, and may heaven bless you.

[*Exeunt Chiefs and women—children remain.*]

MR. C. Come children, Susan will take you to the schoolroom, and introduce you to the other children.   [*Exeunt Susan and children.*]

[*Enter Mr. Elliott, conducted by Catharine.*]
[*Exit Catharine, to the school-room.*]

MR. C. *(To Mr. Elliott.)* How are you pleased, with our young Cherokee?

MR. E. Sir, I am greatly surprised. Whilst at the table, I had a fine opportunity to converse with her, and have discovered her to be quite superior; her manners are gentle, her disposition is affectionate, and her mind appears capable of high improvement. She is dignified and would be an ornament, to any boarding school in New-England.

MR. C. We all love her as our own daughter; she is of great use to the mission.

MRS. H. I have scarcely been able to restrain my tears, when I sometimes have overheard her converse with the little girls, on the concerns of their souls; she is so pleasant to them, and endeavours so earnestly to make them understand their catechism; and it is enough to melt a heart of adamant,[3] to hear her persuade the little creatures to kneel around her, whilst she implores the forgiveness of their sins, and the enlightening influences of the Holy Spirit.

MRS. C. Such is our regard for this interesting creature, that we often tremble lest, by some providence or other, we shall be deprived of her society.

MR. E. I am highly interested in her character, and should like to become acquainted with the rest of your native scholars.

MR. C. You shall be gratified, sir,—and as you are fatigued, we will call the children here, and not put you to the trouble of going to the school-room. I will blow the horn.

(Blows the horn.)
[Enter Susan and Catharine, conducting the children.]

SUSAN. Mr. Elliott—Sir, I have the pleasure to present to you, our native scholars who by the benevolence of the American people, have been taken from the abodes of ignorance and vice—but are now in a way to become enlightened.

MR. E. My young children, I hope you are all well.—*(They all advance and make obeisance.)* You are fond of living in this missionary family I conclude. *(They all look pleased and make obeisance again.)*

MR. C. Sit down children, and wait for further orders.

(They all take seats—the boys on the one side, the girls on the other side.)

MR. E. They are fine looking healthy children. I hope they are all resolved, to make fine men and women. *(They all look pleased.)* I should be gratified to hear them read and spell, but I fear we have not time. I shall be satisfied for the present, if they will sing an hymn.

MR. C. Come children, arise and sing the hymn, beginning with these words.

"How glorious is our heavenly king."

*(The children arise and sing the hymn through—are assisted by Su-
san, Catharine, &c.)*

"How glorious is our heavenly king,
Who reigns above the sky!
How shall a child presume to sing
His awful majesty?

How great his power is, none can tell,
Nor think how large his grace;
Not men below, nor saints, who dwell
On high before his face.

Not angels, who stand round the Lord
Can search his secret will;
But they perform his heavenly word,
And sing his praises still.

Then let me join this holy train,
And my first offerings bring;
The eternal God will not disdain,
To hear an infant sing.

My heart resolves, my tongue obeys,
And angels will rejoice,
To hear their mighty Maker's praise,
Sound from a feeble voice."[4]

MR. E. You have sung sweetly, my children. It is delightful to hear mortals praising their heavenly Father—but you must remember another
hymn observes—

"He does not care for what you say,
Unless you feel it too."[5]

(They all make obeisance and sit down.)
[Enter Mr. Hoyt, leading the little Osage Captive.][6]

MR. H. Here my friends, is the little Osage Captive, whom we have long expected—she has at length arrived.

MRS. H. and Mr. C. *(take her by the hand, and with affectionate looks observe)*—How do you do, my dear?

CAPTIVE. Pretty well. *(Courtesying.)*

(Susan and Catharine kiss her; Catharine is affected and wipes her eyes.)

MR. H. *(Presents her to the children.)* Here my children is the little girl, whose history Mr. Cornelius told you. You recollect her father and mother, were scalped, before her eyes; and she was taken captive by the enemy. And when Mr. Cornelius first saw her, she had travelled on foot, five hundred miles. Her name is Lydia Charter;[7] this name was given her, in honour to the lady near Natches who paid one hundred dollars, to redeem her from captivity.

LYMAN. Mr. Hoyt, where did you find her?

MR. H. About four miles off. The Indian who owned her, brought her there, and sent me word. When they told her I was to be her father, she reached me her bonnet very prettily; and when we were riding along, she gave me some of her nuts of her own accord; and then she leaned her head on my bosom, and went to sleep. I already feel an affection for her. I trust you will all be good to her. Recollect she is only four years old.

SARAH. May she take a seat by me?

LUCY. I wish her to sit by me.

MARIA. May she be my sister?

JULIA. I intend she shall have my play things.

CAROLINE. Mr. Hoyt, whose sister shall she be?

ELIAS. What if she should be sister to us all? Then we shall all be satisfied.

MR. H. There my boy, you have hit the nail on the head; she may be sister to all of you; and you may all love her, just as much as you please. Here Lyman and Sarah, you are the oldest—each take her by the hand, and lead her; and you may all go and play, or if you please you may go and sit under the great tree; and Charles may tell you a story—he has a fine memory, and can tell you several.

(Lyman and Sarah lead her, and—Exeunt children.)

MR. E. I am highly pleased with the school. The children behave well—with much more propriety than I expected.

MR. H. It is my calculation to set out soon to attend to a council of Chiefs, that is to assemble at brother Hicks' tomorrow. I have an invitation from two Chiefs who are on their way thither.

SUSAN. Whilst Mr. C. is getting your horse, I will step and put up some articles, which you will need, sir.

[Exit Susan.]

MRS. H. *(to Mrs. C. and Cath.)* Let us prepare for supper. *[Exeunt Ladies.]*

MR. H. *(to Mr. C.)* Will you assist me in getting ready to go.

MR. C. Yes sir. Mr. Elliott, you will in the mean time, be somewhat gratified, should you walk and take a view of our situation. I will soon overtake you.

[Scene closes—curtain drops.]

SCENE FOURTH.

Twelve Chiefs in Council at Mr. Hicks'.
[The King is placed on a rug, at one side of the room, with his back supported with a roll of blankets; Mr. Hicks is by his side, on the same rug. The other Chiefs, are placed in chairs in front of the King. They are all deep in thought, when Mr. Hoyt enters. At length Mr. Hoyt is discovered by Mr. Hicks, who beckons to him. Mr. Hoyt advances. Mr. Hicks takes him by the hand, without rising.]

MR. HICKS, *(to the King.)* This is Mr. Hoyt the Missionary from Chick-amauga.[8]

KING. *(Takes him by the hand without rising.)* Welcome, sir—we are friendly to you—sit in council with us.

(Each Chief in his turn, takes Mr. Hoyt by the hand without rising.)

MR. HICKS. Take a seat with us, our good brother.—*(Sits a chair and Mr. Hoyt sits down.)*

(The Council is then opened by the King.)

KING. My Chiefs—This Council is called for the purpose of talking on the importance of having Missionaries and schools, in our several nations. Let brother speak his mind to brother, and let us see if our sons and our daughters, cannot be made equal to the children of white men.

SECOND CHIEF. My brethren—When I was at the great city of Washington, and had a talk with the President our father, I saw the great men of the land; I heard their talks: They put me in mind of the stately trees, of the forest that look so noble, and whose branches extend far and wide, to shelter the more humble trees, that grow within their reach. I thought, what makes these men so noble? I found it was education. I saw their women: They would appear by the side of our women, like the rose—the honey-suckle—and the ivy—by the side of the cowslip, the daisy, and the snowdrop. I thought, what makes these women so conspicuous? I found it was education. I thought our sons and daughters might be made like them.

THIRD CHIEF. When I have been looking at our young men, and seeing them bounding like the Antelope, over mountains, and through rivers, in search of prey, an[d] in quest of pleasure; I have thought, why cannot they be tamed? Although their fathers set them the example, we are tired of the chace—we admire cultivated fields, and our land can be made equal to the gardens of white men. Our daughters are sprightly as the larks—their voices are shrill as the Linnet's—clear as the running brook, and soft as the Nightingale's. I am for schools.

FOURTH CHIEF. Educate bad men and you make them worse. Look at the white traders—how they cheat us. They give our men strong water, that makes them foolish—then they get away their lands and take their cattle. If we have schools, let us have such schools, as will make our children better people.

FIFTH CHIEF. Look at the Senecas—see the Oneidas—there are the Wyandots—yonder is the Stockbridge tribe—all, all, forsaking Indian ways, and learning the religion of the good white men, and for the hunting chase, are making beautiful their cornfields.

SIXTH CHIEF. Many moons ago, several brothers of us, travelled through the country: We went to Washington—to New-York—tarried three days in New-Haven, and thus we went on from city to city, until we arrived at Boston: We saw great men, and beautiful women: We looked at their cottages: Once in a few miles, they had houses to worship in—to worship the great spirit, who is the giver of all good. It grieved us to think that beautiful country was once ours, and we obliged to wear the name of savage: Let us be savage no longer.

SEVENTH CHIEF. Let us not move to the Arcansas, and sell our lands here—Let us invite schools and Missionaries. Let us build houses for our women and children—Let us work on our lands; and very soon our country will be beautiful, and very soon, at our approach—instead of "there comes the savage," we shall receive the friendly hand, and the great man's bow.

EIGHTH CHIEF. At Chickamauga there is a school—there are Missionaries—the children are happy—they love to work—they read and write—the Missionaries are good to them—they clothe them—they feed them—but they are full—they cannot take more children—we must have schools in our own settlements—we must have them thick.

NINTH CHIEF. My brethren—I would not wish to be considered as an opposer—but let us be considerate—can our young men be tamed?— See how they skip like the Rein-Deer, across the plain—See them climb the mountains—Look at our young women—How gay they are, no birds in the forest so gay—They go beyond the Peacock—I wish to be considerate—I am agreed if all are agreed—Let us be considerate.

TENTH CHIEF. My mind is fixed—No girl in our nation so fine as Catharine Brown—Her father is a great warrior—is rich—allows her as much wampum as she chooses—He sent her to Chickamauga— She is now modest—pleasant—charming as a bright summer's morning.

ELEVENTH CHIEF. Take a young tree—Place it by your door—Trim it every day—You can make it stand straight as an arrow, or you can make it bend to the north, to the south—to the east, to the west, just as your mind is—It is so with our children. Not long since, some of our young men shook hands, and all agreed not to drink any more— not to be wild—agreed to invite schools—They said they were tired of Indian ways. If fathers, mothers, and young men, walk in the good way—the young women, will soon follow—I am agreed.

MR. HICKS. My brethren—you already know my mind on the subject. Nothing but a conviction of the utility of the proposal, would have made me consent to part with my darling son. Leonard,[9] my beloved son, has gone far away to receive a christian education. Before this time he has reached Cornwal, in Connecticut. There is in that place, a school—which has the charge of youths of many nations, kindred and tongues. There the good men preach—and there the good men pray. There the good women clothe them—young and old are doing what they can to educate Indians and heathen. They are friendly to Indians—let us be friendly to them.

KING. *(Arises and makes a bow to Mr. Hoyt.)* Brother, will you give us a talk—we are ready and willing to hear your talk. *(Sits down.)*

MR. HOYT. I perceive, brethren, you are all anxious to have learning and religion introduced in your several nations. This belief affords me much satisfaction. We have long believed you to be men as well as ourselves; that you have minds equally capable of improvement, and souls susceptible of endless felicity. We shall rejoice to see your hitherto injured race brought forward—shall rejoice to see you civilized, and evangelized. There is no enjoyment, nor any privilege, which is in our possession, but that we wish you an equal share: we are willing to do you all the good we can. You have many friends living, at the north, who all wish you happiness here, and hereafter. When your friends have been informed of the cruelty, deceit, and wickedness of the white men that surround your border; when we have been told how these abandoned men would intoxicate and demoralize your people, and steal your cattle; and when your characters have been misrepresented by them, to your disadvantage, we have mourned and wept in compassion to you. And when, by constant and repeated abuse, they make "your poor men wretched, and induce your rich men to move away," still farther from the light of the gospel "our hearts sink within us, and we feel constrained to weep—we seek where to weep; we enter our closets and weep there." Think not, my brethren, that all white men are your enemies. No; many gentlemen and ladies, of the first respectability in the United States, lay your case deeply to heart. They ask themselves where, and what should they have been, had they not been instructed and enlightened—they then say, as we would wish others to do unto us, let us do even so to them; and upon that principle they are making great exertions to promote your welfare, and it will be highly gratifying when they are informed you have so much anxiety on the subject.

(The King then arises, and gives him the friendly hand.)

KING. I give you this friendly hand, and you may tell your people that we are friendly. We thank you for your good talk—we believe all you say. I shall delegate some of my best men to go with brother Hicks, and visit the city of Washington immediately. They must pray the good President, our father, to send us instructors; and you must beseech your good people to send us missionaries.

(Each chief then arises, and advances to Mr. Hoyt, and gives him the friendly hand.)
[Exit Mr. Hoyt—Chiefs take seats.]
[Enter a company of Indian women, singing the following hymn, which it is supposed they have learnt of Mr. Hicks.]

"The sun sets at night, and the stars shun the day,

147

But glory remains when the light fades away;
Begin ye admirers of Jesus' love,
Who died to redeem us, and raise us above.

Remember the night when his sorrows began,
The horrors of darkness that fell on the man:
Why so faint and so slow does your gratitude move,
To the Lamb that was wounded that sinners might live.

Remember the spot where in anguish he lay,
The sins which he bore from his people away;
Now faith rises high, we exult in his love,
Who died to redeem us, but now is above.

We'll go the land where our Saviour is gone,
And Saints shall rejoice in the fruits of the son,
And the angels shall sing Hallelujah, Amen,
All glory and praise to the Lamb that was slain."[10]

[The scene ends—curtain drops.]

SCENE SIXTH.

*[The missionary family (children excepted) are assembled for reading,
at the time when Mr. Hoyt returns from the talk.]*
[Enter Mr. Hoyt.]
[Susan arises and takes his hat, &c. and sits a chair.]

MRS. HOYT. We have been quite impatient to have you return, sir. How
have you been prospered, and what news do you bring us? How do the
Chiefs stand affected towards civilization, and towards christianity?
MR. HOYT. I have been well—have been highly gratified with my journey; and I have much pleasing intelligence to communicate; but I
must defer it for the present. Catharine, when I was coming across
the plain, I saw two Cherokees coming down the road, whom I took
to be your father and mother. They are coming to make you a visit,
I suppose.

CATH. Ah, indeed! I shall be happy to see them; there they come. *(She runs to meet them—they enter.)* How do you do, my parents?

FATHER. *(Catches hold of her hand very joyfully.)* My daughter, you still alive, and, like old father and mother, in good health.

MOTHER. You been well all the time?

CATH. Yes ma'am, only when I have been home-sick to see father and mother. Walk in, my parents, the family will be happy to see you. *(They advance—Mr. and Mrs. Hoyt go to meet them, and pass the usual compliments.)*

MR. HOYT. Walk in, my friends; we make you very welcome—you must be fatigued, you have come such a distance. *(Mrs. H. hands a chair—they sit down.)*

FATHER. Yes sir, our old age feels travelling; rather more than we did when young folks.

MOTHER. Ah, we found our daughter alive, and brisk—that's paid us—we rested already—we been so lonesome—the moons great while going away—we thought the year never come—but now we reached here—she still alive, we feel young again.

MR. HOYT. Catharine, step and get a pitcher of beer to refresh your friends. [*Exit Catharine.*] Your daughter is very dear to us; she has improved surprisingly since her residence here. We intend to have her well educated before she leaves us.

FATHER. You must be quick about it then; we come after her. *(The family all look surprised.)*

MR. HOYT. Come after her! We can't spare her; we shall be very reluctant to part with her.

MOTHER. I can't spare her any longer; you have more girls—I have none but her—she must go.

MR. C. She wants more education before she leaves us.

FATHER. Education! She has more than her old father and mother has now. I don't care how much she gets. I like education—but I like my daughter better. She must go.

MRS. C. I hope you will be persuaded to let her stay one year more.

FATHER. No my good madam, she must go back with us—quick as she get ready.

[*Enter Catharine with a pitcher of beer, which she hands to her parents—They drink—She sits down the pitcher, &c.*]

MRS. H. Catharine, your parents have brought us such ill tidings, that we quite regret their having come at this time.

CATH. Indeed madam! What can it be? The tidings must be very unwelcome, to make their presence disagreeable to me.

MR. H. They intend to take you home with them; and we all feel very reluctant to comply with their request.

CATH. *(Looks surprised.)* Indeed! How unexpected! Take me home! But you will consent my parents, to my staying one year more?

FATHER. No you must go—We going to cross the Mississippi, and move to the Arkansas—We want you go with us—We old people.

CATH. But I just begin to know a little, and desire greatly to stay one year more.

MOTHER. We can't spare you—Your mother is old—You all the daughter we have to make us happy.

CATH. I love my parents. But the thought of leaving these dear Missionaries, is very painful.

FATHER. The thought of leaving you here, hurts us as bad—I like Missionaries too—I wish we live here—but we must go to Arkansas— Come fix away.

CATH. *(Sees they are in earnest—begins to weep.)* I beg of you my beloved parents, let me stay one year more—or even six months longer, and I will come to the Arkansas.

MOTHER. No, you must go.

CATH. But when I get more education, I will come to you, and shall be better able to comfort you in the decline of life. Shall be better able to read you the scriptures of truth; and the precious promises which they contain.

MOTHER. If you don't go I die.

CATH. But to leave these dear Missionaries—the preaching of the word—the sacraments, these most precious privileges; is to me worse than death. Were I to die, I should hope to enter the mansions of the blessed, where all sin and sorrow cease, and trials have no more room forever. If you take me to the Arkansas, I shall go where none of these privileges exist, where all is ignorance and vice, where all go astray. I shall have none to guide me, I shall be alone in that wilderness world.

FATHER. *(Grows impatient.)* You like these folks better than father or mother, do you? You shall go. If you don't go, I will disown you forever—You shan't be my daughter any more.

CATH. What shall I do? Ah me, how trying to offend such beloved parents. Yet to leave this dear people, is a trial equal in magnitude. What can I do?

FATHER. *(is somewhat smoothed.)* I tell you what you can do—If you will go to the Arkansas, when Missionaries come there, you may live with them, as long as you please. I guess some will come. We tell the good spirit every day we want Missionaries—I guess some will come.

CATH. I cannot now determine what I will do. I must be alone; give me a short time to consider, and I will return and tell you what I will do. I wish only to learn my duty, and I will do it, be it ever so painful.

[*Exit Catharine.*]

FATHER. How can she think of staying—She knows we want her to prop up our old age.

MRS. H. She only asks permission to stay one year more, or even six months. She greatly desires more education, and she can easily obtain it by remaining here.

MOTHER. We willing she have more, if we no go to the Arkansas—but we can't go without her.

MR. HOYT. Can't you put off moving another year—she is of great use here—she will be of greater use still, wherever she may reside, if she only has more education.

FATHER. We must go as soon as we can—the white people determined to have the country. They steal our cattle, hogs, sheep, they get all they can—we no want to quarrel—rather live in peace—so we go—let them have the land—The good spirit take care of us—so we go soon—she must go with us.

MR. HOYT. We will take good care of her and send her to the Arkansas if you will let her stay.

MOTHER. I glad you like her—I thought you would—I glad she likes you—But she must go—don't ask us any more about it—we be vex't I fraid—You get our temper up, we make her ashamed of us—say no more—she be back soon—she no stay long away from her father and mother that love her so.

[*Enter Catharine with a composed countenance.*]

MR. HOYT. Well my child, what is your conclusion.—We wish you to stay. Your parents wish you to go.

CATH. I have concluded to go, sir. It appears to me to be my duty. When I first retired, the tumult of my soul was very distressing. To leave this beloved spot, with its many blessings, was an idea almost insupportable; and yet I feared the providence of God was about to send me far, far away. A flow of tears, relieved my bursting heart; at the throne of Grace, I became calm and undisturbed. I began to consider. I recollected I had given myself to my God, and he had engaged to be my portion forever. His word has passed, that his children shall have no more trials, than they shall be able to endure; and that they shall not be tempted, except there be a way for an escape. I recollected, that Joseph, was sent by a mysterious providence, far away from the house of Israel; and obliged to dwell in a land of idolaters. Yet God was with him, and ever preserved him from partaking of their sins. I hope in God. I will also put my trust in him, and endeavour to go on my way rejoicing.

MRS. H. Then the path of duty appears plain.

CATH. Yes madam. And since it does, I can now, with some degree of magnanimity, bid Brainard, with all its beloved inhabitants, farewell.

MRS. H. By your own feelings of tenderness, you can judge what ours are on the occasion.

CATH. Oh, spare me any further trial. My first object now, is to have the event passed, as easy as possible. I must make ready, my parents are impatient.

[*Exeunt Catharine and Susan.*]

FATHER. She acts like my daughter now—She always did mind her father and mother—I thought she would go.

MOTHER. I thought she would get right yet.

MRS. H. This is an unexpected separation—I fear it will quite overcome us.

MR. H. I hope the same power will support us, that has so remarkably reconciled her to the trial.

MRS. C. I hope you will suffer Catharine to own pen, ink and paper, that she may converse with us, although at a distance.

FATHER. Certainly, certainly—any thing to please you—any thing to please her, if she only go.

MOTHER. She may read, write—work much as she please, if she only go—when she does, we shall think of the good Missionaries—we thank them—we love them.

FATHER. You good folks—we thank you—we thank you for all you done for her.

[*Enter Catharine, with Bonnet, Shawl, and Gloves, accompanied by Susan.*]

MOTHER. You ready so soon, my daughter—how quick you have been.

CATH. Friend Susan assisted me. *(She turns to Mr. Hoyt.)* The parting moment has at length arrived, and if we can unite in singing an hymn, and supplicating the divine protection, I shall hope to pass on my journey, with considerable composure.

MR. H. With pleasure my dear child. Susan call in the children.

[*Exit Susan.*]
[*Enter Susan with the children.*]
(They all unite in singing the parting hymn.)

"Blest be the tie that binds
Our hearts in christian love,

The fellowship of kindred minds,
Is like to that above.

Before our fathers throne,
We pour our ardent prayers;
Our fears, our hopes, our aims are one,
Our comforts and our cares.

We share our mutual woes;
Our mutual burdens bear;
And often for each other flows,
The sympathizing tear.

When we asunder part,
It gives us inward pain,
But we shall still be join'd in heart,
And hope to meet again.

This glorious hope revives
Our courage by the way,
While each in expectation lives,
And longs to see the day.

From sorrow, toil and pain,
And sin, we shall be free;
And perfect love and friendship reign,
Through all eternity."[11]

MR. HOYT. *(Takes her hand.)* Catharine, as painful as it is, I must first
say the trying word, farewell. May the righteous Jehovah, ever be your
guide and guard; and if we never again meet in this world, may we
all spend an eternity together, blessed and happy.

CATH. I thank you sir—be it even so. *(Lets go of his hand and points to the
ladies, who are weeping.)* From the tender embrace, and the parting
kiss, I must tear myself away; the indulgence of which, will be two
much for my already tried feelings. Ye fathers—ye more than mothers—my beloved brothers and sisters—farewel. *(She puts her handker-
chief to her face, and hastens out.)*

FATHER. Come my woman, let us follow—Good bye friends—I thank you for all you have done.

[*Exeunt Father and Mother.*]

MR. H. "Precious babe in Christ; a few months ago, brought out of the dark wilderness; here illuminated by the word and Spirit of God; and now to be sent back to the dark shades of the forest, without one fellow-traveller, with whom she can say, 'Our Father.' Oh, ye who with delight, sit under the droppings of the sanctuary, and enjoy the communion of saints, remember Catharine in your prayers."

[DRAMA ENDS.]

Excerpt from *Traits of the Aborigines of America* (1822)

Lydia Sigourney

                            Amid the group
Of thy new gathered family, is one,
Whose humble aspect and mild eye reveal
That in her heart the Spirit of God hath wrought
A holy work. With gentlest hand she leads
Those younger than herself, repeating oft,
"How good, how merciful is He who took
Us from our low estate."

                            Patient she strives
By prayers, and by instructions, to arouse
Reflection in the hearts of those she styles
Her wretched people. Modest, tender, kind,
Her words and actions; every vain desire
Is laid obedient at the feet of Christ.
And now no more the gaiety she seeks
Of proud apparel; ornaments of gold
She gladly barters for the plain attire
Of meek and lowly spirits. Catharine, hail!
Our sister in the faith! Can those who love
The image of their Saviour, lightly prize
His lineaments in thee?

                            How beautiful
Is undefiled Religion, mild enthroned

Upon the brow of youth. Its touch dispels
All dissonance of feature, every shade
Which darkens this dull clay, each narrow line
Of cold division, and with Truth's clear beam
Reveals the graces of the pure in heart,
Who shall see God.

Inscription

FOR THE GRAVE OF CATHARINE BROWN (1825)

Anonymous

Zion's Herald, Feb. 16, 1825

> Here, midst the scenes where once untaught and wild,
> She rov'd neglected, simple nature's child,
> Her ashes rest, whose name, now widely known,
> Asks no memorial from the crumbling stone.*
> Sprung from a race, degraded, fierce and rude,
> And nurtur'd midst the forest's solitude,
> Yet o'er her tomb no heathen rites were paid,
> Nor pagan darkness gather'd all its shade.
> But Christian hands prepar'd her last abode,
> And mingled tears of joy and sorrow flow'd
> While "dust to dust" was laid, with pious care,
> And calmly rose the hallowed voice of prayer.
> Light beam'd around, while faith stood smiling by,
> Wav'd her bright wings, and pointing to the sky.
> Spoke of Immanuel's love, and power, to save
> His saints triumph'd o'er the vanquish'd grave.

---

* "A neat monument of wood, erected by her bereaved relatives, covers the grave where she was laid. Though a few years hence, this monument may no longer exist, to mark the spot where she slumbers, yet shall her dust be precious in the eyes of the Lord, and her virtues shall be told for a memorial of her."—*Memoir*, p. 140.

And why this scene? Around her resting place,
Repose the savage fathers of her race;
Untam'd barbarians, who, while ages pass'd
Fell like the leaves before the autumn blast;
Ne'er felt, in life, the peace of sin forgiv'n.
Nor, dying, triumph'd in the hopes of heaven.

Oh! Why did she, now slumbering by their side,
Exult with raptures to their hearts denied?
Why liv'd she not, like them, mid strife and care,
And sunk, at last, in silence and despair?
Caught she some glimpses, with a prophet's eye,
When the Great Spirit pass'd in thunder by?
With bolder thought, burst she *their* narrow bound,
To rove in fields of light *they* never found?

No—but glad tidings of a SAVIOUR's name,
To cheer the solitary desert, came;
His servants here, with *Brainerd's* zeal, have stood,
To point the savage to a Saviour's blood;
Spread to his view the holy page, and show
The glorious refuge from eternal wo.
She heard—believ'd— and, earliest-born, confess'd
Her lov'd Redeemer's name— and now is bless'd.

Great Son of God! who, on thy Father's throne,
Art reigning now, with glory all thine own!
What boundless power, what matchless love, are thine.
How rich the trophies of thy grace divine!
Where'er thy gospel sheds its heavenly light,
Where'er thy Spirit comes, with quickening might,
The fiercest heart, relenting, owns thy sway,
The darkness flies, and sorrow melts away;
Death wears no more despair's appalling gloom,
But tranquil hope sits guardian of the tomb.

The Grave of Catharine Brown (1825)

H.S.

Religious Intelligencer, 17 Sept. 1825

Pour forth thy voice, oh buried maid!
 And gently warn the sister throng,
Who while their raven locks they braid,
 And lightly weave the heathen song,
Shall o'er thy grave a vigil keep,
And true to nature, fondly weep.

Here should the man of pallid brow,
 Stern hater of thy nation, hie;
Thy sainted spirit hovering low,
 With hymns of dulcet melody,
In his cold heart no change might trace;
No pity for a wasted race.

But hither should the christian rove,
 Whose hand the word of truth hath sent,
The Mission of his Master's love,
 Warning the sinner to repent:
Strike thy high harp, and let his ear,
One strain of angel rapture hear.

"They rise! they rise!—to heaven they soar!
 Souls who have learnt salvation's song,
From every kindred, clime, and shore,
 To heaven's unfolded gate they throng;
Oh! Let they ride of bounty flow,
Till all the earth its God shall know."[12]

Memoir of Catharine Brown, a Christian Indian of the Cherokee Nation

RUFUS ANDERSON, A.M.

Assistant Secretary of the American Board of Commissioners for Foreign Missions.

Boston:
Samuel T. Armstrong, and Crocker and Brewster.
New York: John P. Haven.
1825.

Preface.

THIS Memoir was commenced as a biographical article for the Missionary Herald. In its progress, however, the materials were found to be so abundant, as to suggest the inquiry whether a distinct publication were not expedient.

Such a publication being advised, by the Prudential Committee of the Board of Missions, it is now respectfully offered to those who feel interested in the success of missionary efforts.[14]

The author is not conscious of having exaggerated a single fact, nor of having made a single statement not drawn from authentic documents. His object has been to give a plain and true exhibition of the life and character of a very interesting convert from heathenism.

The hope is cherished, that this little volume will augment the courage, animate the zeal, and invigorate the efforts, of the friends of missions, in their benevolent attempts to send the Gospel of Jesus Christ to all nations.

Missionary Rooms,
Boston, Mass. Dec. 1824.

Contents

....

Chapter IV.

FROM HER TAKING CHARGE OF A SCHOOL AT CREEK-PATH, UNTIL HER SICKNESS.

Chapter V.

HER SICKNESS AND DEATH.

Chapter VI.

HER CHARACTER.

MEMOIR
OF
CATHARINE BROWN

Chapter 1.

··

HER HISTORY UNTIL SHE ENTERED THE MISSION SCHOOL AT BRAINERD.[15]

CATHARINE BROWN was born about the year 1800. The place of her nativity was a beautiful plain, covered with tall forest trees, in a part of the country belonging to the Cherokee Indians, which is now called Wills-Valley,[16] and is within the chartered limits of the State of Alabama. It is between the Raccoon and Lookout mountains, twenty-five miles southeast of the Tennessee river. David, the brother of Catharine, says, that the name, by which the place is known among his countrymen, is *Tsu-sau-ya-sah*, or *the ruins of a great city*. But, if such ruins ever existed, all traces of them have long since disappeared.

The Indian name of Catharine's father, is *Yau-nu-gung-yah-ski*, which signifies *the drowned by a bear*. He is, however, known among the whites by the name of *John Brown*. The Cherokee name of her mother is *Tsaluh*. The whites call her *Sarah*.—Neither of Catharine's parents understand the English language. They are now about sixty years of age. Since the decease of the daughter, whose history and character are to form the subject of this memoir, they have removed beyond the Mississippi river, to the Arkansas Territory, whither a part of the Cherokee nation of Indians have emigrated, within the last fifteen or twenty years.[17]

Mr. Brown is represented as possessing a mind more than commonly discerning; yet as having, when the missionaries first saw him, but few ideas on the subject of religion. He believed in a Supreme Being, the author of the visible creation, and that there is a state of rewards and punishments, after the present life; and appeared conscious, that there were things implied in this short creed, of which he had no distinct apprehension; such as the character of the Supreme Being, the nature of the rewards and punishments, and the manner in which the one is to be obtained, and the other avoided. He seemed to have no notion of forgiveness of sin upon any terms. When told of these things, he said he had never heard of them before.

Concerning the *mother*, less is known to the writer of this memoir. Her religious knowledge, if equal to that of her husband, did not probably exceed it. She is represented as having been more attentive to neatness and good order, in the internal arrangements of the family, and more conversant with the duties of domestic life, than her countrywomen generally.

Ignorant as were the parents of Catharine, on the most important subjects, they were among the more intelligent class of their people. Till within a few years, the Cherokees had scarcely begun to feel an impulse towards civilization. Indeed, as a nation, they were almost entirely destitute of the means of intellectual, or moral culture. In a very few instances, a youth was sent to school in the white settlements, bordering on the Indian territory; and still more rarely, perhaps, an outcast from civilized society would undertake for a short time, and from interested, and probably sinister motives, to instruct among the natives. In 1801, a Moravian mission was established at what is now called Springplace, and one or two excellent men have, since that period, resided there.[18] But, their means having been limited, their influence could not be extensive. Very commendable exertions, in support of a school among the Cherokees, were also made, for a few years subsequent to 1803, by the Rev. Gideon Blackburn.[19]

Excepting these efforts, there was, until the year 1816, nothing done for the Cherokees by the Christian church, nothing by the civilized world. They inhabited a country, which is described as susceptible of the highest cultivation. But most imperfect was their agriculture. They possessed a language, that is said to be more precise and powerful, than any, into which learning has poured richness of thought, or genius breathed the enchantments of fancy and eloquence. But they had no literature. Not a book existed in the language. The fountains of knowledge were unopened. The mind made no progress.

After these statements, the reader will be prepared to credit what will be said, in the progress of this memoir, respecting Catharine's intellectual condition, when she first came under the care of the missionaries.

It is pleasing to observe here, that her moral character was ever irreproachable. This is the more remarkable, considering the looseness of manners then prevalent among the females of her nation, and the temptations to which she was exposed, when, during the war with the Creek Indians, the army of the United States was stationed near her father's residence. Were it proper to narrate some well authenticated facts, with reference to this part of her history, the mind of the reader would be filled with admiration of her heroic virtue, and especially of the protecting care of Providence. Once she even forsook her home, and fled into the wild forest, to preserve her character unsullied.[20]

These occurrences took place before the establishment of a school at Brainerd, while Catharine was young, ignorant of the world, without any clear views of morality, and destitute of the knowledge and love of God. Strange that so great a sense of character should then have influenced her resolutions! But she was a chosen vessel of mercy, and a hand, which she then knew not, was doubtless extended for her preservation.

Early in the autumn of 1816, a missionary, sent by the American Board of Commissioners for Foreign Missions, made his appearance in a general Council of the Cherokees, and offered to establish schools among them. His offer was favourably received. After consultation, a principal chief came forward, took him by the hand, and said: "You have appeared in our full Council. We have listened to what you have said, and understand it. We are glad to see you. We wish to have the schools established, and hope they will be of great advantage to the nation." This missionary was the Rev. Cyrus Kingsbury, who, after commencing and aiding in the formation of the first establishment of the Board among the Cherokees, took up his residence among the Choctaws, was the chief agent in forming the stations of Elliot and Mayhew, and is now the superintendent of the Choctaw mission.

The place selected for the first school, was then called Chickamaugah; but it subsequently received the name of Brainerd, in memory of David Brainerd,[21] that devoted friend and benefactor of the American Indians, who stands pre-eminent among modern missionaries.[22] Early in the following spring, Mr. Moody Hall and Mr. Loring S. Williams, with their wives, arrived as assistant missionaries; and, soon after their arrival, a school was opened, with fair prospects of success.

Information of these proceedings soon spread through the nation. It came to the ears of Catharine, then living at the distance of a hundred miles, and excited in her a desire to attend the school. She besought her parents to send her, and they granted her request. Accordingly, on the 9th of July 1817, when she was about seventeen or eighteen years of age, she became a member of the missionary school at Brainerd.

Chapter II.

FROM HER ENTERING THE SCHOOL AT BRAINERD, UNTIL HER REMOVAL BY HER PARENTS.

CATHARINE was of the middle stature, erect, of comely features, and blooming complexion; and, even at this time, she was easy in her manners, and modest and prepossessing in her demeanour.

"It was, however, manifest," says Mr. Kingsbury, "that, with all her gentleness and apparent modesty, she had a high opinion of herself, and was fond of displaying the clothing and ornaments, in which she was arrayed. At our first interview, I was impressed with the idea, that her feelings would not easily yield to the discipline of our schools, especially to that part of it, which requires manual labour of the scholars. This objection I freely stated to her, and requested that, if she felt any difficulty on the subject, she would seek admission to some other school. She replied, that she had no objection to our regulations. I advised her to take the subject into consideration, and to obtain what information she could, relative to the treatment of the scholars, and if she then felt a desire to become a member of the school, we would receive her.

"She joined the school, and the event has shewn, that it was of the Lord, to the end that his name might be glorified. I have often reflected, with adoring gratitude and thankfulness, on the good providence, which conducted that interesting young female to Brainerd, and which guided her inquiring and anxious mind to the Saviour of sinners."

Sometime before this, it is not known precisely how long, while residing at the house of a Cherokee friend, she had learned to speak the English language, and had acquired, also, a knowledge of the letters of the alphabet. She could even read in words of one syllable. These acquisitions, which were of no particular service at the time they were made, are to be noticed with gratitude to God, as the probable means of leading her to Brainerd. They excited desires, which she could gratify no where else.

Her teachers declare, that, from her first admission to the school, she was attentive to her learning, industrious in her habits, and remarkably correct in her deportment. From reading in words of one syllable, she was able, in sixty days, to read intelligibly in the Bible, and, in ninety days, could read as well as most persons of common education. After writing over four sheets of paper, she could use the pen with accuracy and neatness, even without a copy.

From the testimony of different persons it appears, that, when she entered the school, her knowledge on religious subjects was exceedingly vague and defective. Her ideas of God extended little further than the contemplation of him as a great Being, existing somewhere in the sky; and her conceptions of a future state were quite undefined. Of the Saviour of the world, she had no knowledge. She supposed, that the Cherokees were a different race from the whites, and therefore had no concern in the white people's religion; and it was some time before she could be convinced, that Jesus Christ came into the world to die for the Cherokees. She has been known, also, to remark, subsequently to her conversion, that she was much afraid, when she first heard of religion; for she thought Christians could have no pleasure in this world, and that, if she became religious, she too should be rendered unhappy. How much her opinions and sentiments on this subject were, in a short time, changed, will abundantly appear as we proceed.

That the reader may be duly sensible of the singleness of heart and Christian devotedness of the men, under whose instruction this interesting female had placed herself, he is informed, that, not long after her introduction to them, they adopted the following resolution, which developes an economical principle, carried through all the missions to the Indians, under the direction of the American Board of Commissioners for Foreign Missions.—"That, as God in his providence has called us to labour in the great and good work of building up his kingdom among the Aborigines of this country, a work peculiarly arduous, and which will be attended with much expense; and above all, considering that we have solemnly devoted ourselves, and all that we have, to the prosecution of this work; we declare it to be our cordial, deliberate, and fixed resolution, that, so far as it respects our future labours, or any compensation for them, we will have no private interests distinct from the great interests of this institution. And, that if it meets the views of the Prudential Committee, we will receive no other compensation for our services, than a comfortable supply of food and clothing for ourselves and families, and such necessary expenses as our peculiar circumstances may require; observing at all times that frugality and economy, which our duty to the Christian public and the great Head of the Church demands."

Catharine had been in the school but a very few months, before divine truth began to exert an influence upon her mind. This was manifested in an increased desire to become acquainted with the Christian religion, and in a greater sobriety of manners. A tenderness of spirit, moreover, was, at the same time, observed in several others.

Such was the state of things, when the Rev. Elias Cornelius, then acting as an agent of the American Board, made his first visit to Brainerd.[23] His conversation and preaching had considerable effect on the Cherokees, and on the white people in the neighbourhood of the station. On the last Sabbath of his preaching, which was the first Sabbath in November 1817, four persons were much affected during the service, among whom was Catharine. It is proper to add, that she did not seem, at any time, to be greatly influenced by a fear of the punishment threatened against sin. Her chief object of solicitude seemed rather to be, that she might know the will of God, and do it. She appeared to seek the kingdom of heaven with great earnestness, and spent much time in reading the Scriptures, singing, and prayer, and was often affected to tears. Her whole deportment, as a member of the mission family, is represented as having been unexceptionable.

In December, she indulged a hope, that she had been pardoned and accepted, through the Lord Jesus Christ. And it is no small proof of the excellent practical tendency of her religion, that, of her own accord, she very soon began to pray with her associates, and to assist in teaching the Lord's Prayer and the catechism to the younger girls in the school.

The Rev. William Chamberlain, now residing at a missionary station called Willstown, not far from the place of her nativity, states, that, after the interesting period just mentioned, her desires for the salvation of her people, were strong and ardent. She wept and prayed for them, in secret places, as well as in the company of her female friends at their weekly prayer-meetings. Among the rest, the case of her brother David, then on the Arkansas river, was specially interesting. One morning, having retired to the neighbouring woods for devotion, she became so deeply engaged in prayer for this dear brother, that the time passed insensibly, and she remained in her sacred retreat till the sun was near setting. She had been favoured with unusual nearness of access to her heavenly Father, and returned home with an humble confidence, that He would fully answer her prayers. After David had gone to New England to complete his education, having previously given satisfactory evidence of piety, she related these facts to a confidential friend, and said she wished to remember them with gratitude.

Catharine is regarded as the first, who was hopefully converted from among the Indians, by means of the missionaries sent out by the American Board of Missions. It may well be supposed, therefore, considering her amiable manners and promising character, that she was dear to them all. How painful, then, must have been any prospect of her removal into the western wilderness, where she would behold no pious example, and hear no monitory voice; and this, too, at the commencement of her Christian career, before her religious knowledge and habits were matured.

At the commencement of the year 1818, her father came to take her home. He expressed entire satisfaction with the treatment, which she had received at the school; but said he contemplated removing beyond the Mississippi, and wished to have her with him. This intimation was not less painful to Catharine, than it was to the missionaries; but it came under circumstances, which seemed to demand an acquiescence. "Perhaps," said her teachers and spiritual guides, "the Lord is taking her from us, that she may be more useful in promoting his cause in some other place." We shall see, ere long, that they ultimately found occasion to give praise to God, not only on account of the brief separation, which now took place, but also for the more painful separation, which happened in the latter part of the same year.

Catharine desired to receive, before her departure, the seal of the covenant of grace, in the holy ordinance of baptism. As no reasonable doubt could be entertained of her piety, her request was cheerfully granted. On the 25th of January, Mr. Kingsbury preached from Gal. iii, 28,[24] on the fellowship of those, who are in Christ, of whatever colour, or nation. The assembly was unusually large and solemn. After the sermon and a prayer, the sacred ordinance was administered to the deeply affected convert. She was the first Indian baptized by the missionaries of the Board. This event occurred about eight months after the opening of the school at Brainerd.[25] Since then, about one hundred adult Cherokees have received the same ordinance, preparatory to admission to the visible church.

The month of February was spent by Catharine at her father's house. But, circumstances conspiring to prevent an immediate execution of the purpose to remove to the Arkansas country, she was, to the no small satisfaction of herself and the mission family, permitted to revisit Brainerd, and continue there a few months longer, before commencing her undesired journey. While at home, she had been closely questioned, with respect to her religious faith, by some irreligious white people. They endeavoured, though in vain, to perplex her mind, by objections against the Scriptures. But her parents were pleased, that she had learned so many good things, and expressed a desire to be themselves instructed.

Her return furnished an opportunity for admitting her to full communion in the visible Church of Christ. On the 29th of March, about two months after her baptism, she, with others, ratified a solemn covenant with the Most High, at the sacramental table. Seven of the communicants were Cherokees. The assembly was solemn and attentive; and there was reason to believe, that some of the bystanders had a great desire to be with the little company, which commemorated the love of Jesus, particularly one negro woman. This person, being asked how she felt on that occasion, replied, "I felt as if that (meaning the communicants,) was my company, and that they had left me alone in the wicked world." "Our red brethren and sisters," say the missionaries, "declared, that their joys, while at the table, exceeded every thing they had before conceived."

It has not been common for missionary stations among Pagans, to be favoured so early, as was Brainerd, with the converting influences of the Spirit of God. Generally, in these latter days, the faith and patience of a missionary, under such circumstances, have been considerably tried, before he has seen the fruits of his labours; though, in due season, there has seldom failed to be a harvest amply compensating him for all his toils. But among the Indians of North America, who have not incorporated the worst vices of civilized life with their own, the preacher of the Gospel has some peculiar advantages. They possess not, as do most heathen nations, a complicated system of false religion, transmitted from their fathers, which must be overthrown, before the Gospel can prevail. They are, to a great extent, "without a sacrifice, and without an image, and without an ephod, and without a teraphim."[26] There is scarcely any thing among the Indians themselves, to oppose the prevalence of the Gospel, except their unfortified ignorance and depravity. The greatest obstacles to missionary success among them, arise from a foreign influence, industriously, and sometimes powerfully, exerted.

In May, Jeremiah Evarts, Esq., at that time Treasurer of the American Board of Commissioners for Foreign Missions, arrived at Brainerd, on a visit of inspection and superintendence. By extracting two or three passages from a letter, which he then wrote, to Dr. Worcester, Corresponding Secretary of the Board, the reader will have an interesting view of the internal economy of the missionary establishment, with which Catharine was connected.[27]

"It was on Friday evening, the 8th inst., just after sun-set, that I alighted at the mission-house. The path, which leads to it from the main-road, passes through an open wood, which is extremely beautiful at this season of the year. The mild radiance of the setting sun, the unbroken solitude of the wilderness, the pleasantness of the forest with all its springing and blossoming vegetation, the object of my journey, and the nature and design of the institution, which I was about to visit, conspired to render the scene solemn and interesting, and to fill the mind with tender emotions.

"Early in the evening, the children of the school, being informed that one of their northern friends, whom they had been expecting, had arrived, eagerly assembled in the hall, and were drawn up in ranks and particularly introduced. They are neither shy, nor forward in their manners. To a stranger they appear not less interesting than other children of the same age; but, if he considers their circumstances and prospects, incomparably more so.

"At evening prayers, I was forcibly struck with the stillness, order, and decorum of the children, and with the solemnity of the family worship. A portion of Scripture was read, with Scott's practical observations;[28] a hymn was sung, in which a large portion of the children united; and Mr. Hoyt led the devotions of the numerous family. If all the members of the Board could hear the prayers, which are daily offered in their behalf at this station, (and I presume at all others under their superintendence;) and if all patrons and contributors could hear the thanks, which are returned to God for their liberality; and especially if they could see a large circle of children, lately rescued from heathenism, kneeling with apparent seriousness, and engaging in the solemnities of Christian worship, one of them [Catharine Brown] already a hopeful convert, and others thoughtful and inquiring;—if all these things could be seen, one may safely predict, that the exertions and sacrifices of the friends of missions would be increased four-fold. These things are not the less real, however, because they cannot be seen by every friend to the cause."

The Rev. Ard Hoyt, mentioned in the above extracts, joined the mission in the January preceding, and, in June, succeeded Mr. Kingsbury as superintendent of the Cherokee mission, the latter having removed to the Choctaw nation.

A farther extract from the letter of Mr. Evarts will not only confirm much, that has already been said respecting Catharine, but will add some other particulars.

"Her parents are half-breeds, who have never learnt to speak English; yet if you were to see her at a boarding-school in New-England, as she ordinarily appears here, you would not distinguish her from well-educated females of the same age, either by her complexion, features, dress, pronunciation, or manners. If your attention were directed to her particularly, you would notice a more than ordinary modesty and reserve. If you were to see her in a religious meeting of pious females, you would not distinguish her, unless by her more than common simplicity and humility. When she joined the school in July last, (having come more than one hundred miles for that sole purpose,) she could read in syllables of three letters, and was seventeen years old. From her superior manners and comely person she had probably attracted more attention, than any other female in the nation. She was vain, and excessively fond of dress, wearing a profusion of ornaments in her ears. She can now read well in the Bible, is fond of reading other books, and has been particularly pleased with the Memoirs of Mrs. Newell.[29] Last fall she became serious, is believed to have experienced religion in the course of the autumn, and was baptized in January. Since that time, she has been constantly in the family; and all the female members of it have the most intimate knowledge of her conduct, and receive a frank disclosure of her feelings. It is their unanimous opinion, that she gives uncommon evidence of piety. At meetings for social prayer and religious improvement, held by them on every Thursday afternoon and Sabbath evening, Catharine prays in her turn, much to the gratification of her sisters in Christ. Her prayers are distinguished by great simplicity as to thought and language, and seem to be the filial aspirations of the devout child. Before Mrs. Chamberlain took charge of the girls, Catharine had, of her own accord, commenced evening prayer with them, just as they were retiring to rest. Sometime after this practice had been begun, it was discovered by one of the missionaries, who, happening to pass by the cabin where the girls lodge, overheard her pouring forth her desires in very affecting and appropriate language. On being inquired of respecting it, she simply observed, that she had prayed with the girls, because she thought it was her duty. Yet this young woman, whose conduct might now reprove many professing Christians, who have been instructed in religion from their infancy, only ten months ago had never heard of Jesus Christ, nor had a single thought whether the soul survived the body, or not. Since she became religious, her trinkets have gradually disappeared, till only a single drop remains in each ear. On hearing that pious females have, in many instances, devoted their ornaments to the missionary cause, she has determined to devote hers also. In coming to this determination, she acted without influence from the advice of others."[30]

Time fled rapidly away, in pious employments and in Christian intercourse, and brought the long expected, much dreaded separation. It shall be described in the words of those, who, next to the interesting sufferer, felt it most.

"November 4. The parents of Catharine Brown called on us. They are on their way to the Agency. The old grey-headed man, with tears in his eyes, said he must go over the Mississippi. The white people would not suffer him to live here. They had stolen his cattle, horses, and hogs, until he had very little left. He expected to return from the Agency, in about ten days, and should then want Catharine to go home, and prepare to go with him to the Arkansas. We requested him to leave his daughter with us yet a little while, and go to the Arkansas without her; and we would soon send her to him, with much more knowledge than she now has. To this he would not consent; but signified a desire, that some of us would go along with him. It is a great trial to think of sending this dear sister away with only one year's tuition; but we fear she must go. The Lord can and will order otherwise, if, on the whole, it is for the best."

While her parents were gone to the Agency, Catharine made a farewell visit to Springplace, the seat of the Moravian mission, about thirty-five miles from Brainerd. The feelings, with which she parted from Mr. and Mrs. Gambold, the venerable missionaries there, were such as might be expected, from her high regard for their characters, and her prospect of never seeing them again.[31] She returned to Brainerd on the 9th; and, on the 20th, the missionaries thus describe her removal.

"We had a very affecting scene, in the departure of our sister Catharine. Her father and mother, returning from the Agency to go to the Arkansas, stopped yesterday for the purpose of taking her with them. She knew that she needed more information to be prepared to go alone into the wilderness, and intreated them to leave her with us a little longer. She is their only daughter; and they would not consent on any terms. The struggle was very severe. She wept and prayed, and promised to come to them, as soon as she had finished her literary education, and acquired some further knowledge of the Christian religion. We engaged that she should be provided for while here, and assisted in going to them. Her mother said, she could not live, if Catharine would not now go with them. Catharine replied, that to her it would be more bitter than death to leave us, and go where there were no missionaries. Her father became impatient, and told her, if she would not mind him, and go with them now, he would disown her forever; but if she would now go, as soon as missionaries came to the Arkansas, (and he expected they would be there soon,) she might go and live with them as long as she pleased. He wished her to have more learning.

"Never before had this precious convert so severe a trial; and never, perhaps, did her graces shine so bright. She sought for nothing but to know her duty, and asked for a few minutes to be by herself undisturbed. She returned, and said she would go. After she had collected and put up her clothing, the family were assembled, a parting hymn was sung, and a prayer offered. With mingled emotions of joy and grief, we commended her to the grace of God, and they departed.

"Precious babe in Christ! a few months ago brought out of the dark wilderness; here illuminated by the word and Spirit of God; and now to be sent back into the dark and chilling shades of the forest, without one fellow traveller, with whom she can say, 'Our Father!' O ye, who with delight sit under the droppings of the sanctuary, and enjoy the communion of saints, remember Catharine in your prayers."

Thus was she removed from a place, endeared to her by some of the most pleasing associations of her life; and she departed, expecting to return no more. A day of sorrow must it have been to the members of the school, whose warmest attachment she had most effectually secured. The chief consolation of her religious friends was, that the whole had been ordered by infinite Wisdom.

Early in the following month, information was received at Brainerd, that two children, who had been taken captive by the Cherokees from the Osage tribe of Indians, were in the lower part of the nation, and that one of them was supposed to be the sister of *Lydia Carter*, the interesting "Little Osage Captive,"[32] who was then a member of the school. There being some reason to believe, that the man, in whose possession they were, might be induced to surrender them to the care of the missionaries, Mr. Hoyt, accompanied by his son, set out in quest of the unfortunate children. They travelled between two and three hundred miles, and encountered many hardships on their way. But, though they found the children, and ascertained that one was indeed the sister of Lydia, they failed in their great object. The man, who professed to be the owner of the children, would not relinquish them.[33]

The journey was not, however, in vain. Mr. Hoyt had the happiness of meeting with Catharine, at her father's house. This occurrence is thus noticed, in the journal of the mission.

"In this tour, father Hoyt spent two nights and a day at the house of Catharine Brown's father. He was received with great cordiality by the whole family; and Catharine's joy was so great, that he says, 'I felt myself more than paid for the fatigues of the whole journey, by the first evening's opportunity.' Catharine said, it had been very dark times with her, since she left Brainerd. All around her were engaged for the riches and pleasures of the world; and because she could not unite with them, as formerly, they were telling her, they supposed she thought herself very good now; that she expected to go to heaven alone; &c. Her greatest burden was, a fear that she should be drawn away from the right path, and at length be left to do like those around her. She felt herself too weak to leave the society and instruction of Christians, and go into the world alone."

While Mr. Hoyt was at her father's, he preached to a small audience of Cherokees, and one Indian woman was so much affected, that she wept during the whole service. After the departure of Mr. Hoyt, this woman sent for Catharine to read and explain the Bible to her, and to pray with her, which was repeatedly done. There is reason to believe, that a salutary and abiding impression was produced; for, after Catharine's return to Brainerd, this poor female came all the way, a distance of more than a hundred miles, to hear, as she said, more about the Saviour.

This chapter will be closed with two letters from Catharine to her friends, which are the earliest, of which her biographer has any knowledge. And this occasion is taken to remark, that nearly all the letters, which will find a place in this memoir, were written from the overflow-

ings of her heart to persons with whom she was intimately acquainted, and hence with little study, or effort. The greater part of them have
never before been published. They are generally copied from the originals, which are in a plain, intelligible running hand, and the orthography is very seldom incorrect. Alterations in the sense, are never made;
and corrections in the grammar, but rarely.

The first of the letters was written in the anticipation of her dreaded removal from her Christian friends, sixteen months from her first
coming to Brainerd.

To Mrs, Williams, at Elliot.[34]

Brainerd, Nov. 1, 1818.

My dearly beloved Sister,

I HAVE been wishing to write to you ever since you left us. You can
hardly tell how my heart ached when I parted with you, expecting
never to see you again in this world; but when I remembered that you
were in the hands of the Lord, and that he would dispose of you as
he pleased, it gave me joy equal to my sorrow.

O how I rejoiced, to think that you were going to carry the glad
tidings of salvation to a people who had never heard of the dear
Saviour. I do hope and pray that the Lord will bless your labours
among them, as he has here.

We were very lonesome when you left us, especially at our prayer
meeting; but I hope our hearts were united in love. I was very sorry to
hear that you were sick; but it rejoiced me to hear that you were
recovering, O, my dear sister, I will join with you in praising the Lord
for his goodness in restoring you to health, I shall never forget you, or
your kind endeavours to bring me to a knowledge of the Saviour.
Sometimes I feel the love of God shed abroad in my heart, and feel as
if I should be willing to give up every thing in this world to Christ. O
how good is it to enjoy the presence of God; O that I might always
enjoy it: but my heart is so bad and so prone to leave the God I love,
that I am afraid he will leave me. O my dear sister, do pray for me.

All the Cherokee brothers and sisters are well. Three of the scholars, viz. Lydia Lowry, Alice, and Peggy Wilson, we hope have obtained an interest in the Saviour. Mr. Wilson came here, and wished to take his daughters on a visit to Mr. Brown's. Nearly a week after, he sent word that he was not going to send them back to school again. We felt very much grieved to hear it.

I expect my father here every day. I do not know whether I shall go to the Arkansas, or not. I feel grieved when I think of leaving my Christian friends, and of going far from all religious people, into a wild howling wilderness, where no star shines to guide my wandering feet to the Babe of Bethlehem; where no warning voice is heard to keep me in the straight path that leads to heaven. When I look to that dark region, I start back; but when I think of my two brothers there, and my dear parents, who are soon to go, I feel reluctant to stay behind, and leave them to perish alone.

Tell Mr. Williams and Mr. Kingsbury, that I remember them most affectionately, and also all the dear brothers and sisters at Yello Busha.

From your loving sister,
Catharine Brown.

To Mr. and Mrs. Chamberlain, at Brainerd.

Fort Deposit, Dec. 12, 1818.

My dearly beloved Brother and Sister Chamberlain,

I JUST sit down to address you with my pen. But is this all? Am I so soon called to bid you adieu, and see your faces no more in this world? O my beloved friends, you know not the love I bear to that blessed spot, where I have spent so many happy hours with you; but it is past never to return.

Dear friends, I weep; my heart is full; tears flow from my eyes while I write; and why is it so? Do I murmur? God forbid. Ought I not to praise the Lord for what I have received, and trust Him for every thing? O yes, his ways are best, and he has graciously promised, that "all things shall work together for good to them that love him."

But do I love him? Have I that love to him, which will enable me to keep all his commandments? Do I love him with all my heart? O that the Lord would search me, and lead me in the way of eternal life.

Since I left you, I have led a very lonesome life, and not heard the Gospel preached but once; that is, when father Hoyt was here, and Milo. They came here on Tuesday evening. I was sitting in my room, and heard a knocking at the door. I bid them come in; and who but Milo appeared. I inquired if any body was with him. He said his father was at the door. That rejoiced me very much, and I enjoyed very much while they were here. Blessed be God for sending them here to instruct us.

I am here amongst a wicked set of people, and never hear prayers, nor any godly conversation. O my dear friends, pray for me: I hope you do. There is not a day passes but I think of you, and the kindness I received during the time I staid with you. It is not my wish to go to the Arkansas; but God only knows what is best for me. I shall not attempt to tell you what I have felt since I left you, and the tears I have shed when I called to mind the happy moments we passed in singing the praises of God. However, I bear it as well as I possibly can, trusting in our dear Saviour, who will never leave nor forsake them, that put their trust in him.

It may be possible, that I may see you once more; it would be a great happiness to me if I don't go to the Arkansas; perhaps I may; but if I should go, it is not likely we shall meet in this world again:— but you will excuse me, for my heart feels what I cannot express with my pen. When I think and see the poor thoughtless Cherokees going on in sin, I cannot help blessing God, that he has led me in the right path to serve him.

Father will start to the Arkansas about some time after Christmas; but, I am not certain that I shall go.

I thank you for your kind letters. Do write to me every opportunity.

I shall conclude with my love to all my brothers and sisters at Brainerd. Sister Flora, do kiss all the children for me. I shall expect letters from all the little girls. O may we meet at last in the kingdom of our blessed Saviour, never more to part. Farewell, my dear brother and sister, farewell.

From your affectionate sister in Christ,
    Catharine Brown.

Chapter III.

. . . .

FROM HER RETURN TO BRAINERD, UNTIL SHE TAKES
CHARGE OF A SCHOOL AT CREEK-PATH.

THOSE, who will but observe, may often witness very affecting instances of the particular and merciful providence, which God exercises towards his children in this world. Both the removal and the return of Catharine may be regarded as such instances.

What was the precise influence upon her own character, of her being taken from Brainerd, cannot be determined; though there is little doubt but her faith and patience were, by this means, increased. But the consequences of her removal to others, are more obvious. It led the way to the formation of schools, and to the stated preaching of the Gospel, at Creek-Path, the place of her father's residence, and to the hopeful conversion of nearly all her family; thus illustrating the maxim, that our greatest blessings may spring from our severest afflictions.

Her return was scarcely expected by the missionaries, when, on the 23d of May 1819,[35] her father brought her again to Brainerd, and committed her to their care, until her education should be completed, intending to remove immediately, with the remainder of his family, beyond the Mississippi. This purpose, as has been previously intimated, was not executed. Mr. Brown did not proceed to the Arkansas country until more than four years after this time, and not till the beloved daughter, for whose society he was so desirous, had been laid in the dust. The causes of this delay are unknown to the author of this memoir.

Catharine ascribed the change in the intentions of her parents respecting her, wholly to the special providence of Him, who heareth prayer. The appointed time for their departure drew near. She was convinced that it was not best for her to go. Her continual intercessions were, that her parents might be induced to leave her behind. And her prayers were answered. After one of her seasons of private devotion, she returned to her family, with a delightfully confident hope, that God had listened to her requests; and, as she entered the room where her parents were sitting, she found they had been consulting on the expediency of sending her back to Brainerd; and had actually resolved upon her return. This was just half a year from the period of her removal from that consecrated place.

On this occasion, the missionaries very naturally exclaim;—"How unsearchable are the ways of God! We thought it a very afflicting providence that this lamb should be snatched from the fold of Christ, to go, as we thought, where she would be exposed to be devoured by wolves; and were ready to say in our hearts, when her father required her to go with him, 'not so.' But in this very way, God has given her an opportunity to set an example of filial obedience, by submitting to the authority of a father, in a most painful requisition, and of manifesting her love to the Saviour, in her willingness to forsake all for him; and, at the same time, has granted her the object of her pious and fervent desire."

With how much delight she revisited the scenes of her first aspirations after God and heaven, will appear in a letter, which was written a few days after her arrival at Brainerd.

To Mr. and Mrs. Hall, at Knoxville.

Brainerd, May 30, 1819.[36]

My dear Brother and Sister,

WITH pleasure I spend a few moments in writing to you this evening, to tell you of my safe arrival on the 23d of this month. O how great was the joy that I felt, when meeting the dear family at Brainerd, with whom I have long desired to be. Yes, dear brother and sister, God has returned me back once more, where I can be with Christian friends, and get more instruction. If it is the Lord's will, I hope to stay here two years longer. O that I might improve the great privileges, which I now enjoy.

It appears strange to me, that I am not more interested in the cause of Christ, when he has done so much for me. But I will now give myself up entirely to Him. I should be willing to leave every thing for God, and to undergo any sufferings, if it would but make me humble, and would be for his glory.

My heart bleeds for my people, who are on the brink of destruction. O pray for me, my dear brother and sister. I long to see you and your little one. I am your affectionate sister,

Catharine Brown.

Of her employments, from this time till the end of the year, the documents, on which the principal reliance is placed, contain no important notices. Doubtless she was occupied in making useful acquisitions; and, so far as her duties as a member of the school would permit, in communicating the knowledge she had acquired to others.

Two or three letters may properly be inserted here.

To Mr. and Mrs. Williams.

Brainerd, July 5, 1819.

My dear Brother and Sister Williams,

ALTHOUGH I have long omitted answering your affectionate letters, my heart has been often with you. Yes, dear brother and sister, I do not forget you, and all the pleasant meetings we had together, when you were here. But pain is mixed with pleasure, when I think they are gone, no more to return! When I remember the kind instruction I received from you, before you left this place, my heart swells with gratitude. I feel much indebted to you, but more particularly to that God, who sent you here to instruct the poor ignorant Indians in the way that leads to everlasting life. Oh, my dear friends, may the Lord ever bless you, and make you the instrument of doing great good where he has called you.

You may pass through many trials; but remember, beloved brother and sister, all our trials here will only make us richer there, when we arrive at our home. A few more days, and then I hope our weary souls will be at rest in our Saviour's kingdom, where we shall enjoy His blessed presence forever.

When I wrote you before, I expected to go to the Arkansas, and never to see this place again. But the Lord has in mercy ordered it otherwise. He has permitted me to live with the dear missionaries here again, though my parents could not bear to think of leaving me behind. My mother said, if I remained here, she did not expect to see me again in this world. Indeed, she wished she had never sent me to this school, and that I had never received religious instruction. I told her, if she was a Christian she would not feel so. She would be willing to give me, and all she had, up to Christ. I told her I did not wish to stay on account of my own pleasure; but that I wished to get more instruction, so that it might be for her good, as well as for mine.

I felt very sorry for my poor parents. I thought it was my duty to go in obedience to their commands, and commit myself to the will of God. I knew the Lord could change the hearts of my parents.

They are now perfectly willing, that I should stay here two years longer. I left them in March. They expected to set out in that month for the Arkansas. They had already prepared for the journey. But the Lord has so ordered, that they have concluded not to go until next fall. I don't know whether they will go then. I hope you will pray for them, and also for me, that I may be useful to my dear people. My heart bleeds for their immortal souls. O that I might be made the means of turning many souls from darkness unto marvellous light.

My dear brother and sister, I love you much, and feel that the time is short when we shall sit down with our Saviour, and experience that love which no words can describe.

Give my love to my dear brother and sister Kingsbury, and also to all the dear missionaries there. From your affectionate sister in Christ,
Catharine Brown.
P. S. Please to accept this small present for my little darlings; and learn them to say, "Aunt Catharine."[37]

To Mr. Moody Hall, at Taloney.[38]

Brainerd, Oct. 25, 1819.

A FEW moments of this day shall be spent in writing to my dear brother. It seems a long time, since you left us. I long to see you. I long to hear from you. I hope the Lord is with you this day, that you enjoy the presence of our dear Redeemer. My sincere desire and earnest prayer to the throne of grace, is, that your labours may be blessed, and that God would make you the instrument of saving many souls from eternal destruction.

O how I feel for my poor Cherokee brethren and sisters, who do not know the blessed Jesus, that died for us, and do not enjoy the blessings that I do. How thankful I ought to be to God, that I have ever been brought to the light of the Gospel, and was not left to wander in darkness. O I hope the time is at hand, when all the heathen shall know God, whom to know is life everlasting.

My dear brother, may we be faithful to our Master, knowing that in due season we shall reap, if we faint not. Our pilgrimage will shortly be ended, and all our trials will be over. Do not forget me in your daily prayers, for I need very much the prayers of God's children. My heart is prone to leave my God, whom I love. From your unworthy sister in Christ,

Catharine Brown.

To Mr. and Mrs. Hall,
On their removal from Brainerd.

Brainerd, Nov.——, 1819.

How solemn, my dear brother and sister, is the idea, that we must soon part. Perhaps the next time we meet will be in eternity, before the bar of God. O my dear brother and sister, if we are prepared to meet our God in peace, we shall surely be happy. But, my beloved friends, how can I be permitted to meet you in heaven! My heart is so prone to sin against God, that I am sometimes afraid he will leave me. Forget not to pray, that all these doubts may be removed from me, and that my soul may be washed in the blood of Jesus Christ.

I love you much, and feel that the time is short when we shall sit down with our Saviour. Farewell, my dear brother and sister. May the Lord go with you. From your sister

Catharine.

In the same month, in which the last letter was written, we find David Brown, the brother of Catharine, employed, in connexion with another young Indian named John Arch, to assist the Rev. Mr. Butrick, one of the missionaries at Brainerd, in preparing a Cherokee spelling-book, which was afterwards printed for the use of the schools.[39] Of course, David had previously entered the school. And we may safely conclude that she, who had prayed so earnestly for him, when he was absent, would not fail to exert herself for his spiritual good, when present. Her efforts, in conjunction with those of the missionaries, were not ineffectual. David became thoughtful—deeply impressed—convinced of his sinfulness and his need of salvation by Jesus Christ—and, early in the year 1820, hopes were entertained, that he had become truly pious.

Soon after this, hearing that their father was ill, these young converts from heathenism went home to see him. They remained at home about seven weeks. Catharine says, "David seized his Bible as soon as he reached home, and began to read and interpret to his father and mother, and the other members of the family, exhorting them to attend to it as the word of God, to repent of their sins, which he told them were many and great, and to become the followers of the Lord Jesus Christ." With his father's consent, he maintained the worship of God in the family, morning and evening, and craved a blessing and gave thanks at the table. He also conversed freely with friends and neighbours, boldly professing himself a Christian.

The impression made by this visit, in connexion with the previous efforts of Catharine, was such, that when Mr. Brown, after recovering from his illness, brought his children back to Brainerd, he delivered to the missionaries the following letter, signed by himself and others, headmen and chiefs.

"We, the headmen, chiefs of the Creek-Path town, Cherokee nation, have this day assembled ourselves together for the purpose of devising some plan for the education of our children. We daily witness the good effects arising from education, and therefore are extremely anxious to have a school in our neighbourhood, as the distance from this part of the nation to Chickamaugah is so great as not to suit our convenience. We therefore solicit your aid in carrying our plan into execution. We can raise twenty, or perhaps twenty-five children. You will please write us immediately on the receipt of this. Given under our hands, this 16th of February 1820."

In consequence of this request, the Rev. Daniel S. Butrick, who had acquired some knowledge of the Cherokee language, left Brainerd for Creek-Path, on the 11th of March, and, at a place about two miles from Mr. Brown's residence, the natives having erected a convenient house for the purpose, he soon after opened a school, under very favourable auspices.

Mr. Butrick was accompanied and much assisted by John Arch, a converted Cherokee of good promise, whose name has already been mentioned. This young man was born and bred among the mountains, near the confines of South Carolina, in the most ignorant part of the nation. Happening to be at Knoxville, Tenn. in December 1818, he saw Mr. Hall, who informed him of the school at Chickamaugah. Returning home, he took his gun, and set off in search of the place. After travelling a hundred and fifty miles, he arrived at the station, told the missionaries he had come to attend the school, and offered them his gun, which was his only property, for clothes. We are informed his appearance was so wild and forbidding, that the missionaries hesitated to receive him, especially as he was supposed to be not less than twenty years of age. But he would not be refused. They took him upon trial. It was not long before he discovered an anxious solicitude respecting his soul, and soon gave the most satisfactory evidence of piety. His thirst for knowledge was ardent, and his application and proficiency in learning were gratifying. In ten months he could read and write well. Sometime after he became serious, he was falsely accused, by some one of his schoolmates, of doing an improper act. Conscious of innocence, he could not well brook the charge. That evening and night he was missing, and the next morning it was concluded that he had absconded. But in the course of the forenoon, he made his appearance. On being questioned respecting his absence, he made this reply: "I felt angry, and knew that it was wicked. But I could not suppress it. I therefore went to seek the Saviour, that he might reconcile my heart." It appeared, that he had spent the night in devotional exercises. He was at length admitted to the church, and, from that day to the present, has sustained a good Christian character. He has been much employed as an interpreter, both at the different stations, and in the evangelical labours of the missionaries in various parts of the nation.[40]

While Mr. Butrick was prosecuting his incipient labours at Creek-Path, Catharine and David were employing themselves diligently at Brainerd. Once, in particular, it is recorded, that, after a prayer-meeting, conducted by the missionaries, these two young Cherokees, aided by a pious Indian woman of great age, collected a little group of their people, who had come to spend the Sabbath there, and held a religious conference, with prayer and praise, all in the Cherokee language.

These united labours were, however, interrupted, on the 11th of May, never to be resumed, by the departure of David for the Foreign Mission School in Cornwall, Conn. He left Brainerd only a few days after his admission to the church.

David had been desirous, for some time, of being fitted to preach the Gospel to his countrymen, and was encouraged to aim at such a preparation, first by his sister Catharine, and then by the missionaries. He arrived at Cornwall, sometime in the summer; was connected with that highly favoured school about two years; was then removed to Andover, Mass. where he remained a year, and, without becoming a member of the Theological Institution in that place, enjoyed many of its distinguished advantages. In consequence of the state of his health, and of the great need of his services among those of his countrymen, who reside in the Arkansas country, he returned to them, early in the year 1824. The addresses, which he delivered in many of our principal towns and cities, on the wrongs and claims and prospects of the American Indians, will not soon be forgotten by those who listened to them.[41]

Since his return, a letter has been received, by the Corresponding Secretary of the American Board,[42] which, coming from one so nearly related to Catharine, and giving an amiable view of her family, will interest the reader.

Point Pleasant, Arkansas,[43] *Sept. 20, 1824.*

Dear Sir,

LONG before this time, you must have heard of my speedy passage from Washington City to Arkansas, and of my delightful and joyful meeting with my brethren and kindred according to the flesh. My father and mother embraced me with tears. We were unable to converse, for more than an hour: our mutual joy was so great, that we could not speak for some time. My friends ran as far as they could see me, in order to meet me, and embrace me. The scene was somewhat similar to that of Jacob meeting with his beloved son Joseph.[44]

I was glad to find so much religious feeling among my friends. My parents are very useful in this country, by making known to others the way of salvation. Since my arrival I have had no rest. My friends and relatives are so numerous, that I am constantly on a visit. Dwight, and the residence of my brother Webber, I have made my homes.[45] At Dwight I have all my books. On the Sabbath, I interpret English sermons, and sometimes preach myself in the sweet language of *Tsállakee,* [the Cherokee.] Never were there greater prospects of success among the Cherokees, than at present.

I expect to revisit my mother-country soon, on my father's business, and once more to be at Brainerd, and Creek-Path, beneath the tall trees of *Tsu-saw-ya-wa-sah.* In November and December please to write me at Brainerd, and inform me whether the Board can send us a printer, who is accomplished in his art. Pray send us one.

My fond remembrance to your family. Time and distance can never erase from my bosom the marks of friendship and attention I received in Boston.

David Brown.

About the time of David's departure for New England, Mr. Butrick's school, at Creek-Path, had so increased in the number of its scholars, that there was no more room for the admission of other applicants. The people therefore desired another school. They said, if a female would come to instruct their daughters, they would build a school-house for her. At the same time, it was evident, that a spirit of deep seriousness and anxious inquiry was beginning to prevail among them.

These facts being known at Brainerd, the missionaries thought it their duty to advise Catharine to go and take charge of the contemplated school. In this advice she acquiesced, though not without a painful diffidence of her qualifications for such a service. When it was known at Creek-Path, that she was to take charge of the school, the most enthusiastic joy was occasioned among the people. They seemed to feel, that the preparations could not be made too soon. Not less than fifty Cherokee men, besides negroes and boys, assembled immediately to build a house, which, in two days, was nearly completed according to their stipulation.

Every thing being in readiness, Mr. Brown came for his daughter. She was at Taloney, the missionary station where her friends Mr. and Mrs. Hall resided, and he waited at Brainerd for her return; during which time it was perceived, that the venerable old man was anxiously inquiring after the truth. On the last of May 1820, a little less than two years and eleven months from her first entering the school, as an untaught heathen girl, Catharine bade an affectionate adieu to Brainerd, to take charge of the school for females near her paternal home. The following entry was made at this time, in the journal of the mission.

"31. Catharine left us, in company with her father, to go to Creek-Path, to teach a school of females.

"How very different the scene from that, which passed here not quite two years since, when her father required her to leave the society of Christians, and to accompany him to the then dark shades of the Arkansas! Now, he does not ask her without our consent; will not take her except by our advice; and she is going, not into the wilderness unprepared to teach, but into a place where divine light has already begun to spring up, prepared, as we think, to instruct others. Yet, it is highly probable, that this removal will not be productive of so much good as the former. So unsearchable are the ways of God, and so incompetent is man to judge. It now appears, that her first removal was the means of sowing the seed, which is now springing up at Creek-Path with such hopeful promise."

The remaining letters written during the period embraced by this chapter, will now be inserted. The first was originally published at the close of the narrative of the "Little Osage Captive."

To a Lady in Connecticut.

Brainerd, Jan. 12, 1820.

Dear Sister in Christ,

I THANK you much for your affectionate letter, which I received on the 23d of December. O, how great, how rich is the mercy of our dear Redeemer, who has made us the subjects of his kingdom, and led us, as we trust from death unto life. My dear sister, I can never express my gratitude to God, for his goodness towards me, and my dear people. Surely it is of *his own glorious mercy*, that he is sending to us the Gospel of the Lord Jesus, in this distant land, where the people had long set in darkness, and were perishing for lack of the knowledge of God. Blessed be his holy name! O my sister let us rejoice continually in our Lord and Saviour, and as we have put on Christ, not only by outward profession, but by inward and spiritual union, let us walk worthy of our high and holy vocation, and shew the world, that there is something in true religion. And may the Lord give us strength to do his will, and to follow continually the example of our meek and lowly Jesus. I thank you for the present you sent me, which I received as a token of love. The mission family are all well, and also the dear children. Many of them are serious, and we hope they love and pray to God daily. O that I were more engaged for God, to promote his cause, among these dear children, and my people. I am going soon to visit my parents, which is an hundred miles from here, and expect to stay two months. I hope you will pray for me, that the Lord would bless my visit, and renew the hearts of my dear parents.

Your sincere friend and sister in Christ,
Catharine Brown.

To Mrs. Isabella Hall, at Taloney.

Brainerd, March 8, 1820.

My dear Sister,

IT is with pleasure I take time this morning to assure you, that my love for you is still as great as ever. You cannot tell how painful it was to me to hear that you had been sick. But we know, that the Lord is good, and that all things will work together for good to those who love him, and put their whole trust in him. O could we see each other, how would we talk, and weep, and sing, and pray together.

But our Heavenly Father has separated us. Perhaps we loved each other more than we loved him, and did not pray to him, and praise him, and thank him, as we ought to have done. And is it not so, dear sister? Did we not neglect our duty, and grow cold and careless, when we were together? Now we are sorry, and the Lord will forgive us. Still, dear sister, we can pray for each other. Think you not that our prayers often meet at the throne of grace? O then let us pray on, and never cease to pray for each other, while he lends us breath; and when we meet in heaven, we shall see him whom our soul loveth.

Let us praise the Lord for what he is doing. My dear brother David is now rejoicing in his blessed Redeemer. He has a great desire to do good among our people. I expect he will leave us, in two or three weeks, for Cornwall, to study divinity, and prepare to preach the Gospel of Jesus Christ. I do hope and pray that the Lord will go with him, and enable him to do much good in the world.

He and myself spent seven weeks with our dear parents, and returned to school the last week. I hope to continue here some time longer, but know not how long. My dear mother feels that she cannot spare me much longer, I wish to learn as much as I can, before I go.

And now, my dear sister, may we both be faithful to our Lord, and do much in the world. And when time with us shall be no more, may we be permitted to meet in that world, where Christians will be collected to sing through eternity the song of Moses and the Lamb.[46]

From your sister

Catharine Brown.

To Her Brother David,
While on his way to New England.

Brainerd, May 16, 1820.

My very dear Brother,

I CANNOT express my feelings this evening, when I read your kind letter. My heart is full. But we know, dear brother, that our Saviour orders all things right. I am very sorry to hear that you have lost your horse. What will you do now? But let us not be troubled about these things. If it is best that you should go on, the Saviour will provide for you in some way. Let us only, my dear brother, put our whole trust in God, and be humble at the feet of Jesus. We can do nothing of ourselves. We are like little children. If we rely on our own strength, we shall fall.

It is impossible for me to express what I felt, the morning you left us. But I thought, that if I should never see you again in this world, I should meet you in a better, where there will be no separation. O how thankful we ought to be to God, who has brought us from darkness into the light of the Gospel.

But many of our dear people are yet deprived of this great privilege. They know not the Saviour, whom we have found so precious. Yes, even our dear parents are yet living without any hope in God. O my brother, let us never cease to pray for them. God will surely hear us, if we ask in faith.

Dear brother, forget me not in your prayers. Your sister C. will never forget you. When you are far from this place, your poor sister C. will be praying for you. Good night, dear brother, till we meet again.

Catharine Brown.

Chapter IV.

FROM HER TAKING CHARGE OF A SCHOOL
AT CREEK-PATH, UNTIL HER SICKNESS.

WE now enter upon the last three, and the most interesting years of Catharine's life, in which we shall behold her in new circumstances; her character more fully developed, and her graces shining with greater lustre.

In order that she may speak for herself as much as possible, that part of her private diary will be inserted, which was saved from the destruction, to which many of her papers were devoted, a little before her sickness. It was obtained from Mrs. Gilbreth, a sister of Catharine, and a faithful copy was transmitted by Mrs. Potter, the wife of the Rev. William Potter, missionary at Creek-Path.

Extracts from Her Diary.

"Brainerd, May 30, 1820. Tomorrow morning I shall leave this school, perhaps never to return. It is truly painful to part with my dear Christian friends, those, with whom I have spent many happy hours in the house of worship. I must bid them farewell. This is the place, where I first became acquainted with the dear Saviour. He now calls me to work in his vineyard,[47] and shall I, for the sake of my Christian friends and of my own pleasures, refuse to go, while many of my poor red brothers and sisters are perishing for lack of knowledge? O no. I *will not* refuse to go. I will go wherever the Saviour calls me. I know he will be on my right hand, to grant me all the blessings, that I shall need, and he will direct me how to instruct the dear children, who shall be committed to my care.

"31. This morning I set out from Brainerd, with my dear father. Travelled about twenty miles. Thought much of my beloved Christian friends. Whether I shall ever see them again, is uncertain. The Lord only knows.

"June 2. Have been very sick to day; but, blessed be God, am now a little better. Hope I shall be able to travel tomorrow. The Lord is very kind and merciful to all those, who put their trust in him. Last night I slept on the floor without any bed. Felt quite happy in my situation. Though very sick in body, yet I trust my heart was well.

"5. Have arrived at my father's, but am yet very unwell. Have a bad cold. Am sometimes afraid I shall not be able to teach school at Creek-Path. We slept two nights on the ground with our wet blankets, before we reached our home.

"20. Blessed be God, who has again restored me to health. It is two weeks to-day since I commenced teaching a girl's school. O how much I need wisdom from God. I am a child. I can do nothing. But in God will I trust, for I know there is none else, to whom I can look for help.

"Sept. 5. This day I received a letter from brother David. I rejoice much to hear, that he has arrived safely at Cornwall. May the Lord be with him, and make him useful as long as he lives, and at death may he be received at the right hand of God. This is the prayer of his affectionate sister Catharine."

Before proceeding further with the extracts from the diary, it seems proper to insert some notices not found in that document.

Catharine commenced her school with about twenty scholars, and the number soon increased. Not only the daughters, but the mothers also, manifested a strong desire to receive instruction. Several of her pupils, in consequence of previous tuition, could read in the New Testament, when they came under her care. These it was her delight to lead to a more perfect acquaintance with that sacred volume. But most of the children began with the rudiments of learning. This school she continued three quarters of a year, much to the satisfaction of her scholars, their parents, and the missionaries. She finally relinquished it only because the arrival of Mr. and Mrs. Potter gave her an opportunity to surrender her charge into other hands, and at the same time opened the way for her prosecuting higher studies, with a view to greater usefulness to her people.

The spirit of serious inquiry at Creek Path, to which there was an allusion at the close of the last chapter, increased after the arrival of Catharine, especially among her own kindred. Doubtless she was not backward, with the meekness of humility and with the earnestness of affection, to warn and exhort. And she had the joy of beholding her father, mother, a brother, and two or three sisters, unitedly seeking the pardon of their sins, and that peace, which the world giveth not. After a suitable trial, and due instruction, all these her relatives, with others of their countrymen, publicly professed faith in Christ, and were united to his visible Church.

It is gratifying to be able to remark, that no one of them has hitherto dishonoured the Christian profession, and that all who survive, are believed to be the humble followers of the Lord Jesus. One has "fallen asleep," and of him an affectionate record will be found in the diary of Catharine.

Shortly after the last paragraph extracted from her diary was written, nearly the whole family made a visit to Brainerd. The hearts of the missionaries were made glad, by the sight of this little band; and oh! how must the heart of Catharine have exulted with joy, while she presented her beloved relatives, one after another, as the friends and followers of her blessed Saviour!

It will be remembered that a letter from the chiefs at Creek-Path, desiring the missionaries to establish a school among them, was inserted in the last chapter. Mr. Brown was now the bearer of another letter from the same chiefs, signed by their Chairman, or Speaker, in which they thus express their approbation of the school, and their good wishes with respect to missionary efforts:

"Friends and Brothers,

"we are glad to inform you, that we are well pleased with Mr. Butrick, who has come forward as a teacher to instruct our people. We believe he does discharge his duty; and we hope his coming will be of great advantage to our people. Our wish is, that you may prosper throughout our nation, in your laudable undertaking. It is out of our power to see you, in any short time, on account of the National Council, and other business we are obliged to attend at this time. It is our wish that the school should continue at this place. Mr. John Brown, sen. will deliver this, who will present you our hands in friendship. We hope we shall see each other before long. We are glad to see our children advancing so well. We conclude with our best respects.

    WAU-SAU-SEY, *Bear-meat*, Speaker."

Here some remarks may properly be introduced, on the traits of character, which Catharine exhibited, during a part of the time embraced in her diary. These remarks are taken from the letter of Mrs. Potter, which enclosed that document.

"In the spring of 1821, while making the necessary preparations for a settlement at Creek-Path, Mr. Potter and myself, for two months, made Mr. Brown's house our home. Here we had an opportunity of noticing Catharine's daily deportment, as a member of the domestic circle.

"For sweetness of temper, meekness, gentleness, and forbearance, I never saw one, who surpassed her. To her parents she was uncommonly dutiful and affectionate. Nothing, which could contribute to their happiness, was considered a burden; and her plans were readily yielded to theirs, however great the sacrifice to her feelings. The spiritual interests of the family lay near her heart, and she sometimes spent whole evenings in conversation with them on religious subjects.

"Before our arrival, she had established a weekly prayer-meeting with the female members of the family, which was also improved as an opportunity for reading the word of God, and conversing upon its important truths. Such was her extreme modesty, that she did not make this known to me, until more than a week after my arrival; and the usual period had passed without a meeting. She at length overcame her diffidence, and informed me what their practice had been, in a manner expressive of the most unfeigned humility. These meetings were continued while we remained in the family, and I believe they were highly useful. A monthly prayer-meeting among the sisters of the church was soon after established, in which Catharine took a lively interest; nor did she ever refuse, when requested, to take an active part in the devotional exercises.

"Soon after we removed to our station, Catharine became a member of our family, and of the school. All her energies were now bent towards the improvement of her mind, with a view to future usefulness among her people. Both in school, and in the family, her deportment was such as greatly to endear her to our hearts, and she was most tenderly loved by all the children.

"She was not *entirely* free from the inadvertences of youth; but always received reproof with great meekness, and it never failed to produce the most salutary effect.

"She was deeply sensible of the many favours she had received from Christian friends, and often, in the strongest terms, expressed her gratitude.

"She was zealous in the cause of Christ, and laboured much to instruct her ignorant people in the things, that concern their everlasting peace. The advancement of the Redeemer's kingdom was to her a subject of deep interest, and she read accounts of the triumphs of the cross in heathen countries, with peculiar delight. Not many months after we settled here, a plan was devised to form a female charitable society. This plan was proposed to Catharine. She was much pleased with it, and spared no pains to explain it to the understandings of her Cherokee friends. And so successful were her exertions, that, at the meeting for the formation of the Society, at which a considerable number were present, not one refused to become a member. For the prosperity of this Society she manifested the most tender concern till her death; and she had determined, if her life should be spared to reach the Arkansas country, to use her exertions to form a similar Society there."[48]

The extracts from the diary will now be resumed, and will be continued without interruption.

Extracts from Her Diary.[49]

"*Creek-Path May* 1, 1821. Commenced boarding with Mr. and Mrs. Potter. My parents live two miles from this place. I think I shall visit them almost every week, and they will come to see me often.

"2. I love to live here much. It is retired, and a good place for study. Every thing looks pleasant around the school-house. The trees are covered with green leaves, and the birds sing very sweetly. How pleasant it is to be in the woods, and hear the birds praising the Lord. They remind me of the divine command, 'Remember thy Creator.' O may I never be so stupid and senseless [as to forget my Creator,] but may I remember to love and serve him, the few days I live in this world; for the time will soon come, when I must appear before him. Help me, Lord, to live to thy glory, even unto the end of my life.

"I think I feel more anxious to learn, and to understand the Bible perfectly, than I ever did before. Although I am so ignorant, the Saviour is able to prepare me for usefulness among my people.

"5. Saturday evening. Again I am brought to the close of another week. How have I spent my time the past week? Have I done any thing for God, and any good to my fellow creatures? I fear I have done nothing to glorify his holy name. Oh, how prone I am to sin, and to grieve the Spirit of a holy God, who is so kind in giving me time to prepare for heaven. May I improve these precious moments to the glory of my God.

"6. Sabbath evening. How thankful I ought to be to God, that he has permitted me once more to commemorate the love of a Saviour, who has shed his precious blood for the remission of sin. It was indeed a solemn season to me, and I hope refreshing to each of our souls. While sitting at the table, I thought of many sins, which I had committed against God, through my life, and how much I deserved to be cast out from his presence forever. But the Son of God, who was pleased to come down from the bosom of his Father, to die on the cross for sinners like me, will, I hope, save me from death, and at last raise me to mansions of eternal rest, where I shall sit down with my blessed Jesus.

"8. This evening I have nothing to complain of, but my unfaithfulness both to God and my own soul. Have not improved my precious moments as I ought. Have learned but little in school, though my privileges are greater than those of many others. While they are ignorant of God, and have no opportunity to hear or learn about him, I am

permitted to live with the children of God, where I am instructed
to read the Bible, and to understand the character of Jesus. O may
I be enabled to follow the example of my teachers, to live near the
Saviour, and to do much good. I wish very much to be a missionary
among my people. If I had an education———but perhaps I ought
not to think of it. I am not worthy to be a missionary.

"14. Mr. Hoyt called on us this week, on his return from Mayhew. He
gives us much interesting intelligence respecting the Choctaw mission. Mr. Hoyt expected to have brought Dr. Worcester with him, but
he was too sick to travel, and was obliged to stay behind. He hopes
to be able to come on soon. I long to see him. He has done a great
deal towards spreading the Gospel, not only in this nation, but in
other heathen nations of the earth. May the Lord restore his health,
that he may see some fruits among the heathen, for whom he has
been so long labouring.

"29. This day I spent my time very pleasantly at home with my dear
friends. Find that brother John is the same humble believer in Jesus,
walking in the Christian path. I am truly happy to meet my dear parents and sisters in health, and rejoicing in the hope of eternal glory.
O may God ever delight to bless them, and to pour his Spirit richly
into their hearts. I am much pleased to see them making preparations for the Sabbath. They have been engaged to-day in preparing
such food, &c. as they thought would be wanting to-morrow. I think
brother John and sister Susannah have done much good here with
respect to the Sabbath.

"30. This day attended another solemn meeting in the house of God.
Mr. Potter preached by an interpreter. I think more people than usual
attended. All seemed attentive to hear the word of God. Mr. P. spoke
of the importance of keeping the Sabbath holy. I hope it will not be
in vain to all those who were present.

June 4. This day being *the first Monday in the month*, the people met to
pray and receive religious instruction. It was truly an interesting time.
The congregation, though small, was serious. One man and his wife,
who have been for some time in an anxious state of mind remained
after the meeting, and Mr. and Mrs. P. earnestly entreated them to

seek the Lord while he was near unto them. They appeared very solemn, and said they wished to know more about God, that they might serve him the rest of their days. We hope and pray, that they may be truly converted, and become our dear brother and sister in the Lord.

"July 1. This day I have enjoyed much. Was permitted once more to sit down at the table of the Lord, and commemorate his dying love. O how good is the Saviour in permitting me to partake of his grace. May I improve my great privileges in the manner I shall wish I had done, when I come to leave the world.—P.M. Went to Mr. G.'s, where Mr. Potter preaches once in two weeks. Most of the people present were whites, from the other side of the river. It was pleasant to hear a sermon preached without an interpreter.

"Sept. 2. Think I have had a good time to-day, in praying to my heavenly Father. I see nothing to trouble me, but my own wicked heart. It appears to me, that the more I wish to serve God, the more I sin. I seem never to have done any thing good in the sight of God. But the time is short, when I shall be delivered from this body of sin, and enter the kingdom of heaven.

"3. The first Monday in the month. No doubt many Christians have been this day praying for my poor nation, as well as for other heathen nations of the earth. O why do I live so little concerned for my own soul, and for the souls of others? Why is it that I pray no more to God? Is it because he is not merciful? Oh no. He is good, kind, merciful, always ready to answer the prayers of his children. O for more love to my Saviour than I now have.

"4. I am now with my sister, with whom I expect to spend a few days. I hope the Lord will make our communion sweet.

"Visited at Mr.————'s, but had no opportunity of conversing with Mrs.————on religious subjects, as we intended to have done. Mr.————said he had seen so many different ways among professed Christians, that it was hard to tell who was right. I felt too ignorant to instruct such a well educated man; though I knew, that there is *but one* way under heaven, whereby men can be saved, and that is, by coming to Him, who came to seek and to save that which was lost.

"9. Returned yesterday from sister G's. Found the mission family in good health. I cannot express how much I love the missionaries, with whom I live. I do not feel my privileges, until I am away from them, and mingle with worldly people. Then I long to get back to be with Christians.

"I rejoice and bless my heavenly Father, that he has kept my dear brother John, and permitted me to meet him once more in the land of the living. I am sorry to see him so unwell, and fear he will not recover. But the Lord's will be done, and not mine. I know that he will do all things for the good of those who love him.

"Left home, in company with brother John and sister Susannah, [his wife,] for the purpose of visiting the Sulphur Springs in Blount county, Alabama.

"21. About noon we came to a spring, which is said to possess the same qualities with those we intended to visit, and we concluded to make it the place of our abode for a few days. We therefore pitched our tent a few yards from the water, and at night spread our blankets on the ground, and slept very well.

"22. Feel very uneasy respecting my brother, he is so unwell. May the Lord be with us in this lonely place.

"23. Brother John drinks the water, and bathes in it, but has yet received no benefit. I do not feel so well as I did before I came here, and almost wish to return immediately. Perhaps it is lying on the ground, that makes me feel sick. But if brother John had a comfortable place to sleep, I should not care for myself. The Lord knows what is best for us.

"24. We expect a boy with our horses to-day, and hope to reach home tomorrow. Saw Mr. J. R. to-day in a very low state of health. Conversed with him a little on the subject of religion. This I really felt was my duty, as I thought it likely I should never have another opportunity. He said, he was very wicked, and afraid to die. I told him we were all wicked, but the Saviour, who was willing to die for us, would pardon our sins, if we would only give ourselves to him. He replied, that when he was in health, he did not do his duty towards God, but if he recovered he would try to do better. As he was not able to converse much, I commended him to God, and left him. God is able to make him his dear child, and to prepare him for heaven.

"Jan. 3, 1822. This was truly a solemn and interesting day to me, one which will never be forgotten. My dear father and mother were baptised in the name of the Holy Trinity. How kind is our Creator, in his willingness to take notice of us sinful worms of the dust, and allowing us to become acquainted with Jesus Christ. O may we walk close with God, and be enabled to set such an example to others, that they may be led to glorify our Father, who is in heaven.

"14. Have not attended school since last vacation, having been at home taking care of my sick brother. He has failed very fast, the past week. I fear he will not live many days. The will of the Lord be done.

"16. My dear brother is very low. Perhaps he will soon depart from this sinful world, and fly to the arms of his blessed Redeemer. Had some conversation with him in the evening. His mind seemed to be in a happy state. He asked me, whether, after his decease, I thought we should stay here, or go to the Arkansas. I told him I hoped he would be restored to health. He said he thought that was very doubtful, and added, that he thought brother Webber would come for us after his departure. My heart was full. I could make no reply.

"18. Mr. Butrick and John Arch, who have been visiting us for a few days past, left us this morning, with the intention of going through the nation, preaching Jesus Christ to those, who are in darkness. This will probably take three months. May the Lord go with his dear servants on their long journey through the wilderness, and bless their labours to many immortal souls. I cannot sufficiently express my gratitude to God, for sending out missionaries to this distant land, that we, who were wanderers in the wild woods, might find the road to heaven. How kindly are they inviting us to come and partake of the rich feast, which has been provided for all who will accept it. Yet how few are willing to comply with the invitation! Frequently do I weep for my Cherokee brothers and sisters, when I consider their awful situation while out of Christ; and willingly would I offer myself for their assistance, were I qualified for a religious teacher. I hope God will prepare me to do some good among the heathen. O that it may be my greatest desire to do the will of my heavenly Father. I am determined to pray for my people, while God lends me breath;

and when I die, may my Saviour receive me to my heavenly home, to join with millions of saints in singing the praises of redeeming love through a never-ending eternity.

"29. Eternity seems near. A few days more, and if I am indeed a child of God, I shall walk the golden streets of the New Jerusalem. O happy day, when I shall see all the Christians, who have ever lived, and when God himself shall be my joy.

"30. Brother John is senseless most of the time. I fear he is to remain but a little while in this world. But in that case he will soon go to his Father in heaven. May we be submissive, knowing that he, who sent us into this world, has a right to call us hence whenever he sees best. Our great consolation is, that our dear brother will soon be freed from pain, and rest in the bosom of his dear Jesus.

"31. Had the pleasure of seeing Mr. and Mrs. Potter at this place. I love them, as *my own* brother and sister.

"Feb. 2. My dear brother very sick. O thou blessed Jesus, take him not away by this sickness. Restore him to health, that he may live long, and be a great blessing to our nation. But O may I be submissive to thy holy will.

"Sabbath morning. Painful is it to record, that my dear brother John appears, this day, to be on the borders of eternity! Lord, come near to us at this time. Help us to give up our dear brother into thy hands.

"Evening. Brother John is no more! O distressing thought, he has gone to return no more! But we shall soon go to him. I trust, indeed, we have much reason to believe he has gone to Christ his Saviour. Through his sickness he seemed reconciled to the will of God, and said he was not afraid to die. He said, that though his sufferings were great, they were nothing in comparison with Christ's sufferings. About a week before he died, he spoke to the family as follows:—'It is now more than a year since we began to follow Christ, and what have we done for him? Do we live like Christians? I fear we do not. I do not hear you talk to the people about our Saviour, when they come to visit you. We are professors of religion, and why is it that we do not show it to others? You should always remember to keep the Sabbath holy. You are too much occupied in domestic concerns on the Sabbath, so that you cannot get time to converse about God.' He asked me, if the missionaries did their cooking on the Sabbath. I told him, their preparations were made before the Sabbath. He said, 'that is what we ought to do.' He frequently requested me to read and explain the Bible to him, which was my great delight."

Here ends her diary. And the reader will doubtless wish that all had been saved, breathing, as it does, so much good sense and unfeigned piety.

Of her brother John, the journal of the mission at Brainerd contains the following eulogium, penned on hearing of his death.

"Two years ago he was in heathenish darkness. About that time, his brother and sister told him of the Bible, and some of the important truths it contained; and he soon felt an unconquerable desire to read it. He could then talk and understand familiar English. Soon after, a school was opened in his neighbourhood, and he applied himself, with the most unwearied diligence, to study. In the course of six months, he learned to read intelligibly; read the New Testament through once, and about half through again; wrote a number of legible letters to his friends; became a hopeful convert to the Christian religion, and a member of the Church of Christ, which he continued to adorn by an exemplary life, till his departure from these dark and afflictive scenes, to join, as we trust, the Church of the first-born in heaven."

Soon after the decease of this brother, Catharine accompanied her father to Huntsville, in the state of Alabama.

Here, either at that time, or later in the season, she spent two or three months, in the family of Dr. Alexander A. Campbell, a pious and esteemed physician. Dr. Campbell had seen her at her father's house before she went to Brainerd, and was so favourably impressed, by her personal appearance, that he subsequently procured for her a Bible, and some other religious books, which were forwarded, but never received.

Nearly five years had elapsed since that interview. Dr. Campbell's own words, extracted from his letter to the Rev. Mr. Potter of Creek-Path, shall describe the impression, which she now made upon him, and upon others in Huntsville.

"She was not now the wild, untutored girl she was then. She was graceful and polite, and humility and benevolence beamed from her countenance. Some of my acquaintance were unwilling to believe she was an Indian.

"At your request, I returned with her to her nation to see a diseased Indian child, and though it was at the expense of neglecting important professional business, I was amply repaid, by the interesting conversation I had with her, on literary and religious subjects.

"At first, she was backward to enter into free conversation. A diffident reserve was a prominent trait in her character. But when we became well acquainted, I found her perfectly agreeable and intelligent on any ordinary subject. But her favourite theme was the Saviour. She dwelt much, also, on the situation of her people, and manifested the greatest solicitude for their spiritual interests; often expressing the hope, that I would come and live among them, and teach them respecting the Lord Jesus.

"During the summer of this year, she spent several months in my family. A part of that time she was suffering very severely from a bilious fever, which she bore with all possible patience and resignation, never showing that peevishness and fretfulness so common in persons recovering from that disease. She always looked upon her afflictions as resulting from the chastising hand of God, and designed for her improvement.

"She received very marked attentions from the visitors at my house, and many of the principal families in the town sought an acquaintance with her, appeared sensible of her worth, and esteemed her friendship highly. These attentions, so far from exciting her vanity, had the effect to humble her the more. She appeared ever to think much less highly of herself, than others thought of her. I have often been astonished to see how the flattering addresses and high encomiums of people of elevated standing in society, seemed to render her more distrustful of her own worth."

This, though evidently the warm language of friendship, is justified by the concurrent testimony of all the intimate friends of Catharine.

In September 1822, at the earnest request of her parents, she left the family of Mr. Potter to reside with them. Being engaged, at that time, in some favourite studies, it was a great trial to leave the school. But so tender was her regard for her aged parents, that she made not the least objection.

Near the close of the year 1822, the Rev. Reynolds Bascom, accompanied by several Indian youth from the Foreign Mission School at Cornwall, arrived at Creek-Path, on his way to Elliot, where he designed to spend a few months in missionary labour.

"Here," says Mr. Bascom, "I had an opportunity of seeing the precious fruits of missionary instruction and divine grace, in the intelligence, amiable manners, and Christian temper, of Catharine, and other members of the little church which had been formed in the place, chiefly among her family connexions.

"The impression made on my mind by my first interview, which was at her father's house, was that of uncommon simplicity, modesty and meekness. We arrived after the family had dined, and she received us and spread a table for our refreshment, with the unaffected kindness of a sister. The gracefulness of her figure, and the sweetness of her expression, have often been the subject of remark; and I was the more delighted with her humility, as I greatly feared I should discover an unhappy influence from the misjudged praise, which had been heaped upon her. The fact was, she gave me evidence, by her habitual behaviour, of being a sanctified child of God."

It was soon after her removal to her paternal home, that the disease, the seeds of which had, probably for several years, been germinating in her constitution, began to assume an aspect, which excited some alarm.

In consequence of this, she took a journey to Brainerd, in February 1823, with the view of consulting Dr. Butler, a medical gentleman residing at that station.[50] She hoped, also, to derive benefit from the journey. These hopes were disappointed. A cold, tempestuous storm arose, soon after she left home, to the whole of which she was unavoidably exposed; and the slight cough, to which she had, for some time, been subject, was very much increased. She spent three weeks at Brainerd, and then returned to Creek-Path, intending to obtain permission from her parents to place herself again under the care of Dr. Butler. But her increased illness rendered her unable to encounter the fatigues of another journey.

The narrative must now be interrupted, in order that several letters, written during the time embraced by this chapter, may be introduced. A part of the first, and the fourth, were published in the narrative of the "Little Osage Captive." The third made its first appearance in the New Haven Religious Intelligencer.

To Her Brother David, at Cornwall.

Creek-Path, Aug. 12, 1820.

My dear Brother,

YOUR dear lines I received this evening, for which I thank you. I hope they will not be the last you will write me. O dear brother, how much it would rejoice my heart to see you this evening, and converse with you face to face! But our good Lord has separated us, perhaps never to see each other again in this world. I often think of the morning you left Brainerd. It was a solemn hour, and I trust it was a sweet season to our souls. We wept, and prayed, and sung together before our dear Saviour; and longed for that blessed day, when we should meet, to part no more. What is a short separation in this world? Nothing compared to an eternal separation! How thankful we ought to be then, my dear brother, that we have a hope to be saved through the blessed Lamb of God. Yes, I trust when our bodies shall die, our souls shall be raised above the sky, where we shall dwell together, in singing the praises of Him who bought us with his precious blood. I hope we shall meet our parents, and brothers, and sisters there. Since you left, the Lord has reached down his arm, to take sinners from darkness, into the marvellous light of the Gospel. Dear brother, let us praise and rejoice continually in the Lord, for his goodness to our dear people, in giving them hearts to love and praise his holy name. Surely the Lord is with us here. We feel his presence. Our dear father and mother are inquiring what they shall do to be saved. Mother says she is grieved to think her children are going to leave her behind. But she says she will pray as long as she lives, and that the Saviour will pardon her sins, that she may go with her children to heaven.

I hope you will write to our parents as often as you can. I sometimes think the Saviour has given them new hearts, especially our dear father. He appears quite changed.

Soon after you left Brainerd, I was called here to take charge of a school of females, about two miles from home. I take great delight in teaching. The number of girls in school is twenty-eight. They are very good children, and learn fast. Sister Anna is assisting me in the school. She rejoices with us to hear from you in this distant land.

O dear brother, I hope you will pray for me. Pray that I may do good to the immortal souls of my pupils. Sometimes the work appears too great for me, and I am almost discouraged. But I know, He that has called me to work in his vineyard, is able to keep me.

I could tell you a great many good things, if I had time. But I must stop, after asking your prayers for all your Creek-Path friends. I hope when you return to your nation, you will find many Christians. Farewell, dear brother; may the Lord be with you, and prepare you for great usefulness in the world. This is the prayer of your sister
> Catharine Brown.

To Mr. and Mrs. Hall.

Creek-Path, Nov. 19, 1820.

My dear Brother and Sister,

THIS is the first opportunity I have had to answer the kind letter, which you wrote some time since. I thank you for it, and hope you will forgive me for not writing sooner. I think of you every day, and long to see you once more in this world. I often think of the happy hours we used to spend together, while I was with you at Brainerd. But the happy hours are gone, I fear never to return. I hope, if we may not meet in this world, we may in heaven, where we shall never be separated. O, my dear friends, do you not sometimes long to see that glorious day, when Christians shall be gathered from all parts of the world to sing the praises of our dear Redeemer? What a day it will be for Christians! And shall we be among the number?

Sometimes I fear I shall not be, my wicked heart is so prone to sin. But I know the blood of Christ is sufficient to wash away all my sins, and prepare me for his eternal glory. I will, therefore, commit myself to God. It is all that I can do.

O how good it is to lie at the feet of Jesus, and feel ourselves purified by his blood. Then we have no reason to fear what the world can do unto us.

My dear friends, I cannot tell you how much I love you, because you were willing to leave your native land, and your dear people, to come into this heathen part of the world, to instruct me and my people in the way of salvation. May the Lord reward you for this labour of love. Probably you must have some trials to pass through, as other missionaries do; but we ought to rejoice, that we are accounted worthy to labour for God. Our days will soon be past, and if we are the children of God, we shall soon be at rest in the bosom of our dear Saviour.

My father, mother, brothers, and sisters, wish to be remembered affectionately to you. Write often. I am always happy to hear from you.

From your sister,

Catharine Brown.

To Her Brother David.

Creek-Path, Feb. 21, 1821.

My dear Brother,

I RECEIVED your kind letter some time since, and it gave me great satisfaction to hear from you. I should have written to you before this time, but did not know how to send to Brainerd. I am truly happy to hear that you feel so well contented with your situation in school, and that you are well pleased with your dear instructor. Our dear parents are in good health. They have removed from the place where they lived before, and are now living with brother John. I think they have truly passed from death unto life. They seem to be growing in grace and in the knowledge of Him who has redeemed their souls from hell.

Indeed, you cannot imagine how different they seem from what they did when you left us. All they desire now, is to do the will of our dear Saviour. This work is the Lord's, and no doubt he will keep them and carry them safe through this sinful world, until he receives them to his heavenly kingdom, O, dear brother, truly the Lord has heard our prayers for the souls of our parents. We have great reason to rejoice. May we not say,—not unto us, but to thy name be all the praise? You have doubtless heard that brother John has joined the church. Dear brother David, my heart is full while I am writing. How shall I express my gratitude to God for bringing him to a knowledge of the Saviour. He says sometimes he feels happy in praying to God, and feels willing that he should do with him as seemeth good in his sight.

My brother David, when we look back and see what the Lord has done for our family in the course of a few years, O let us call upon our souls, and all that is within us, to praise our God for his great blessings to us.

I sometimes long to see your face once more in this world, to converse and pray with you before our Saviour. I often think of the happy hours, which we spent when we were at Brainerd, when we first tasted the sweetness of religion, and when we used to take each other's hand to walk and sing our favourite hymn,

"Come we that love the Lord."

We then knew the happiness of saints, and felt that religion was not "designed to make our pleasures less." But now our heavenly Father has separated us for a time in this world; I hope for his glory, and for the good of perishing souls around us. We have much to do for our Saviour. As we hope we are children of the most high God, let us be good soldiers, and not be weary in well-going, for in due season we shall reap if we faint not. Father and mother send love to you, and to the scholars in Cornwall. I hope you will write to us soon, and let us know how you do.

Adieu, dear brother, till we meet again,

Catharine Brown.

To the Same.

Creek-Path, 1821.

My dear Brother,

ALTHOUGH we may be separated many hundreds of miles, the God of the Universe, whom we serve, will often give us the enjoyment of himself, which you know is of far greater value than all this world can afford. Last Sabbath was a very solemn and interesting day to us. Rev. Mr. W. from the state of New York was here—a very pious and engaged Christian. We were much refreshed by his kind instructions. I think it was truly a pleasant day to my soul. The sacrament was administered, and we were permitted once more to sit at the table of the Lord, and commemorate his dying love. Mr. S. was baptised. Also an infant of Mrs. F. named Samuel Worcester. The congregation were attentive and some of them were affected to tears. I hope the time is not far distant, when all the heathen shall be brought to the knowledge of the Redeemer. We have recently formed a Female Society[51] in this place. The members pay fifty cents a year. I trust you will pray that we may be blessed, and that we may be instrumental in the great work of building up the cause of the Redeemer. I can never be sufficiently thankful to God for sending us missionaries, to teach us the way we should go. We love them as our own brothers and sisters. That you may enjoy the light of our Saviour's countenance, while in this short journey of life, and finally be received to mansions of eternal glory, is the prayer of your sister,

Catharine Brown.

To Mr. and Mrs. Hall.

Creek-Path, June 1, 1822.

My dear Brother and Sister Hall,

SWEET and reviving is the thought, that we are not to continue long in this world, but hope soon to rest in the city of our God. My dear brother and sister, be patient in all your trials and hardships, remembering that you are labouring for God, and not for man alone. The Saviour will give you an unfading crown of glory in due season. I often think of the glorious day, when I shall meet you, and all good missionaries, in the kingdom of our Saviour. I shall then be always with those dear friends, who have told me so much about heaven, and taught me to love and serve Christ. I hope you will not forget to pray, that I may possess more of the spirit of Christ.

The pupils in the school here generally make good improvement. The religious prospects are encouraging. Meetings on the Sabbath, and weekly conferences, are well attended. The church appears well. Last Sabbath I, for the first time, met my parents at the table of the Lord.

I have many things to tell you; but my health will not allow me to write much at one time. The little I have written gives me pain. My health has been feeble for some weeks past, but my complaints are not alarming. I shall try to visit you next vacation, if life is spared. Will my dear brother and sister write soon to their affectionate
Catharine.

To Her Brother David.

Huntsville, Aug. 30, 1822.

My dear Brother,

I AM sorry to tell you, that I have but a few moments of time to write this evening. I came here the 13th inst. and expect to return in a few weeks.

I left our friends all very well, and walking in the fear of God. I should have written long before this, had I not been sick; but my health is now much better than it was when I left home. Brother David, remember that your sister Catharine loves you much, and prays for you every day. I trust you will not return before you are prepared to preach the Gospel. Let me know your feelings in this respect when you write again, and I shall know how to pray for you. I do not expect you to go through all the studies, that ministers generally do in New

England, but wish you to be qualified enough to withstand the enemies of God, and teach the truths of Christianity. If your health does not permit you to study, and your hesitation of speech still continues, I should not think it was your duty to pursue your studies.

However, I know the Lord will make every path of duty plain before you. Do not think we are unhappy. It is true we were greatly tried, last winter, in losing our dear brother. But, blessed be God, it was not more than we are able to bear.

We feel it was good for us to be afflicted, knowing that the Lord is good, and will always do what is right. I have not time to write all I wish to send you. When I return home, you shall have a long letter from your affectionate sister
    Catharine.

To the Same, at Andover.

Creek-Path, Jan. 18, 1823.

My dear Brother,

YOURS of Nov. 2, 1822, was received a few days since. I am much gratified to hear, that you are to continue in New England another year. I hope you will be the better qualified for usefulness to our countrymen, when you return. I pray for you daily, that God may be with you and bless you in your undertaking.

I feel anxious to see you, yet I am willing to have you stay until you have received further education. How has your mind been exercised since you entered the interesting Seminary at Andover? Are you living in the enjoyment of the religion of Christ? We must, dear brother, live near to God, and be engaged in his cause, if we would be his followers. Let us, then, not calculate to live in idleness and ease, unconcerned for the salvation of souls.

We are under great obligations to honour God before the world, and to be active in his service. Let us not hide our talents in the earth, for the Lord will require them of us. There is a crown of glory laid up for those who are faithful unto the end.

It is now eleven months, since our dear brother John departed from this lower world, and entered the unseen regions of eternity, where I hope he is now walking in the streets of the New Jerusalem, filled with holy love. Oh boundless love, and matchless grace, of our Lord and Saviour Jesus Christ! How happy shall we feel when we land on the shores of eternal felicity. There we shall meet our dear brother, and all who have gone before us, and shall reign in the paradise of God forever and ever.

I often think of our relations in the Arkansas. I long to hear of their conversion. Let us not neglect to pray for them daily; particularly for brother W. The Lord, I hope, will renew his heart, and make him abundantly useful to the cause of missions.

We rejoice to see brother A. once more in our dwellings. After a long journey from the Arkansas country, he arrived here, much fatigued, in the latter part of November. He intends to spend a few months with us, and then return with sister Susan. I do not feel very well about her going into the wilderness, and far from Christian society, where she will perhaps have no religious instruction.

Her mother has removed thirty or forty miles from the missionary station [at Dwight.] But we commend her into the hands of the Almighty, who is able to keep her from evil, and from all the temptations of this delusive world. I am glad to hear from our relations in that country. Brother Walter was expecting to set out in a few days for the city of Washington, and had thoughts of visiting some of the northern States before he returned. It is likely you may see him in New England. He has placed brother Edmund in the missionary school at Dwight, to continue three or four years. He has become very steady and attentive to his books. I hope the Lord will give him a new heart, and prepare him for usefulness.

Brother W. has given up trading, and has commenced farming. He has purchased land in the Osage country, at the Salt Springs. Whether he intends removing his family to that place, I know not. It is my prayer, that he may be brought to bow to the sceptre of King Jesus, in whom is life everlasting. As for our going to the Arkansas, it is not decided. Perhaps we shall know better, when you return. You know mother is always very anxious to remove to that country, but father is not. For my own part, I feel willing to do whatever is duty, and the will of our parents. I feel willing to go, or stay. The Lord will direct all things right, and in him may we put all our trust.

We had the pleasure of seeing your schoolmates McKee and Israel Folsom. They called on us on their way to the Choctaw nation. They said there were many good people at the north. They had rather live among the Yankees, than any other people. I hope they will be very useful to their nation.

Mr. Potter has gone to Brainerd on some business, and I shall stay with Mrs. P. until he returns. We expect him home this week. I hope he will bring a large packet of letters from our Brainerd friends. Mrs. P. is engaged in teaching school while her husband is absent. Several of the scholars are very attentive, and make good progress in their studies. Sarah is in the first class. She is a good girl to learn, and is much beloved by her teacher. She has begun to read the Bible in course, and has read partly through the Memoirs of Miss Caroline Smelt. When I wrote to you last, I was in a declining state of health, and for that reason I left my studies to have more exercise. The Lord has been pleased to restore me to my usual health, and I now feel pretty well.

I spent two months in Huntsville, last spring, in the family of Dr. Campbell. Mrs.————is a very pious and engaged Christian. I became acquainted with several pious families in Huntsville, who, I believe, feel interested in the cause of missions. The pious ladies made up clothing for the children in Creek-Path. We hope this is only the beginning of a missionary spirit in that place.

I am glad to tell you, that our female Society is growing in its numbers. We have collected nearly double the sum this year that we did last. The Society has concluded to send our money for this year to the Arkansas mission.

I am glad the people are so willing to assist in advancing the Redeemers kingdom in our heathen land. May the glorious period soon arrive, when all the nations of the earth shall be brought to the knowledge of the truth as it is in Jesus. Oh, dear brother, though we are widely separated in person, yet we are near in spirit, and can unite our prayers for the approach of this happy day. O let us do with our might what our hands find to do. I am now in my little study. I have spent in this room many happy hours in prayer to my Heavenly Father. But Oh, how cold and stupid my heart is! How little I feel for the salvation of souls!

> Oh, for a closer walk with God,
> A calm and heavenly frame;
> And light to shine upon the road,
> That leads me to the Lamb.

Please to write soon, and tell me every thing respecting your present situation.
    Catharine Brown.

To the Same.

Brainerd, Feb. 10, 1823.

My dear brother David,

    I AM at Brainerd, on a visit from Creek-Path. My heart is filled with gratitude to God, in being permitted to see these dear missionaries once more, and unite with them in praise to our Lord and Saviour. I feel truly attached to Brainerd, where I first found the Saviour; and O how I love the dear sisters, with whom I have spent many happy hours, both in school, and in walking to the house of worship. But those happy hours are past. We must be contented, and look forward to that day when we shall meet to part no more.

    I left home last week, in company with Mr. Boudinot, and sister Susan. Hope my journey will be beneficial to my health. If our dear father and mother are willing, I intend to pursue study again, as soon as I return home.

    There is some seriousness among the people in our neighbourhood. Several are very anxious to receive religious instruction. When I return, I think I shall make it my business to go round, once in two weeks, to read and explain the Scriptures to the females.

I cannot but hope the Lord will continue to have mercy on our people, and will bring many to the knowledge of the truth as it is in Jesus.

I hope you will write to our dear parents soon. They are always happy to hear from you.

From your affectionate sister
Catharine Brown.

Chapter v.

HER SICKNESS AND DEATH.

THE attention of the reader is now invited to the closing scenes in the life of Catharine, where her faith in her Saviour will be seen to have been signally triumphant over the terrors of the grave.

After she returned from Brainerd, she seems generally to have considered her removal from the world as not very distant, and to have spent much time in reflecting on death and its consequences. These subjects she not unfrequently made the topics of conversation. One instance of this kind is described by Mrs. Potter.

"Entering her room, one evening, at an early hour, I found she had retired with unusual debility. She requested me to read, from some medical author, the symptoms of consumption. I complied; and, after comparing them with her own, she expressed a belief, that she had that disease. I inquired what were her feelings in view of this conclusion. She replied, with tears, 'I am not prepared to die.' You have a hope, I said, of happiness beyond the grave? 'Yes, I have a hope resting on the promises of the Saviour; but I have been unfaithful!'

"We were both too much affected to say more, and remained for some time silent. At length Catharine sweetly raised her voice and said, 'Sister Potter how beautiful is this hymn;' and then she repeated

'Why should we start and fear to die!
    What timorous worms we mortals are!
Death is the gate of endless joy,
    And yet we dread to enter there.

'The pains, and groans, and dying strife
    Fright our approaching souls away;
Still we shrink back again to life,
    Fond of our prison and our clay.

'Oh, if my Lord would come and meet,
    My soul should stretch her wings in haste;
Fly fearless through death's iron gate,
    Nor feel the terrors as she passed.

'Jesus can make a dying bed
    Feel soft as downy pillows are,
While on his breast I lean my head,
    And breathe my life out sweetly there.'[52]

"I inquired if she could adopt this as the language of her heart, and she answered, with great meekness, that she hoped she could."

It does not appear, that, after this, her mind was again seriously disturbed by apprehensions respecting *her own* future well-being.

But when she saw her aged parents in an infirm state of health, and needing all the attentions of an affectionate daughter, and when, moreover, she reflected how many of her dear people remained ignorant of the only Saviour of sinners, she clung to life, and her earnest prayer was, that she might recover. We are informed, that her trials from these sources were, at one time, very severe.

She said to a beloved friend, "I know, that it is my duty to submit entirely to the will of God. He can carry on his work without me. He can take care of my parents. Yet I am anxious to recover. I wish to labour more for my people."

How strong her desires were for the improvement of her people, is further evident from this fact, that though David was the only surviving brother, who had the same mother with herself, and though he was dearer to her than any one else, except her parents, she was, for some time, unwilling he should be informed of her sickness, lest he should be induced to leave his studies, and come home to see her. Much as she loved him, she said she had rather he would remain in New England, until he was prepared to preach Christ to his countrymen.

In April she was visited by that kind friend of herself and family, Dr. Campbell. He strongly advised, that she should remove to his house, thinking it probable that he might then relieve her. Her friends all consented, only desiring her to remain at home a few days, till the departure of her brother Webber, who had come from the Arkansas. But his stay was unexpectedly prolonged a month. During this time, Catharine failed so rapidly, that she was unable to ride to Limestone,[53] where Dr. Campbell then resided.

On this occasion, Catharine thus wrote to Mrs. Campbell.

Creek-Path, April 17, 1823.

My dear Mrs. Campbell.

MY heart was made truly glad this morning, by the arrival of Dr. Campbell. I have long been very anxious to see him, on account of the low state of my health. For two months past, it has been declining, and I am now reduced to extreme debility. This affliction I view as coming from my heavenly Father. I deserve correction, and hope to bear the chastising rod with humble submission.

I have a wish to recover, that I may be useful to my poor countrymen, but know, that all human means will be ineffectual without the blessing of God. I pray that Dr. Campbell may be the instrument in his hands of restoring me to health. If the weather were pleasant, I should be disposed to return with him.

I thank you for your present, and wish I had something valuable to send in return. Dr. Campbell will hand you a little ribbond. When you wear it, remember Catharine.

Mrs. P. sends love, and hopes to receive a visit from you ere long. Much love to the children.

Farewell, my friend, my sister. May heaven grant you its choicest blessings, and reward you an hundred fold for all your kindness to me. Again I say, farewell. May we meet in heaven. Yours affectionately.

Catharine Brown.

As she approached nearer to eternity, her faith evidently grew stronger, and she became more and more able cheerfully to resign, not only herself, but her parents, her friends, her people, her all, to the disposal of her Lord.

May 15th she was reduced very low by a hemorrhage from the lungs, and for a few days was viewed as upon the borders of the grave.

Before this alarming symptom, it had been proposed to send again for Dr. Campbell. But her parents were persuaded first to try the skill of some Indian practitioners. Their prescriptions were followed, until the hemorrhage occurred. Then her alarmed parents sent immediately for Mr. Potter, hoping he could do something to relieve their darling child. Providentially the Rev. Reynolds Bascom, of whom mention has been already made, had just arrived from the Choctaw nation, on his way to the northern States; and having been afflicted in a similar manner himself, he was able to administer effectual remedies.

It is pleasing to be able to insert here the notices, which Mr. Bascom made, at the time, respecting his interview with her, in this hour of trial.

"May 15. Rode to brother Potter's, before breakfast. Soon after our arrival, a message came, that Catharine Brown had been taken with bleeding at the lungs, and brother Potter was requested to visit her. We accordingly rode over to her father's house immediately after breakfast, and found her entirely prostrated by a copious hemorrhage. After bleeding her in the arm, she experienced a sensible relief.

"16. Visited Catharine, with brother Potter, and found it necessary to bleed her again. Conversed and prayed with her, and left her in a peaceful frame of mind.

"19. Left Creek-Path for Brainerd. Brother Potter rode with us to Mr. Brown's. Catharine appeared sweetly composed. Her countenance was cheerful, and her soul filled with tenderness and filial trust in God. After conversation and prayer, I asked her what she would have me say to her brother David.

"She replied, 'Tell him not to be uneasy about *me*. If I do not meet him in this world, I hope to meet him in heaven. I have a great desire to see him, but the Lord may not permit us to meet here.' These words were spoken in a low, but audible whisper, and with the significant emphasis of a heart filled with faith and love.

"I have rarely, if ever, seen a more lovely object for the pencil, than she appeared to me on her dying bed. The natural mildness of her features seemed lighted with a beam of heavenly hope, and her whole aspect was that of a mature Christian, waiting, with filial patience, the welcome summons to the presence of her Lord."

Mrs. Potter says,—"Death was now disarmed of his terrors. She could look into the grave without alarm. She confessed her sins with great meekness, and mourned that she had not been more faithful in the service of God; yet rejoiced to resign her soul into the hands of her Redeemer.

"Once, when I visited her, she affectionately took my hand and said,—'My dear sister, I have been wishing to see you, for several days. I have thought a great deal of you and Mr. Potter. I love you much, but am going to leave you. I think I shall not live long. You have done much for me. I thank you, and hope the Lord will reward you. I am willing to die, if it be the will of God. I know that I have experienced his love. I have no desire to live in this world, but to do good. But God can carry on his work without me. I hope you will continue the meetings of females. You must not be discouraged. I thought when I should get to the Arkansas, I would form a society among the females, like ours. But I shall never live to get there. I feel for my dear parents, but the Lord will take care of them.'

"At another interview she said,—'I feel perfectly resigned to the will of God. I know he will do right with his children. I thank God, that I am entirely in his hands. I feel willing to live, or die, as he thinks best. My only wish is, that he may be glorified. I hope, should I ever recover, I shall be more faithful in the cause of Christ, than I have ever been.'"

A request was sent to Dr. Campbell to visit her as soon as possible. But he was unable to come till the 21st, by which time Catharine was so much enfeebled, as to be entirely confined to her room. She could not even raise herself without assistance. The physician gave it as his opinion, that she could live but a few days, unless she was removed to

Limestone, it being impossible for him to attend on her at so great a distance. Whether such a removal was possible, was at first doubted. But a kind Providence furnished unexpectedly such facilities for the measure, that it was determined on.

Before entering on an account of her removal, some further notices of the state of her mind will be given.

Just before her leaving home, she requested a friend to write thus, on her behalf, to her brother David. "I am entirely resigned to the will of God, and hope you will feel the same resignation. I am perfectly willing to die, or to live, as the Lord shall direct. This world is nothing but sin. I have no wish to live in it but to do good. If it be the Lord's will to take me now, I am willing to go."

"Religious confidence and tranquillity," says Dr. Campbell, "were at this time her sweet companions. How happy she seemed in my view, so near the confines of the eternal world, about to relinquish all earthly cares and sorrows for the enjoyment of her dear Redeemer's presence!

"On the 23d, she seemed to have the most cheering evidence of her interest in the Lord Jesus. Thus she exclaimed,—'Now I am ready to die. Oh, how delightful is the view of my Saviour! How happy shall I be, when I arrive at my Father's house.'

"On being asked, what would be her feelings, if it was the will of God she should live, she replied; 'The Lord's will be done, and not mine. If I can promote his cause in any way, I am desirous to live. But if I am taken away, I hope my brother David will be useful, in bringing our benighted nation to a knowledge of Jesus.'

"Her soul appeared full, and more than full, of love to God. She spoke much of his goodness to her, and expressed much regret, that she had done so little in his cause. The day preceding this, she had expressed a wish to go to Huntsville, and unite with Mrs. L. and C.[54] in forming an association for prayer, and in endeavouring to do something for the cause of Christ."

Catharine was now unable to endure the motion of a carriage, even for a short distance. It would be necessary, therefore, in proceeding to Limestone, to carry her on a litter to the Tennessee river, which was six miles distant; then to take her in a boat down the river, forty miles, to a village named Trienna;[55] and from thence, on a litter again, about five miles, to Dr. Campbell's. But, in order to the successful prosecution of this enterprise, the aid of some person, through the whole distance, who was acquainted with the English language, was indispensable. And it should be thankfully noted, that, just when the question of removal was agitated, Mr. William Leech,[56] a pious acquaintance from Hunts-ville, providentially arrived at Creek-Path, and very kindly tendered his services.

Monday, the 26th of May, was the time appointed for commencing the journey.

"Numbers," says Mrs. Potter, "assembled to take, as they feared, and as it proved, a last look of their beloved friend. After a prayer, in which she was commended to the divine protection, the canoe was announced to be in readiness, and we followed the litter, borne by her affection-ate people, to the river. Old and young were bathed in tears, and some were obliged to use their influence to prevent a general and loud lam-entation. Catharine alone was calm, while she bade farewell to those she tenderly loved."

Mr. Leech says, that small groups of her acquaintance were frequently seen on the road, waiting her approach. When she arrived where they were, they would hasten to the side of the litter, take her by the hand, and often walk away without speaking a word, the tears all the while rolling down their cheeks.

Two or three extracts from Mr. Leech's narrative of the voyage and journey, from the time of her embarkation on the river, will be inserted.

"About 4 o'clock, P.M. on the 26th, we began to glide quite pleasantly down the stream, accompanied by several of Catharine's relatives. Our design was to stop as soon as it became dark, until the moon arose. But we could discover no suitable place for landing, till daylight was gone, and then the difficulty was increased. The margin of the river was gen-erally covered with brushwood. In some places, the shore was a deep mire; at others, there were bluffs and rocks. This made landing difficult and dangerous in the dark; and along this part of the river were scarce-ly any settlements.

"At length the danger of running was such, as to determine us to get upon the land in some way. We accordingly steered towards the shore, and providentially discovered a good landing-place, near which was also a house, where our party was kindly entertained, and our various wants supplied. Had we passed this place, we should not have found such another, for twenty miles.

"When the moon was sufficiently risen, we again started. The night was beautiful, and the rocks and mountains, towering up from the river's brink, looked grand, by the moonlight, as we passed along. The next day the heat of the sun was excessive, and we did not reach Trienna till one o'clock in the afternoon.

"Here we were all strangers. I had, however, a letter from Dr. Campbell to a young gentleman, which I delivered. He obtained a carriage, but Catharine was too weak to ride in it. How to procure people enough, in this land of strangers, to carry her in a litter to Dr. C.'s, a distance of five miles, I knew not. But our situation becoming known, men were soon at hand to carry her, free of all expense.

"And here I would observe, that every person, who saw her, was, so far as I could discover, much interested in her behalf.

"When we were ready to start, our young friend, to whom I brought the letter, placed the mother and sister of Catharine in the carriage, and went himself with them. Thus we were assisted on our way, the Lord putting it into the hearts of strangers to afford us every facility in their power, and we arrived at Dr. Campbell's, a little before dark, on the 27th."

Here, not less than at her father's house, she found friends, who were ready to make any sacrifice for her comfort, and with whom she could freely converse on the subject, which lay nearest her heart. Under the skilful care of Dr. Campbell, she soon began to amend, and hopes were entertained that she would even partially recover.

Early in June, her dear friend, Mrs. Potter, came from Creek-Path to see her.

This lady, in a letter to the Corresponding Secretary of the American Board, says: "She then seemed to think she might recover; but manifested no wish to live, unless it should be for the glory of God. She said, 'When I enjoy the presence of the Saviour, I long to be gone.'

"While at Dr. Campbell's, I wrote a letter to her brother David, informing him of her illness. When about to close the letter, I went to her bed-side and said, 'Catharine, what shall I say to your brother for you?'

"After a short pause, she replied, 'If you will write, I will dictate a short letter.'

"Then raising herself in the bed, and wiping away a tear, that was falling from her eye, she, with a sweet smile, began to relate what God had done for her soul while upon that sick bed.

"To my partial eye, she was, at that moment, an interesting spectacle, and I have often wished, that her portrait could then have been taken. Her countenance was softened with the affectionate remembrance of an endeared brother; her cheek was a little flushed with the exertion of speaking, her eye beamed with spiritual joy, and a heavenly smile animated the whole scene. I shall never forget it, nor the words she then whispered in my ear."

The reader will naturally desire to see the letter, which was dictated and penned under circumstances so interesting. It was written in exact accordance with her dictation, and was as follows.

Limestone, June 13, 1823.

My dear Brother,

MRS. POTTER has told you the particulars of my illness. I will only tell you what I have experienced on my sick-bed.

I have found, that it is good for me to be afflicted. The Saviour is very precious to me. I often enjoy his presence, and I long to be where I can enjoy it without sin. I have indeed been brought very low, and did not expect to live until this time. But I have had joy, such as I never experienced before. I longed to be gone; was ready to die at any moment.

I love you very much, and it would be a great happiness to me to see you again in this world. Yet I don't know that I shall. God only knows. We must submit to his will. We know, that if we never meet again in this world, the Lord has prepared a place in his heavenly kingdom, where I trust we shall meet, never to part. We ought to be thankful for what he has done for us. If he had not sent us the Gospel, we should have died without any knowledge of the Saviour.

You must not be grieved, when you hear of my illness. You must remember, that this world is not our home, that we must all die soon.

I am here under the care of Dr. Campbell, and his very kind family. My mother and sister Susan are with me. Since I came here, I have been a great deal better, and the doctor sometimes gives encouragement of my getting well. But we cannot tell. I am willing to submit myself to the will of God. I am willing to die, or live, as he sees best.

I know I am his. He has bought me with his blood, and I do not wish to have any will but his. He is good, and can do nothing wrong. I trust, if he spares my life, he will enable me to be faithful to his cause. I have no desire to live in this world, but to be engaged in his service.

It was my intention to instruct the people more than I had done, when I returned from Brainerd; but when I got home, I was not able to do it.

It was a great trial to me not to be able to visit our neighbours, and instruct them. But I feel that it is all right. It is my prayer that you may be useful, and I hope the Lord *will* make you useful to our poor people.

> From your affectionate sister
> Catharine.

How much soever her hopes, and those of her friends were raised at this period, with respect to her recovery, they were of brief duration. Though every attention, which an unwearied kindness could bestow, was given her, and prayer was offered continually on her behalf, her Lord and Master was pleased to hasten her departure. She had entered the last six weeks of her life, and thenceforward her descent towards the grave, was regular and unremitted.

Dr. Campbell now thought it his duty to inform her parents and herself, that his hopes, even of her partial recovery, were gone.

Upon communicating this intelligence to her father, who a little before had come to Limestone, the good old man, after a solemn silence of several minutes, observed, "The Lord has been good to give me such a child, and he has a right to take her when he thinks best. But though it is my duty to give her up, it is hard to part with her."

Catharine received the notice without manifesting the least alarm, only requesting the doctor to inform her, how long she might probably live.

On the morning of July 17th, she was supposed to have commenced her last agonies, and Dr. Campbell was immediately called to her bedside.

"I found," says he, "some appearance of anxiety on her countenance, which was the result of new sensations of bodily distress, and not of any agitation of mind. As soon as she could speak, (for she was sometimes speechless,) extending her hand to me, she calmly observed, 'I am gone.'

"Some hours after this, when her distress returned, and her respiration became very difficult and painful, she said, in reference to her sufferings, 'What shall I do?' I inquired, if, in this trying hour, she could not confidently rely on her Saviour? She answered, 'Yes.'

"Through the day her mind was perfectly tranquil, and though several times, when her mother and friends were weeping about her, the tears would start into her eyes, she would quickly suppress them. She seemed to spend most of the time in prayer.

"The night was one of considerable distress, owing to her difficulty of breathing. In the morning she looked toward the window, and asked me if it was not day. I replied, that it was. She then turned her eyes towards heaven, and an indescribable placidness spread over her countenance.

"Perhaps she thought, that the next morning she should behold, would be the morning of the resurrection.

"As death advanced, and the powers of nature gave way, she frequently offered her hand to the friends around her bed. Her mother and sister weeping over her, she looked steadily at the former, for a short time, filial love beaming from her eyes; and then,—she closed them in the sleep of death.

"She expired without a groan, or a struggle. Even those around the bed scarcely knew, that the last breath had left her, until I informed them she was gone.

"Thus fell asleep this lovely saint, in the arms of her Saviour, a little past 6 o'clock, on the morning of July 13th, 1823."

Her afflicted relatives conveyed her remains to Creek-Path, where they were, on the 20th, deposited near the residence of her parents, and by the side of her brother John, who had died about a year and a half before, in the triumphs of the same faith.

Her age was about twenty-three; and six years had elapsed from her first entering the school at Brainerd. She was then a heathen. But she became enlightened and sanctified, through the instrumentality of the Gospel of Jesus, preached to her by the missionaries of the cross; and her end was glorious.

A neat monument of wood, erected by her bereaved relatives, covers the grave where she was laid. And though, a few years hence, this monument may no longer exist to mark the spot where she slumbers, yet shall her dust be precious in the eyes of the Lord, and her virtues shall be told for a memorial of her.

Chapter VI.

HER CHARACTER.

A SUMMARY view will now be taken of the character of Catharine Brown, as it is exhibited in the documents, which have been the basis of the preceding memoir.

Her Mental Characteristics.

The mind of Catharine was of a delicate texture, well proportioned, and happily balanced. Its perception was clear, its judgment correct, and it was well endued with that invaluable quality in the intellectual economy, good sense. In the acquisition of knowledge, it moved easily, and, considering her circumstances and health, wrought with success. In communicating to others what she knew, she had, owing to the clearness of her apprehensions, more than common felicity.

And who has not remarked her delicate sensibility, her exact views of dignity and propriety, her high principles of action, and her gentleness and sweetness of manner? With her advantages of person, and her excellencies of mind, she needed only greater opportunities, to have attained that high degree of refinement and grace, which is so much admired in the more elegant portion of civilized society.

But, until she came to the age, at which the females of our nation have nearly, or quite, completed their education, she derived no benefit whatever from the perusal of books, and enjoyed very little intercourse with civilized people. Her mind, like the wilderness in which she had her home, was uncultivated. But a small degree of intellectual, and scarcely any moral truth, had enlightened it. Bacon, and Newton, and Locke, and St. Paul, and a multitude of others possessing powerful intellects, who had brought the grandest truths in the natural and

243

moral worlds within the comprehension of infantile genius, had, so far as she was concerned, lived in vain. In short, even at that late period, she had every thing to learn.

She lived but six years after her admission to the school at Brainerd. A desire for knowledge evidently brought her there; and that same desire, strengthened and sanctified by grace, attended her through life.

ii. Her Attainments.

1. Concerning those attainments, which are *not of a moral nature*, it will be needless to enter into a lengthened specification. It may, indeed, be impossible for us, into whose minds knowledge has been industriously poured from our earliest years, to form a just conception of her intellectual state, before she had access to the ordinary sources of information, or to ascertain, with precision, what revolutions occurred in her apprehensions of things. But there can be no doubt that most, even of the elements of learning, came before her in the garb of novelty, and that the field of her vision expanded, till she at length found herself introduced into quite a different sphere, from that, which had interested the curiosity of her opening youth.

It is affecting to think of the great mental changes, which were necessary, even to place her on a level with the ordinary intelligence of civilized life. But it is delightful to contemplate these changes as more than accomplished. To a few of the more important of them the attention of the reader is, for a moment, invited.

Her acquaintance with the geographical *features of the earth*, must have been exceedingly vague and limited, hardly extending beyond the wilderness, that embosomed her father's house. After her introduction to the missionaries, that acquaintance was extended to the great natural divisions of the world, its physical aspect, and its civil departments.

Her *astronomical* views, untutored as she was, may easily be conjectured. But she was instructed to contemplate worlds and suns and systems, in uncounted numbers, wheeling, at the command of their Creator, through immensity.

Her apprehensions respecting the *human race* were so imperfect, that she supposed her own people a distinct order of beings. But soon she learns, that God "hath made of one blood all nations of men."

How exceedingly confined, also, how next to nothing, must have been her knowledge of *history*. Ages that were past, must have been to her almost as much a blank, as ages that were to come. But soon the Bible, the wisest, most sure, most comprehensive history of man, is placed in her hands; and she has besides, access to a variety of the most useful human compends.[57] Being thus favoured, it may well be presumed, that the more interesting events of antiquity rose, in rapid succession, above her mental horizon.

Such changes as these elevate the mind immeasurably above the standard of the mere child of nature, and, when beheld in any human soul, must be, to a philanthropist, a subject of grateful contemplation.

2. The greatest and infinitely the most important acquisitions of Catharine, however, had respect to *moral* subjects,—to God, and a future state, to the character, duty and highest interest of man, and the provisions made for his salvation. On all subjects of this class, her ideas, when she came to Brainerd, were very confused and imperfect; and in regard to some of the most momentous of them, she was in total ignorance. She went there an untutored pagan. Scarcely a ray of moral light had gleamed upon her soul. The visible creation was indeed open and bright before her. But how little of the divine perfections does fallen man discern there, until they are pointed out by the finger of revelation!

Of the *moral perfections of God*, such as his holiness, justice, and goodness, she had no conceptions at all, when she entered the mission school. Her knowledge of God, like that of most of her countrymen, was confined almost to the narrowest possible limits. *Galunlahtiahi*, or *the Great Being above*, was thought to possess a material form, and his most prominent attribute to be physical strength. The Indian languages are said to have no word that signifies *spirit*, nor the pagan Indians any idea of a spiritual substance. The spirituality of Jehovah, his holy character, his love of holiness, his hatred of sin, the strictness of his law, his righteous government over the world, and his illimitable benevolence, were things of which Catharine knew little, or nothing.

But soon we find her mind richly furnished with all these views of God. His moral perfections arrest her attention, and she sees, in all their exhibitions, a lovely and attractive glory. What new views of the Eternal must they have been, which drew forth such language as this:—"O, he is good, kind, merciful." "I feel it is good to be afflicted, knowing that the Lord is good, and will always do what is right." "I thank God, I am entirely in his hands." "The Lord's will be done, and not mine." "O happy day, when God himself shall be my joy!" No heathen ever used such language as this. It springs only from the illuminations of Christianity.

Of the *Lord Jesus Christ* she had no knowledge, when introduced to the missionaries; and when told of him, for the first time, she supposed, that what he had done for sinners had no reference to her, or her people.

But the united testimony of all is, that, after her conversion, the Saviour was her favourite theme of contemplation and discourse. He was her ALPHA and OMEGA, her ALL IN ALL. His person, character, and work, appeared to her amazingly interesting. How often does she express a desire to know him better, to love him more, to be more grateful for what he has done, to do more in return, to be with him, to see him, and to sing his praises. "O," she exclaims, "how delightful is the view of my Saviour." "He is precious to me. I often enjoy his presence. I long to be where I can enjoy him without sin." "He has bought me with his blood, and I wish not to have any will of my own. He is good, and can do nothing wrong."

And what new views did she acquire, with regard to the *people* of God. At first, she thought them unhappy, and was fearful they would render her unhappy. But soon she thinks them the happiest people in the world, and longs for their society more than for that of any others. With them she wishes to live, with them to die, with them to be forever. What amount of earthly good would have induced her to forego their company, for a single year, and cast her lot among the giddy sons and daughters of fashionable pleasure?

"I cannot," she remarks, "express how much I love the missionaries with whom I live. I feel not my privileges, until I am away from them, and mingle with worldly people. Then I long to get back, and be with

Christians." "I often think of the glorious day, when I shall meet all good missionaries in the kingdom of our Saviour. I shall then be always with those dear friends, who have told me so much about heaven, and taught me to love and serve Christ." "O, happy day, when I shall see all the Christians, who have ever lived."

We also perceive a great alteration in her views of *herself*. She has declared, that when she came to Brainerd, she did not know she was a sinner; and we are informed, that she was vain of her person, vain of her decorations, and satisfied with herself.

Yet what self-abasing views had she, ever after her conversion. "I see nothing," she observes, "to trouble me, but my wicked heart. It appears to me, that the more I wish to serve God, the more I sin. I seem never to have done any thing good in the sight of God."

"Humility," says Mrs. Potter, "was the most conspicuous trait in her character. I never could discover, that her vanity was excited by the numerous attentions, which she received from different parts of our country. She received them as paid her for Christ's sake. When presents came, her language was, 'These do not belong to me. I do not deserve them. Many Christians have heard, that I love the Saviour, and send me presents on this account. But oh, I feel ashamed that I live so far from him.'

"She received many letters, some of which were highly complimentary; but so far from fostering pride, they always seemed to increase her humility. Once, having received a letter full of expressions of the strongest admiration of her character, she was gently cautioned against being lifted up with vanity. The tears started into her eyes, and she replied, 'I do not wish to be proud;' and added, 'that she believed people had formed too high an opinion of her, and that if they knew her personally, their esteem would be diminished.'

"She was much distressed, that so many of her letters had been published, and, for a season, it was with difficulty, that we could persuade her to write to her correspondents. 'I suppose,' she said, 'the object at *first* was, to show that an Indian could improve. But two or three letters would have answered this purpose, as well as all I have ever written.'"[58]

Mr. Leech says, "I have often seen her in company at Huntsville, and although she was very much caressed, and her society sought, by the most respectable people, yet she always appeared humble. There was nothing about her, that was vain, or assuming. This was not the effect of insensibility to those acts of kindness. She would sometimes say to her particular friends, 'I wish I was more worthy of such friendly attentions.'"

Observe, too, what a revolution was effected in her views of *this world*. An Indian's heaven, even when most distinctly apprehended, has fewer points of attraction, than the earth. Catharine, on coming to Brainerd, evidently regarded it, when she thought of it at all, as a remote, obscure, undefined something, more to be dreaded, than desired. Hence her imagination had contemplated whatever is lovely and attractive, as shining forth only in this world. If she made any comparisons, they only deepened the conviction, that earthly objects were most desirable.

But after her conversion, what a change! Her contemplations are elevated to a superior world of realities. She learns of a higher state of existence, designed for the good of the human race; where the inhabitants are all holy, their employments holy, their joys holy; where the disorders and miseries of earth are not known; where "there shall be no more death, neither sorrow, nor crying, neither shall there be any more pain;" and where there is "no need of the sun, neither of the moon, to shine in it, for the glory of God doth lighten it, and the Lamb is the light thereof." Now, her views of the world are changed. The contrast of earthly with heavenly things, and of the creature with God, hath spoiled the glories of the world.

"How vain," she says, "does this world appear in my eyes. It is nothing but vanity and sin." "Sweet and reviving is the thought, that I am not to continue long in this world, but hope soon to rest in the city of my God." "When I enjoy the presence of my Saviour, I long to be gone." "How happy shall I feel, when I land on the shores of eternal felicity."

To proceed farther in this analysis, is unnecessary. Enough has been said to illustrate the changes, which occurred in her apprehensions on moral subjects. She seems to have possessed much of that kind of understanding, which is denominated, in the word of God, a "spiritual understanding." She appears to have received a spiritual discernment, which enabled her, by the simple reading of the Scriptures, meditation and prayer, to acquire a knowledge of the hidden glories of spiritual things. Hence, the spiritual world, which had been concealed before her conversion, was to her, ever after, a world of beauties, upon which she loved to dwell.

iii. Changes in Her Affections.

The objects of all human affections may be divided into two grand classes, which are designated, in the divine word, as *things earthly*, and *things heavenly*. The earthly things, are the riches, honours, and pleasures of the world. The heavenly things, are whatever bear the marks of a heavenly origin, or of a heavenly destination; such as God, and holy beings, and sacred truth.

When Catharine first became acquainted with the missionaries, her affections were resting wholly on the former class of objects. But how much evidence is there, that, before her decease, there was almost an entire transfer of her affections; that they rested almost wholly on heavenly things.

With respect to the general character of her religious affections, it may be remarked, that they were uniformly tender, often lively, but never enthusiastic. Dr. Campbell observes, "that she never appeared to receive the Christian system of faith otherwise than on the force of evidence, and that evidence drawn from the Bible. The extravagance of feeling, which is the effect chiefly of animal excitement, she could not comprehend, but felt satisfied with possessing that holiness of heart, which leads to supreme love to God."—"She was never enthusiastic," says Mrs. Potter, "yet had seasons of exalted joy, when, to use her own language, 'she felt as though she was in heaven, and was disappointed, when her thoughts returned to earth, and she found herself here!' She had, also, seasons of deep sorrow of heart, when she mourned the hidings of her Saviour's countenance, and groaned under the pressure of in-dwelling sin."

Catharine possessed nothing of that stoical insensibility to pleasure, or pain, for which the Indian character has been considered remarkable. There was never any thing in her deportment like unfeeling hardihood. The very reverse of this was true. She had a heart for friendship, for sympathy, for tender emotion. This is apparent in all her writings, and in her whole history; and is amply confirmed by her intimate friend and companion, Mrs. Potter. She remarks, "Catharine possessed a heart, that could feel for another's wo, and rejoice in another's prosperity."

To the *Saviour* her love was uncommonly strong, and continued so, in every variety of circumstance. Who has not been impressed with this, while reading her journal, her letters, and her recorded sayings, and while contemplating the events of her life? Love to the Saviour, was her ruling principle. She knew his voice. She delighted to sit at his feet. She was overwhelmed with wonder at his condescending goodness. She was enraptured at the thought of beholding his face. Hear her own words. "I will go wherever the Saviour calls me." "How good it is to lie at the feet of Jesus." "O how good is he in permitting me to partake of his grace." "Sweet is the thought of soon beholding the face of the Redeemer."

Here again Dr. Campbell will be quoted. "The Saviour seemed to be continually the anchor of her hope, the source of her constant and greatest happiness, and the object of her most ardent love. With her friends, she was at all times communicative and interesting; but when He became the theme of conversation, the faculties of her soul appeared to receive new vigour, and she became doubly interesting. Every expression shewed, that she was charmed with the goodness of God, in making such provision for fallen, lost man. Although on other subjects she was not generally very animated, her whole soul seemed to feel the importance of this, which produced an earnestness of expression and manner, that constrained those around her to feel its importance too."

Hence she felt, and uniformly manifested, a deep interest in the *cause of Christ*. Especially did she long to have her own people savingly acquainted with the Lord Jesus. For this object chiefly she wished to live. This made her almost unwilling to die. "My heart bleeds for my poor people," was her language; "I am determined to pray for them, while God lends me breath."

Her biographer might enlarge, upon her dependence on God, which led her beautifully to say, "I am a child, I can do nothing; but in God will I trust, for I know there is no one else, to whom can I look for help." He might speak of her tender affection for her friends; of her gratitude for favours shewn her; and of her compassion for the world at large. But enough has been said to shew, that she possessed much, very much of the meek and glowing benevolence of the Gospel.

"Fair spirit, nurs'd in forest wild,
Where caught thy breast those sacred flames?"[59]

iv. Her Christian Conduct.

There is no reason to believe, that any thing in the conduct of Catharine ever approached to what is denominated immoral. And this is very remarkable, considering her early circumstances. Yet, until she came to Brainerd, she was not religious. She did not lead a life of piety. Till then, the only tendency of her mind and heart and conduct, was towards the world. As she neither knew, nor loved "those things which are above,"[60] so neither did she seek them.

But a change occurred in her objects of pursuit; a revolution took place in the general course and tenor of her life. We find new aims, new plans, new habits of action. "Old things are passed away."[61]

Her *habits of devotion* might well render her an example to others. Not only did she delight to be present in the public assembly, not only did she love to gather little circles of her Cherokee friends for social prayer, but she was constant and earnest in her more private approaches to her God and Saviour.

Mrs. Potter observes, "The Bible, was her constant companion. The law of God was her delight and meditation all the day. And I think I may safely say, that no morning, or evening passed, during her residence with us, (which was considerably more than a year,) when she did not retire to hold communion with her God. At these seasons of devotion,

I was not unfrequently permitted to be by her side, and listen to the fervent breathings of her soul. In strains of the deepest humility, she confessed her sins, acknowledged her obligations to her heavenly Father, and with great fervency prayed for complete conformity to the divine will. Her dear people were never forgotten, and her petitions were extended from them to all mankind."

Her *zeal* was not an irregular, evanescent flame. It was permanent, and always active. How faithful, laborious, and successful she was, with respect to her own family, has been noticed in the preceding memoir. A more kind, attentive, and obliging daughter and sister, than was Catharine Brown, or one more faithfully solicitous for the spiritual good of her relatives, is scarcely to be found, it is believed, in any civilized land.

Nor was she ever unmindful of the duties she owed her people, and she seems to have closely watched for opportunities to do them good. Indeed, their conversion to God was her favourite object, to which she clung, with unyielding tenacity, through every vicissitude of health and circumstance, down to the hour of her dissolution.

> "Patient she strives.
> By prayer, and by instruction, to arouse
> Reflection in the hearts of those she styles
> Her wretched people. Modest, tender, kind
> Her words and actions; every vain desire
> Is laid obedient at the feet of Christ.
> And now no more the gaiety she seeks
> Of proud apparel; ornaments of gold
> She gladly barters for the plain attire
> Of meek and lowly spirits."[62]

It cannot be forgotten by the reader, how diligently she pursued her studies, both at Brainerd and at Creek-Path, in order that she might be more eminently fitted for usefulness; nor how meekly she bore those acquisitions, which elevated her above every other female of her tribe.

That there were defects in her Christian character, must be presumed, in the absence of positive proof, from analogy. The best Christians have failings. But what were hers? The materials for this memoir were furnished by a considerable number of persons, who knew her well; and, without seeming to have been conscious of the omission, not one of them has specified a single fault in her character, as a Christian. Mrs. P. has simply said, that she was not entirely free from the inadvertences of youth. It would seem, therefore, and there is reason to believe it was the fact, that her failings, whatever they might be, were not such as are apt to make a strong impression on the mind.

"Through faith in the Lord Jesus," says the first spiritual guide she ever had, the Rev. Mr. Kingsbury, "she was enabled to bring forth the fruits of righteousness, has left a bright example of the power of divine grace over one who was born in the darkness of heathenism, and is now rejoicing with her Saviour."

Conclusion.

SUCH was Catharine Brown, the converted Cherokee. Such, too, were the changes wrought in her, through the blessing of Almighty God on the labours of Missionaries. They, and only they, as the instruments of divine grace, had the formation of her Christian character; and that character, excellent and lovely as it was, resulted from the nature of their instructions. Her expansion of mind her enlargement of views, her elevated affections, her untiring benevolence, are all to be traced, under God, to her intercourse with them. The glory belongs to God; but the instrumental agency, the effective labour, the subordinate success, were theirs.

In her history, we see how much can be made of the Indian character. Catharine was an Indian. She might have said, as her brother did to thousands, while passing through these States, "Aboriginal blood flows through my veins."[63] True, it was not unmixed; but the same may be affirmed of many others of her people. Her parentage, her early circumstances and education, with a few unimportant exceptions, were like those of the Cherokees generally. She dwelt in the same wilderness, was conversant with the same society, was actuated by the same fears, and hopes, and expectations, and naturally possessed the same traits of character. Yet what did she become! How agreeable as an associate, how affectionate as a friend, how exemplary as a member of the domestic and social circle and of the Christian church, how blameless and lovely in all the walks of life! Her Christian character was esteemed by all who knew her, while she lived, and will bear the strictest scrutiny, now she is dead. To such an excellence may the Indian character attain; for, to such an excellence did it actually attain in her.

And why may it not arrive at the same excellence, in other Indians? Are there no other minds among them as susceptible of discipline and culture? no other spirits, that, in the plastic hands of the Divine Agent, can receive as beautiful a conformation? Are there not dispositions as gentle, hearts as full of feeling, minds as lively and strong? And cannot such minds be so fashioned and adorned, that heavenly grace shall beam as charmingly from them, as it did from hers?

The supposition, that she possessed mental and moral capabilities, which are rare among her people, while it adds nothing to our respect for her, does injustice to her nation. In personal attraction, and in universal propriety of manner, she was, undoubtedly, much distinguished. But, in amiableness of disposition, in quickness of apprehension, in intellectual vigour, it is believed there are hundreds of Cherokee youth, who are scarcely less favoured.

In confirmation of this, will be given the description of a school, composed entirely of young Cherokees, from the pen of a clergyman, whose accuracy of judgment, and faithfulness of description, have never been questioned.

"It has never been according to our views of propriety and expediency to be lavish in commendations of our schools; lest we should seem to colour high and exaggerate, or to indulge in pride and vain glory. We think, however, (and we would ever think soberly,) that much might be said in favour of the schools at Dwight, without in any measure departing from 'words of truth and soberness.' I would not draw invidious comparisons, between the schools here and those of other similar institutions. But I would say, that I never saw, at any place, in any country, more interesting groups of children, than those at present under our care: interesting, in almost every point of view, whether we consider them in their relations, their appearance, their behaviour, their progress, or their prospects.

"Those, who, when revolving in their thoughts the idea of Indians and savages, vainly imagine that nothing can belong to the Aborigines of our country, except what is frightful in appearance, and deeply imbued with cruelty and barbarism, would scarcely believe themselves to be in an Indian school, when surrounded by the children, which fill our little sylvan seminary. Were they here, they would see nothing of that coarseness of feature, nor ferocity of look, nothing like that dirty dress, ugly visage, and repelling countenance, and nothing of that hard, unkind, and cruel disposition, which they have been wont to associate with the Indian character. But they would see a lovely group of children, who, by the regularity of their features, their neat and cleanly dress, their fair complexions, (fair indeed for a sultry clime,) their orderly and becoming behaviour, their intelligence and sprightliness, their mildness of disposition, tempered with a manly spirit, and their progress in knowledge, would not suffer by a comparison with most schools in a civilized land, nor disgrace respectable parents, by passing as their sons and daughters.

"Such, dear Sir, are our schools at Dwight, our precious children, not long since brought from the shades of the forest. We love them, and we can but love them, for they are lovely. They are docile in their dispositions, generally quick in their apprehensions, prompt in their obedience, active and sprightly in their sports, and diligent and ambitious in their studies. Of the whole number of sixty, who compose the school in two departments, there are not more than six who cannot read with ease in the New Testament, and spell almost any words put to them. A considerable number can read with propriety and apparent understanding any book, and write a fair and legible hand. Near one fourth of both departments of the school are pursuing the study of geography. Some of the boys have made some progress in grammar and arithmetic, and in some other branches. It may be said with truth, that most, if not all, are as forward, as the children of most district schools in the most favoured part of New England. But what is more interesting to the Christian is their intelligent reading of the Scriptures, singing with delightful voices the praises of God, and making progress in a knowledge of the Gospel."[64]

The uniform testimony respecting all the other schools, which have been established by the American Board, is in accordance with the above.

Catharine was not the only convert from her people. There have been others, both among the old and the young, in whom similar transformations have been wrought. Her brother John was an instance. Her aged and venerable parents, who are much and justly respected by all who know them, are instances. Others still might be named, were it not probable that these pages will fall under their notice. More than fifty Cherokees were added to the church, the first year after the decease of Catharine, the great proportion of whom adorn their profession in a manner resembling what we admire in her.

It is hardly possible, indeed, that any of these converts should become so well known to our community, as she was. Circumstances have changed. The novelty of Indian missions is gone. The multiplication of converts diminishes our curiosity respecting individuals. But excellence and worth of character, are none the less real for being unnoticed and unknown.

Here, then, we find encouragement. The success of past efforts has been rich in its nature, and animating in its amount; and the same kind of instruments, increased in number, are still employed, and employed, too, upon similar materials. The course of divine grace, moreover, is, in some sense, uniform, like the course of nature; so that what Almighty God has done, in past time, is an earnest and a pledge (circumstances being the same,) of what he will do, in time to come. Upon these accounts, among others, we may cherish raised expectations. Should the enterprise, which has been commenced so auspiciously, be prosecuted with prudence, zeal, and in the fear of God, we shall not be extravagant if we look for the general prevalence of pure religion among a people, in the midst of whom, at the breaking up of their long night of paganism, this interesting female shone as a morning star.

The present is emphatically the time for vigorous Christian effort. Probably it is the only time when great success is possible. Various unpropitious causes press heavily upon the poor Indians; and it is believed, that nothing will save them from extinction, as a people, but the general prevalence of true religion. All things else will be vain without this.

The position, that civilization must precede Christianity, is so unsupported by facts, is so opposed to all experience, that one would think it could hardly be advanced by enlightened philosophers, or be received by rational Christians. What is civilization? In Pagan and Mohammedan countries, it is, it ever has been, a state of society, where moral excellence is little known, and domestic and social happiness little enjoyed; where man is a lordly tyrant, and woman is a slave. True civilization is found only in Christian countries; and no where, but as the *result* of Christianity; of Christianity, too, planted, in the first instance, by missionary enterprise.

Bring this religion to act strongly upon the Indians. Give them the full enjoyment of Christian ordinances. Then their "winter will be past, the rain will be over and gone." Agriculture, art, science, legislation, and literature, the germs of which already appear, will grow in rich luxuriance, and the Indian character will be respected by the nations of the earth.

Let the life of Catharine Brown operate as an appeal to the benevolence of the Christian community. Though dead, she speaks: and oh, let her voice fall with persuasive and irresistible eloquence upon every ear.

Shall her people, of whom, by the purifying and ennobling influences of the Gospel, so much can be made, be abandoned to ignorance and wo? Shall beings, who are capable of knowing God, of understanding the grand economy of his grace, of enjoying the imperishable blessings of his salvation, be shut out eternally from such wisdom, and debarred forever from such enjoyment?

Are they not susceptible of whatever is useful, and beautiful, and even sublime, in character? Can they not appreciate, and will they not use, the means of Christian civilization, if placed within their reach?

And may we not expect an abundant reward? Nay, have we not already been amply rewarded? To say nothing of the impulse given to the intellect, the industry, and the enterprise, of the nation, to which the subject of this memoir belonged; or of their accelerated progress in legislation and government; or of the amelioration in the habits and manners of their domestic and social life; or of the rudiments of learning imparted to a multitude of children and youth; or of the amount of sacred truth, the only means of conversion and sanctification, instilled into their minds; or of an inheritance in the heavens secured to many souls:—to say nothing of all this, Were not the holy life and triumphant death of Catharine Brown, an ample remuneration for all the labours and expenditures of the mission to her tribe?

Say, ye missionaries of the cross, should ye repent of your self-denying toils, if this had proved your only reward? Say, ye churches of the Redeemer, would ye recal her sainted spirit from the skies, if what ye have expended for her nation could be refunded? A thousand worlds would not be worth what you have, through the grace of God, secured to her, as is humbly believed, in the regions of the blessed. And when ye, also, stand on the heights of the Zion above, and behold her ransomed spirit "filled with all the fulness of God," and exulting amid the hosts of heaven, will ye have any regrets for the sacrifices it cost you to send the Gospel to her people?

O let sloth be driven away; let the grasp of avarice be loosened; let benevolence assume the dominion; let a spirit of enterprise be kindled; let the messengers of salvation be quickly sent to every tribe that roams the western wilds.

Then "the wilderness and the solitary place shall be glad for them, and the desert shall rejoice and blossom as the rose."[65]

FINIS.

Source Acknowledgments

Sections of the introduction first appeared as "Cherokee Catharine Brown's Epistolary Performances" by Theresa Strouth Gaul, in *Letters and Cultural Transformations in the United States, 1760–1860* (Burlington VT: Ashgate, 2009), edited by Theresa Strouth Gaul and Sharon M. Harris, 139–60. © Theresa Strouth Gaul. Letter from Laura Potter to Jeremiah Evarts Nov. 1824 (ABCFM 18.3.1 v.4); letter from Ard Hoyt to Jeremiah Evarts Mar. 2, 1820 (ABCFM 18.3.1 v.3); letter from Moody Hall to Jeremiah Evarts Feb. 14, 1824 (ABCFM 18.3.1 v.3), all from the American Board of Commissioners for Foreign Missions archive, used by permission of the Houghton Library, Harvard University; courtesy of Wider Church Ministries, United Church of Christ. Catharine Brown Papers, courtesy of the Congregational Library, Boston. Letter from Catharine Brown to William and Flora Chamberlain dated Dec. 12, 1818 (Acc. 117 Brown, Catharine. Correspondence), courtesy of Chattanooga Public Library. Catharine Brown letters in Herman Vaill Collection, courtesy of Yale University Library. *Memoir of Catharine Brown*, courtesy of DeGolyer Library, Southern Methodist University, Dallas, E90.B87 A5.

Notes

Part 1. Collected Writings

1. [return address area:] Rossvill Cherokee Nation / November 2nd [postage:] 25 [address:] Mrs. Matilda Williams / Yello Busha / Choctaw Agency

2. Mathilda Loomis Williams (1793–?) and her husband, Loring S. Williams (1796–1889), were missionaries who participated in the establishment of Brainerd in 1817 (Kidwell, *Choctaws and Missionaries in Mississippi*, 57–58; Walker, *Torchlights to the Cherokees*, 42). The Williamses left Brainerd in May 1818 to establish Eliot Mission, the first American Board mission to the Choctaws (*BJ*, 59).

3. Matilda Williams nearly died from a "bilious fever" in the summer of 1818; her husband suffered from dysentery and fever (*BJ*, 467n96).

4. Lydia Lowrey (ca. 1803–62), the daughter of George Lowrey (1770–1852), who later became assistant principal chief under John Ross. Lydia Lowrey attended Brainerd between April 10, 1818, and October 29, 1819, and was admitted to the Brainerd Church on March 28, 1819 (*BJ*, 524n48, 471n105, 406). Lowrey married Milo Hoyt, the son of Cherokee missions superintendent Ard Hoyt, on February 24, 1820 (*BJ*, 154). A missionary teacher commented that Lowrey was "in some respects thought to be superior to Catherine Brown" (Gaul, "Ann Paine's 1820 Travel Narrative," 155).

5. Peggy Wilson (born ca. 1808) and her sister, Elsey or Alice Wilson (born ca. 1806), had the same father but different mothers. In his letter, Mr. Wilson explained that he was afraid the girls' mothers, who were "in an uncivilized & heathen state," would attempt to claim their daughters from the school and "it would then be out of his power to get them" (*BJ*, 80, 82). Cherokee children belonged to their mother's clan, and fathers had no custodial rights (Perdue, *Cherokee Women*, 82).

6. John Brown (Yau nu gung yah ski, ca. 1761–1826), Catharine's father. A number of Cherokees, including members of Brown's family, had removed to Arkansas to escape the harassment of white Georgians; see McLoughlin for a description of the "removal crisis" of 1817–19 (*CM*, 108). Brown's

father was among those who considered removing, although ultimately the family did not move until after Catharine's death.

7. A mark resembling a parenthesis precedes this word; a mark resembling a parenthesis follows the word *alone* below. It is impossible to know whether Brown or another writer inserted these parentheses. Because she did not use parentheses elsewhere in her writings, I have assumed that a later reader inserted these and omitted them from the transcription above.

8. Moody Hall (1789–?) and Isabella Murray Hall (1791–?) were among the ABCFM missionaries first sent to establish Brainerd Mission (*BJ*, 440n23). They left Brainerd on November 22, 1819, to open a new mission at Taloney in what is now Pickens County, Georgia (*BJ*, 140, 481n32). Sarah Hoyt (1794–1869), the eldest daughter of Ard and Esther Hoyt, worked as a missionary assistant at Brainerd and other missions (*BJ*, 446n50).

9. Isabella Hall's "feeble state" and the fact that she was "frequently confined almost entirely to her bed" are probably related to pregnancy (*BJ*, 72). Hall gave birth to her second child in December 1818 while in Knoxville; she had delivered a son who died minutes after birth eleven months earlier, in January 1818 (*BJ*, 42, 424).

10. This is presumably the daughter that Matilda Williams delivered on August 20, 1817 (*BJ*, 37).

11. Peter Kanouse (b. 1784), a blacksmith and schoolmaster who was returning to New England because of illness, escorted Eliot student Israel Folsom and Brainerd student James T. Fields (born ca. 1801) to the ABCFM's Foreign Mission School in Cornwall, Connecticut (*BJ*, 468n100).

12. Cyrus Kingsbury (1786–1870) was the founder of Brainerd Mission and its superintendent until 1818 (*CM*, 110). Kingsbury left Brainerd in May 1818 with the Williamses to establish the Eliot Mission in the Choctaw Nation, near the Yalobusha River in Mississippi (*BJ*, 59).

13. Betsy Burns enrolled at Brainerd at the age of ten in 1817 and, according to Brainerd records, ended her studies there on October 28, 1819, a date in conflict with this letter's date (*BJ*, 408).

14. Fifteen-year-old Polly Burns began her studies at Brainerd on September 24, 1818, only a little over a month before writing this letter. She left Brainerd in June 1819. Brainerd records describe her as "a respectable young lady" (*BJ*, 411).

15. See 50n23 for information on McDonald.

16. The periodicals prefaced the letter with the following comments, in part: "We have the original in our possession; and have altered the grammar in two sentences only, but the sense in none. Let the reader bear in mind, that this young woman, when she joined the school, could only read in

syllables of three letters; that she then knew nothing of God or duty, of Christ or salvation; and that she enjoyed the benefit of instruction for only fourteen or sixteen months. The letter was written from the over-flowings of her own heart, when she was far removed from Christian society, and from intercourse with any person of a cultivated mind" (Brown, "Specimens of Indian Improvement," 170).

17. William Chamberlain (1791–1849), an itinerant preacher and teacher at Brainerd Mission (*BJ*, 447n52), and Flora Hoyt Chamberlain (1798–1886), the second eldest daughter of Esther and Ard Hoyt and a teacher. They named their first daughter Catharine Brown Chamberlain (*BJ*, 446n50, 404). Brown writes from Fort Deposit in central Alabama, about ninety miles southwest of Brainerd and thirty-five miles southwest of what is now Montgomery. Brown's parents removed her from the Brainerd Mission School because of their plans to move to Arkansas.

18. In this letter only, [illegible] indicates a single character that appears in the midst of the flow of words that does not seem to fit within the context of the sentence. The letter might be an uppercase "I" or a lowercase "l," or it might be something else entirely.

19. Ard Hoyt (1770–1828) was the superintendent of Brainerd Mission from 1818 to 1824 (*BJ*, 446n50). Milo Hoyt (ca. 1800–1863), son of Ard and Esther Hoyt, was a missionary assistant and teacher at the Brainerd school who later married Lydia Lowrey, a Cherokee student (*BJ*, 471n105).

20. The date on this letter appears to be incorrect. The Halls returned to Brainerd from Knoxville, where they had spent some months to improve Isabella's poor health due to pregnancy, on April 2 (*BJ*, 112). It seems most likely that Anderson mistook "Mar." for May, or perhaps Brown misdated the letter.

21. Appears to be a single character blotted out.

22. Sarah Brown (Tsa luh, ca. 1768–?), John Brown's second wife, and the mother of John, Catharine, and David Brown.

23. Appears to be a single character blotted out.

24. Hall left Brainerd on October 6 to begin the construction of a new mission station at Taloney (later renamed Carmel), about sixty-five miles southeast of Brainerd near what is now the town of Talking Rock in Pickens County, Georgia (*BJ* 133, 481n32).

25. The Halls moved to Taloney permanently on November 22, 1819 (*BJ*, 140).

26. Blotted out.

27. Blotted out.

28. At the bottom of the page, another hand (presumably either Moody or Isabella Hall's) has written, "Written on our leaving Brainerd for Taloney."

29. Blotted out.
30. The periodicals prefaced the letter with the following, in part: "The reader will recollect that the writer of this letter was but a short time since an *ignorant heathen*. In an accompanying note, Miss Hoyt remarks, that the composition and writing are wholly Catharine's, except the correction in spelling of a few words. The word [*heathen*] we have supplied" (Brown, "Cherokee Mission," 116). The context of the comments suggests that Sarah Hoyt had sent the letter to the *Religious Remembrancer* for publication.
31. In Cornelius, *The Little Osage Captive*, this letter was not attributed by name to Catharine Brown but was presented as an example of "a letter from a female convert in the school at Brainerd" in a chapter titled "Indian Letters" (147). The date, salutation, and subscription are omitted from the version in *The Little Osage Captive*; they are given here from the edition in *Memoir*.
32. The publication in *Christian Watchman* included both sections of the letter, while the *Religious Remembrancer* included only the first part of the letter.
33. David Brown (ca. 1801–29), Catharine's younger brother, the third child of John Brown and Sarah Brown.
34. Harriet Newell (1793–1812) accompanied her missionary husband to India and Burma but died after childbirth at the age of nineteen. Like the biography that was published after Brown's death (by the same publisher, Samuel Armstrong), *Memoirs of Harriet Newell* collected Newell's letters and diary entries. See Cayton, "Canonizing Harriet Newell" for a discussion of the book's influence and cultural significance.
35. Lucy Fields enrolled at Brainerd in 1817 at the age of eleven and continued there through 1820. Records describe her as "a respectable young lady" (*BJ*, 410).
36. Cornwall, Connecticut, the site of the Foreign Mission School. Between 1818 and 1825 the Brainerd missionaries sent a total of ten Cherokee scholars there for advanced study (*CM*, 139). The American Board closed the school in 1826 in large part due to the controversies created when two Cherokee students married young white women from the local community; see Gaul, *To Marry an Indian*.
37. [address:] Mrs. Isabella Hall / Tellony / Cherokee Nation
38. There is a faint vertical line between the preceding two words.
39. The *Brainerd Journal* records the Halls' ongoing difficulties retaining hired help at the Taloney Mission in the face of Isabella's frequent pregnancies and ill health. On March 30, a few weeks after this letter was written, Isabella delivered a "very feeble" child, "not expected to continue long" (*BJ*, 162). This was Hall's third delivery in three years; only one child survived.

40. Blotted out.
41. One or two characters blotted out.
42. One character blotted out.
43. Catharine and her brother had left Brainerd around January 23 because their father was ill (*BJ*, 152).
44. One or two characters blotted out.
45. The Halls' sole surviving child, Louisa Jennet Hall, born December 27, 1818 (*BJ*, 424).
46. The last two characters of this word are blotted out.
47. Blotted out.
48. The identifier "Mrs. A.H." appears at the end of the letter, and the periodical identifies her as "a Lady in Philadelphia."
49. See 53n88 for information on Butrick. The Creek Path Mission and school were located in Alabama, near today's Guntersville and near Brown's parents' home.
50. David Brown was baptized on April 30, 1820, according to mission records (*BJ*, 168).
51. David Brown left for Cornwall on May 11, 1820, and lost his horse while staying with the Halls at Taloney en route (*BJ*, 174).
52. The nineteen-year-old made the thousand-mile journey to Cornwall by himself with a small amount of money, possibly insufficient to cover the cost of the trip, thus eliciting his sister's concern (*BJ*, 172).
53. Blotted out.
54. There is a lengthy space after the preceding word, *precious*.
55. Another lengthy space follows the word *night*.
56. Jane Murray is quite probably Isabella Hall's biological sister. Brainerd records identify Hall's maiden name as Murray and give her place of origin as Lansingburgh, New York (*BJ*, 424).
57. Only a partial excerpt of the letter appeared in Cornelius, *The Little Osage Captive*, from the words "O dear brother" in the second sentence to the end of the first paragraph. This edition of this letter is therefore based on *Memoir*.
58. The *Brainerd Journal* reports that Brown left Brainerd on May 31, 1820, to teach at the newly established girls' school at Creek Path (*BJ*, 178).
59. Anna Hoyt (b. 1802), Ard and Esther Hoyt's youngest daughter (*BJ*, 404).
60. Hole in manuscript.
61. The word *that* is written in the left margin as if inserted later.
62. Hole in manuscript.
63. Single character blotted out.
64. Blotted out, or perhaps accidentally smeared.

65. A parenthesis appears here. There is no corresponding parenthesis in the letter. Since there are other marginal marks in this letter that were apparently made by a later reader, it seems probable that this parenthesis was also inserted by that person.

66. Blotted out.

67. Canceled by a series of crisscrossing lines.

68. This John Brown is Catharine's nephew, the son of Catharine's half-brother, Richard Brown (*BJ*, 450n19). An entry in the *Brainerd Journal* dated March 9, 1818, notes, "John would be glad to return to school, but the late death of his father had brought great care upon him {in business to which he must attend}" (*BJ*, 48).

69. On August 21 the Brainerd missionaries sent Mary K. Rawlings, a volunteer from a Presbyterian church in a nearby Tennessee town, to Taloney after receiving a letter from Moody Hall "mentioning that they are again destitute of female help" (*BJ*, 185).

70. John Brown (ca. 1795–1822), Catharine's older brother, the eldest son of Sarah and John Brown.

71. Catharine's brother John Brown and his wife, Susannah, were baptized at the Creek Path Church in 1820 at the ages of twenty-five and thirty, respectively (*BJ*, 424).

72. First line of the hymn titled "Heavenly Joy on Earth," first published in Watts, *Hymns and Spiritual Songs*.

73. Cornelius's unattributed version in *The Little Osage Captive* omits the date, salutation, and subscription and includes two series of four asterisks preceding and following the first sentence. This suggests that material was omitted from the transcription. Anderson leaves out the asterisks in *Memoir*, giving the impression of a complete letter. I omit them here.

74. James Spencer (born ca. 1790), a Creek Path leader, was described on a list of Creek Path church members as "a half breed—has a family" (*BJ*, 424).

75. In a letter published in April 1822, Laura Potter dates the formation of this society to November 13, 1821, putting the likely date of this letter in the last months of 1821. Potter describes the society in a letter that was later published (Potter, "Creek Path").

76. [return address:] Rossville C.N. 26th, May 1821. [postage:] 25 [address:] Miss Flora Gold / Cornwall / Litchfield County / Connecticut [across bottom:] Cornwall Bridge Officer

77. In the *Religious Intelligencer*, the letter was prefaced by the following comments, originally printed in the *Connecticut Journal*: "A friend has favoured us with a copy of an original letter from this interesting convert from Heathenism to Christianity. It has never before been published, and is

given, below, as a practical comment upon the cause of Missions. We have endeavored to give an exact copy of the letter, in respect to orthography, punctuation and the use of capitals, and if we mistake not it will be found with some trivial exceptions, as handsomely written, as it would have been by a great majority of the young ladies in any portion of civilized community. It reflects the highest credit upon the head and heart of its author, and will no doubt afford great gratification to all those who have contributed liberally to the cause of the Western Missions" (Brown, "Cherokee Mission," 264).

78. Twenty-two-year-old Flora Gold, the recipient of this letter, was a member of a large, pious, and missionary-minded family that resided in Cornwall, Connecticut, where David was attending school. The Gold family's connection to the Foreign Mission School is recounted in Gaul, *To Marry an Indian*. Brown's two letters to Gold were passed down through generations of the family, suggesting how prized Brown's letters were to their recipients.

79. William Potter (1796–1891) was the principal missionary at Creek Path Mission from 1821 until 1837 (Walker, *Torchlights to the Cherokees*, 46). See 56n136 for information on his wife, Laura Potter.

80. The arrival of William and Laura Potter relieved Brown of her teaching duties and allowed her to resume her studies.

81. Words in this section of the letter are difficult to read or illegible due to a hole in the manuscript.

82. Third verse of Isaac Watts, "How Sweet and Aweful Is the Place," published in *Hymns and Spiritual Songs*.

83. Matthew 18:19 (KJV).

84. Brown's letter is prefaced in the periodical by the following comment: "Mr. Editor, The Following Letter was copied, at my request, by the youth to whom it is addressed. If you think it will be acceptable to your youthful readers, you are at liberty to insert it in your valuable publication. Yours respectfully, Herman Daggett" (Brown, "Cherokee Nation," 343). Daggett (1789–1832) was David's principal at the Foreign Mission School.

85. Susan Brown (ca. 1802–?) was Catharine's half-sister, the daughter of Betsy and John Brown. Susannah Brown (ca. 1790–?) was Catharine's sister-in-law, the wife of her older brother John. Both women became members of the Creek Path congregation in 1822 (*BJ*, 424).

86. Matthew 7:20 (KJV).

87. Brown is referring to the *Guardian, or Youth's Religious Instructor* (1819–24), the periodical in which her own letter is published. The *Guardian* was published in New Haven in the same office as the *Religious Intelli-*

gencer but was aimed at a juvenile audience. Isabella Marshall Graham (1742–1814) was a noted educator and philanthropist. *The Power of Faith: Exemplified in the Life and Writings of the Late Mrs. Isabella Graham, of New-York* (1816), compiled and edited by Graham's daughter, Joanna Bethune, circulated widely (Benson, "Graham, Isabella Marshall," 71–72).

88. The newspaper editor presumably made this insertion. It suggests that the recipient of this letter was someone who knew David Brown in Cornwall.

89. She refers to her brother John Brown, who began showing symptoms of tuberculosis.

90. Paraphrase of Isaiah 55:8 (KJV).

91. Paraphrase of Ephesians 2:8 (KJV).

92. By this, Brown means that ten of the mission students boarded in the home of Mr. Potter.

93. A series of military battles between U.S. government troops and the Creeks in 1813–14. Cherokees participated in the conflict by fighting under the command of Andrew Jackson against the Creeks.

94. [address:] Mrs. Isabella Hall / Taloney / Cherokee / Nation

95. Single character blotted out.

96. Perhaps as many as several characters blotted out.

97. Single character blotted out.

98. Entries in the *Brainerd Journal* for March, June, and July 1821 make note of Isabella Hall's ongoing poor health; a report filed by Moody Hall in October 1821 states, "Sickness has been our most constant lot. Twice has my dear wife been brought to the gates of death" (*BJ*, 512).

99. Single character blotted out.

100. This and the last two letters of *heathen* slightly earlier in the letter are rendered illegible by a hole in the manuscript.

101. The last letter of the word is canceled with an "x."

102. Blotted out.

103. Blotted out.

104. Another reference, with different spelling, to Louisa Jennet Hall.

105. The periodical publications were prefaced by the following comments: "If there is a sordid soul who would make excuse when solicited to support the missionary cause, and who would adopt the common plea that it will do no good—the time is not come—you can never civilize or Christianize the Indians—let him read the following letter, and as he reads, remember that it was written by a child of the forest, one who a short time since was enveloped in heathenish darkness, and who doubtless would have remained in that darkness for ever, had not a few missionaries, like their divine Master, left the ninety and nine to seek a few scattered lambs in the

wilderness. If he can read, unmoved, the affecting account of the triumphant death of a heathen convert, contained in the two following letters,
he must be worse than sordid—he must be an infidel" (Brown, "Cherokee
Mission," 741).

106. The date 1882 is presumably a typographical error; 1822 is the correct date.

107. Likely a reference to John Ross. Brown had many connections with Ross
and his family; see introduction 9 and 50n23. For more on John Ross, see
Hicks, *Toward the Setting Sun*; Moulton, *John Ross*.

108. Hebrews 11:13 (KJV).

109. John Brown died on February 2, 1822.

110. At this point, the newspaper article notes that it omits the letter's recounting of "some previous circumstances."

111. Like other Cherokees during this period, the Browns were slaveholders.
For discussions of Cherokee slaveholding practices during this period, see
Perdue, *Slavery and the Evolution of Cherokee Society*; Miles, *The House on
Diamond Hill*.

112. Along the top margin of the manuscript is written, "Copy of a letter from
C.B. to AAC——." Responding to the call for materials relating to Brown's
life for the memoir, Alexander A. Campbell forwarded two letter copies, this one and the letter to his wife dated April 17, 1823. In a postscript
added at the bottom of page 2 of this letter, Campbell blames any gram-
matical errors or misspellings on his "hastiness" in copying and a "severe
headach" which was "rendered worse by study therefore cannot correct."
See 55n112 for information on Campbell.

113. In a preface to the letter printed in the *Pittsburgh Recorder*, Loring S. Williams writes, "In looking over some files of letters the other day, I found
some from Catharine Brown, the Cherokee convert, whose history is
probably familiar to most of your readers. Though several of her letters,
and her memoirs, have been published, I think I will copy one before me,
(which has never been printed,) for the Recorder. Should you think that
its publication would tend to revive the remembrance of the Divine blessing on our Indian Missions, that it would, in any instance, again tune the
heart in praise, or melt it in compassion for the heathen of our country,
you are at liberty to insert it" ("Catharine Brown," 26). The quality of the
American Periodical Series reproduction of this article consulted for this
edition is quite poor. A number of words are illegible.

114. Kingsbury arrived at Brainerd on May 3 and left to return to the Choctaw
Nation via Creek Path on May 20. This letter's composition therefore falls
somewhere between those two dates.

115. In the digitized copy of the newspaper upon which this transcription is

based, a mark appears at the ends of certain sentences that, while hard to discern, is distinct in appearance from periods. It seems possible this may be an exclamation point, especially since it typically follows phrases beginning with "O."

116. A paraphrase of Matthew 25:23 (KJV).

117. "Be of good cheer" is repeated multiple times in the New Testament. "All things . . ." is a paraphrase of Romans 8:28 (KJV).

118. *Owyhee* is a variant spelling of "Hawaii." The ABCFM established a mission in Hawaii in 1820; Hawaiian classmates of David's were among the missionaries (Harris, *Nothing but Christ*, 47–50).

119. Bethel Mission in Mississippi opened in 1822.

120. [return address:] Rossville CN. / June 8th [postage:] Free [address:] Mr. Moody Hall / Talloney / Cherokee Nation.

121. There is a larger-than-normal space following this word.

122. John and Sarah Brown were baptized in 1822, around the age of sixty (*BJ*, 424).

123. Henry Parker (b. 1791) and Philena Griffin Parker (b. 1792) were sent to help the Halls at Taloney (*BJ*, 424, 265).

124. An abbreviation indicating the current month.

125. David is apparently trying to decide whether to continue his studies for the ministry or return home.

126. The Andover Theological Seminary, a Congregationalist institution that provided graduate training for the ministry, was established in 1808 in Andover, Massachusetts. David Brown studied there for one year before returning to the Cherokee Nation.

127. Walter Webber, Catharine Brown's half-brother, the son of Sarah Brown and her first husband. Walter was a successful trader and respected leader who visited Washington to negotiate on the Cherokees' behalf in 1823. He owned and operated a store near the Dwight Mission in Arkansas; Webber Falls, Arkansas, is named after him (*BJ*, 536n23).

128. Alexander Brown, Catharine's half-brother, the son of Betsy and John Brown. He removed with his mother to Arkansas.

129. Anderson's editorial comment in brackets. Dwight Mission was established in 1820 as the first mission in Arkansas. It was located near present-day Russellville. Susan Brown's mother was Betsy (Wottee), John Brown's third wife, who removed to Arkansas.

130. Edmund Brown (Nā tý, ca. 1802–?), Catharine's half-brother and the son of Betsy and John Brown. Also referred to as Edward, he attended Brainerd from September 2, 1817, through July 9, 1818. Missionary records noted that he "could read & write" and that his character was "respectable"

(*BJ*, 459n62). A visitor to Brainerd wrote in 1818 that "Edward, a brother of Catharine's, and too many boys to be enumerated, would, for their open, manly countenances, correct manners, and decent school acquirements, obtain respect and consideration in any community" ("Mission and School at Brainerd"). He moved to Arkansas with his mother, Betsy (McClinton, *Moravian Springplace Mission*, 457).

131. McKee and Israel Folsom were the sons of Nathaniel Folsom, a Scots Irish trader from North Carolina who had two Choctaw wives (*BJ*, 454n43; Kidwell, *Choctaws and Missionaries in Mississippi*, 18). After finishing studies at the Foreign Mission School, Israel Folsom returned to the Choctaw Nation, where he worked as an interpreter and helped translate the Book of Luke into Choctaw (*BJ*, 468n100).

132. Edited by University of Georgia president Moses Waddel, *Memoirs of the Life of Miss Caroline Smelt* told the story of the pious daughter of a U.S. congressman who died as a teenager (*BJ*, 498n36).

133. "O for a Closer Walk with God," written by William Cowper and published in Richard Conyer's *A Collection of Psalms and Hymns*.

134. [postmark with January date, postage:] 25 [address:] Miss Flora Gold / Cornwall / Connecticut

135. Brown has misspelled the name of Reynolds Bascom here. Bascom (1793–1827), an 1819 graduate of Andover Theological Seminary, and Adin C. Gibbs (born ca. 1797), a member of the Delaware tribe and alumnus of the Foreign Mission School, stopped at Creek Path on their way to the Eliot Mission, where Bascom served as a missionary for a few months and Gibbs was to work as an assistant missionary (*BJ*, 531n81; "Visit of Indian Young Men").

136. Faded ink.

137. Illegible and difficult-to-read words in the previous two sentences are due to holes in the manuscript.

138. Elias Boudinot (ca. 1804–39) wrote a message, omitted in this edition, on the back page of this letter sending regards to the Gold family. Boudinot, also known as Buck Watie, was one of the Foreign Mission School students who returned to the Cherokee Nation in December 1822. He went on to become the editor of the bilingual newspaper *Cherokee Phoenix* and a signer of the 1835 Treaty of New Echota. For more on Boudinot, see Perdue, *Cherokee Editor*; Gaul, *To Marry an Indian*.

139. See previous note.

140. See note to Brown's letter to Alexander Campbell of March 16, 1822.

141. A sign denoting a new paragraph appears before this sentence.

142. The bracketed letters in this and the preceding two sentences are not

present in the manuscript due to a tear along the right margin of the page. In the manuscript, the section of this letter beginning "We were all glad" through the last sentence of the paragraph has a box drawn around it and is marked out with a number of Xs. The postscripts are also marked out by Xs. Anderson probably did this marking as he prepared the material for inclusion in *Memoir*.

143. Two lines appear under *Catharine*.

144. In a letter dated August 26, 1824, Laura Potter wrote to Jeremiah Evarts, "I have recently been permitted by Mrs. Gilbreath to examine the papers of her lamented sister, Catharine Brown, among which I have found some fragments of a diary, kept during the three last years of her life; a part having been destroyed as she informed me ~~during~~ before her last illness. I have transcribed, and now transmit them to ∧you∧ hoping they may be of some service in making out a sketch of her life." The manuscript used to prepare this edition of the diary is Potter's copy. We cannot know whether Potter changed aspects of Brown's writing when making the copy. Errors in the transcription are probably Potter's errors rather than Brown's.

145. Missionaries insisted upon the passage of several months between baptism and communion, which represented full admission into the church. This "probationary period" was meant to "test the validity of the conversion." Baptism followed a lengthy period during which the potential convert's conduct was also closely monitored (CM, 133).

146. Probably a reference to the parable of the workers in the vineyard, found in Matthew 20.1–16 (KJV).

147. Brown had more than twenty students (Perdue, "Catharine Brown," 84).

148. Laura and William Potter took over the teaching duties upon their arrival at Creek Path, after which Brown continued her own studies.

149. Ecclesiastes 12:1 (KJV).

150. Brown refers here to the communion table.

151. Mayhew was an ABCFM mission in eastern Mississippi. Samuel Worcester (1770–1821), corresponding secretary of the ABCFM, was touring the southern missions when he was taken ill. Worcester eventually made it to Brainerd on May 25, but he died there on June 7, 1821 (BJ, 218–19).

152. Missionary-minded Christians made a practice of praying for the missions on the first Monday of the month (A.B., "Concert of Prayer," 19).

153. Blount County is northeast of Birmingham; in the nineteenth century the sulfur springs were a popular healing destination. See Perdue's reading of the "Cherokee overtones" of this visit ("Catharine Brown," 87).

154. A large inkblot obscures some of the letters in the three preceding lines.

155. Probably Anna Hoyt.
156. A hole in the paper.

Part 2. Nineteenth-Century Representations

1. An article published in the *Religious Intelligencer* provides context for the origin of this drama. The author explains that the idea for the drama arose as teachers were casting about for ideas for an end-of-term school exhibition that would "conduce to the children's improvement in manners and morals." Reading of "the affecting circumstances of the departure of Catharine Brown from Brainerd[,] the idea of a dialogue on this subject was suggested, and a worthy lady, who feels deeply interested in the success of missionary exertions, undertook it." The drama was published when the realization struck that "it might convey information to many who seldom visit the sanctuary, or read religious publications. . . . By presenting the subject in this form, many would hear of the school at Cornwall, of the missionary establishment at Brainerd, of the necessities of our red brethren and of their earnest call for missionaries, who would otherwise remain ignorant." The exhibition was successful, drawing a crowd, and "in that village, no expedient was ever devised more efficacious to excite among all classes a curiosity to enquire about what is doing in the religious world" ("Missionary Dramas"). All of the characters in the drama are based on real people, with the exception of Mr. Elliott, Mr. Thornton, and Mr. Olmstead. The name Susan is probably an error for Sarah; the Hoyts had no daughter named Susan, but their eldest was named Sarah. Mr. Hicks is a character based on Charles Hicks (1767–1827), assistant principal chief from 1817 to 1827 and principal chief for a brief period in 1827. Fluent in English and a Christian convert, Hicks acted as an interpreter and intermediary between the American Board missionaries and Principal Chief Pathkiller. Biographical information on the other individuals inspiring the characters has been provided in the footnotes to part 1.
2. [Playwright's note:] The writer is not positive, there are any Choctaws in the school—but thought it not unsuitable to adopt this plan, to bring to view the anxiety of the Choctaws and other nations of Indians, for the speedy arrival of missionaries.
3. "The quality of not being easily destroyed, overcome, or affected. Chiefly in *of adamant*: having a quality of being unmovable, inflexible, or unsusceptible to even strong emotions, esp. of sympathy or affection" ("Adamant, *n.* and *adj.*," OED Online).
4. A hymn titled "General Song of Praise to God" by Isaac Watts, from *Divine and Moral Songs for Children*.

5. Unidentified hymn.

6. The girl known as the "Little Osage Captive" and another child were taken captive during a territorial dispute between Cherokees and Osages. The Brainerd missionaries ransomed the young captive in September 1818 and took her to live at the mission, where she was adopted by William and Flora Chamberlain, who named her Lydia Carter after a Mississippi woman who had donated the money for her ransom. Eventually the missionaries were compelled by the U.S. government to return the child to the Osages, but she died in 1821 of malaria and dysentery before her return could occur (*BJ*, 83, 187, 236). The next year, Cornelius published a popular account of Lydia Carter's life titled *The Little Osage Captive*.

7. Most accounts call her Lydia Carter.

8. [Playwright's note:] The former name of Brainard.

9. Leonard Hicks (b. 1803) began attending the Cornwall Foreign Mission School in 1818.

10. This seems to be a Christianized rewriting of a popular song, "The Death Song of the Cherokee Hunter," by Anne Home Hunter (1742–1821), which was printed in London in 1781 and sung by Maria in Royall Tyler's *The Contrast*, first performed in 1787 in New York (Crawford, "Music of the Federal Era," 1).

11. John Fawcett's hymn, "Blest Be the Times that Bind," from *Hymns Adapted to the Circumstance of Public Worship*.

12. Additional poems printed in newspapers about Brown include "Lines on the Death of Catharine Brown of the Cherokee Nation" in the *Christian Spectator*, Dec. 1, 1823, and "Catharine Brown" in the *Religious Intelligencer*, Jan. 31, 1829, and the *Cherokee Phoenix and Indians' Advocate*, Mar. 11, 1829.

13. Samuel T. Armstrong (1784–1850), a popular printer of religious literature, also published the *Panoplist*, the religious magazine that later became the *Missionary Herald*, the American Board's official journal (Giddings, *American Christian Rulers*, 26).

14. The ABCFM Prudential Committee was responsible for executing the resolutions of the American Board as a whole (Anderson, *Memorial Volume*, 147–48).

15. The descriptions of each chapter's contents are omitted at the beginnings of chapters in this edition; the descriptions are given in the table of contents.

16. In what is now Fort Payne, Alabama, about seventy miles southeast of present-day Huntsville.

17. [Anderson's note 1:] A more particular account of the family of Catharine, may be acceptable to the reader.

Mr. John Brown was the son of a man named Brown, who has long been dead. It is not known whether he was a white man, or partly Indian. The mother of Mr. Brown was a "full-blooded" Cherokee. So, also, was the mother of Mrs. Brown; but her father was white. Catharine's parents were brought up like others of their nation;—no better acquainted with the language, religion, manners, or customs of the white people.

Mr. Brown has had three wives. The first had two children, neither of whom are living. One of these children became a man of much distinction. In the Creek war he had the title of Colonel, as he commanded a large number of Cherokees, who made a part of the army under General Jackson. He was severely wounded at the battle of the *Horse-shoe*; but recovered, and died subsequently of a fever, or consumption. He is said to have possessed uncommon powers of mind, and to have exerted much influence among his people. He is familiarly referred to by the name of *Col. Dick Brown.*

The children of Sarah, the second and present wife of Mr. Brown, were *John,* who died in the Christian faith, February 1822, leaving a widow, *Susannah,* who is a professor of religion; *Catharine,* the subject of this memoir; and *David,* of whose piety hopes have been entertained for almost five years.

The children of the third wife, named *Wottee,* or *Betsey,* who, for some years, has been living in the Arkansas Territory, are *Polly,* (or Mrs. *Gilbreth,*) *Alexander, Susan,* and *Edmund.* Polly and Susan are esteemed pious.

Sarah and Betsey lived with Mr. Brown at the same time. But some difficulty arising, the latter separated from him.

Sarah was the wife of a man named Webber, before she married Mr. Brown. The children, by this marriage, are *Betsey,* (now Mrs. *Looney,*) a professor of religion, and *Walter,* called Col. *Webber.* He was at Washington city, about two years since, and possesses a handsome property. These children were quite young, when their father died. Col. Webber is now about thirty-five years old.

It appears, therefore, that of Mr. Brown's family no less than *nine* have become hopefully pious, within the last seven years, viz. Mr. and Mrs. Brown, John, Catharine, David, Polly, Susan, Susannah, and Mrs. Looney.

The reader will be apt to infer, when he sees individuals called by names and titles, with which he is familiar, that they are very much like other individuals, whom he has known under similar titles; in short, that they are civilized and intelligent persons. Such an inference, however, is not warranted. The mere possession of an English name, in an Indian country, is no evidence that the person thus distinguished is able to speak the English language; much less, that his habits are those of civilized life, or that his mind has been in any degree cultivated.

As to the military titles of captain, major, colonel, and even general, they are conferred as a matter of courtesy, in consequence of some sort of undefined authority, which is exercised over others, and which is supposed to bear some distant analogy to the authority, implied in these titles, among us. Of course, the titles are conferred by the whites. In some instances, when Indian auxiliaries have been employed in active warfare, by European governments, or by the United States, individuals may have received regular commissions. Mr. Brown and his son John, were both denominated Captain. [Editor's note:] The Brown men fought alongside other Cherokees on the side of the United States in the so-called Creek War (1813–14).

18. The Moravian missionary station, Springplace, was located in what is to-day Murray County, Georgia. The mission operated from 1801 through removal, educating some 114 children, including future Cherokee leaders and friends of Brown, such as Elias Boudinot. For further discussion of this mission, see McClinton, *The Moravian Springplace Mission*; Miles, *The House on Diamond Hill*.

19. Presbyterian minister Gideon Blackburn (1772–1838) established two schools in the Cherokee Nation. The schools shut down in 1810 amid allegations of improprieties by Blackburn (*CM*, 57, 78–79).

20. [Anderson's note 2:] "I was pleased to find," says a friend, "that General Jackson, (who commanded in the war with the Creeks,) had a high opinion of Catharine. In the course of our conversation he remarked, *She was a woman of Roman virtue, and above suspicion.*"

21. David Brainerd (1718–1747), an eighteenth-century missionary to the Mahican Indians in New York and the Delaware Indians of Pennsylvania.

22. [Anderson's note 3:] Brainerd is situated within the chartered limits of Tennessee, on the Chickamaugah creek; two miles north of the line of Georgia; seven miles south-east of Tennessee river; two hundred and fifty north-west of Augusta in Geo.; one hundred and fifty south-east of Nashville, and one hundred and ten south-west of Knoxville, both in Tennessee.

23. Elias Cornelius (1794–1832), an ABCFM agent, visited Brainerd in September 1817 (*BJ*, 445n41).

24. "There is neither Jew nor Greek, there is neither bond nor free, there is neither male nor female: for ye are all one in Christ Jesus" (KJV).

25. Brown was baptized on January 25, 1818 (*BJ*, 44).

26. From Hosea 3:4 (KJV). Teraphim were images or idols associated with the household gods of the ancient Hebrews ("Teraphim, *n.*," OED *Online*).

27. Jeremiah Evarts (1781–1831), one of the American Board's founders, played a pivotal role in its operation, serving as its treasurer (1811–22) and as a member of the Prudential Committee (1812–30) and finally succeeding Worcester as the Board's corresponding secretary (1821–31). Evarts also edited the *Panoplist* and its successor, the *Missionary Herald* (Anderson, *Memorial Volume*, 124–25, 411). Dr. Samuel Worcester (1770–1821) preceded Evarts as the ABCFM's corresponding secretary from its creation in 1810 until his death in 1821, which occurred while he was visiting Brainerd (115–16).

28. Thomas Scott (1747–1821) wrote *Commentary on the Whole Bible*, first published in 1788 and continued over 176 weekly installments.

29. Woods, *Memoirs of Mrs. Harriet Newell* (1814), discussed in note 264n34.

30. [Anderson's note 4:] Panoplist, vol. xiv. p. 344.

31. Rev. John Gambold (d. 1827) and his wife, Anna Rosina Kliest Gambold (d. 1821), supervised the Moravian mission and school at Springplace between 1805 and 1821 (*BJ*, 441n24, 507n26).

32. [Anderson's note 5:] The little girl, a narrative of whom was published, in 1822, by the Rev. Elias Cornelius, now Pastor of the Tabernacle Church in Salem, Mass. [Editor's note:] See 274n6.

33. [Anderson's note 6:] The girl was never obtained by the missionaries: but the boy was afterwards placed under their care, through the kindness of Col. Meigs, the United States Agent, and through the benevolent enterprise of Mr. John Ross, a promising Cherokee young man. The boy was named *John Osage Ross*, in honour of Mr. Ross. [Editor's note:] John Osage Ross lived with the Brainerd missionaries from August 1819, when the missionaries redeemed him, until August 1820, when it was ordered that he and Lydia Carter be returned to the Osage tribe (Cornelius, *Little Osage Captive*, 69–72, 111–12).

34. Notes to all subsequent letters by Brown are found in part 1 of this volume, where the reader is encouraged to locate the letter of the same date.

35. According to the mission journal, it was not May 23 but March 23, 1819, that Catharine Brown returned to Brainerd (*BJ*, 111).

36. Based on the evidence of the *Brainerd Journal*, which states that Brown returned to Brainerd on March 23 (not May 23), it is likely that this date is an error and should be March (*BJ*, 111).

37. [Anderson's note 7:] Any person who had witnessed the separation of Mrs. Williams from her Cherokee friends, when she and her husband left Brainerd and set out for the Choctaw mission, in May 1818, could well understand the affectionate expressions in this letter. When the boat was

ready to proceed, and the hour of parting had arrived; when Mr. Cornelius had made the last prayer, and the last hymn had been sung; Catharine was among those who seemed ready to sink under a burden of grief too great to be borne. Mrs. Williams had always been peculiarly dear to her from their first acquaintance, and, like an older sister, had guided her youthful steps in the path of peace.

38. [Anderson's note 8:] Now called Carmel.
39. John Arch (ca. 1797–1825), whose Cherokee name was Atsi or Atsee, enrolled at Brainerd on January 26, 1819, at the age of about twenty-three (*BJ*, 104, 476n6).
40. After his death, Arch also became the subject of a posthumous biography published by the ABCFM.
41. David Brown's lecture tour in 1823–1824 is discussed by Martin in "Crisscrossing Projects." See Brown, "Address of Dewi Brown" for a transcription of Brown's speech.
42. At that time, Jeremiah Evarts (Anderson, *Memorial Volume*, 411).
43. Possibly Point Pleasant, Louisiana, about twenty miles south of the present-day Louisiana-Arkansas border.
44. A reference to Gen. 46:29–30, Jacob's tearful reunion with his son Joseph, whom he believed to be dead, after many years of separation (KJV).
45. The ABCFM's Dwight Mission. Catharine Brown's half-brother, Walter Webber, owned a store nearby (*BJ*, 536n23).
46. A reference to Rev. 15:2–4 (KJV).
47. Probably a reference to Matt. 20:1–16, the parable of the workers in the vineyard (KJV).
48. [Anderson's note 9:] This Society first sent its annual collections to the mission at Dwight, in the Arkansas. But the last year their collection was devoted to the spread of the Gospel among the Osages. The Cherokee woman, who proposed the resolution to appropriate the money in this way, observed to the Society, "The Bible tells us to do good to our enemies, and I believe the Osages are the greatest enemies the Cherokees have." The sum was about ten dollars.
49. The reader will find explanatory notes to Brown's diary in part 1 of this volume.
50. Dr. Elizur Butler (1794–1857), the Brainerd physician. Butler and a fellow ABCFM missionary, Samuel Austin Worcester (ABCFM corresponding secretary Samuel Worcester's nephew), secured a place in history when they were imprisoned in 1831 for refusing to take an oath of allegiance to the state of Georgia. The Supreme Court ordered their release in 1833 (*BJ*, 503n1).

51. [Anderson's note 10:] The Society, of which mention was made [earlier in the volume].
52. The hymn titled "Why Should We Start, and Fear to Die" by Isaac Watts, *Hymns and Spiritual Songs.*
53. A northern Alabama town about twenty miles west of Huntsville.
54. Probably Mrs. Leech, wife of William Leech, and Sarah Boyce Campbell.
55. Present-day Triana, Alabama, is about fifteen miles southwest of today's Huntsville.
56. Leech was the superintendent of the Huntsville Sunday School and an elder in the First Church of Huntsville, founded by Rev. Gideon Blackburn in 1818 ("Huntsville, Alabama"; Praigg, "Alabama").
57. Compendium.
58. [Anderson's note 11:] Her letters were published, by different friends to whom they were addressed, to gratify the laudible curiosity of the community. It is proper to remark, however, that not more than two or three were ever inserted in the publications of the American Board.
59. Written about Pocahontas by Lydia H. Sigourney (1791–1865) in *Traits of the Aborigines of America: A Poem* (1822). The book portrayed the historic betrayal of Native Americans by Europeans, which Sigourney, an ABCFM supporter, called "one of our greatest national sins" (*Letters of Life*, 327). The work's fifth canto, which called upon Sigourney's contemporaries to teach Native people the ways of Christianity and civilization, makes numerous references to the missionaries at Brainerd and Springplace and their Cherokee supporters, including Brown (*Traits of the Aborigines of America*, 275n4–283n11).
60. Reference to Col. 3:1 (KJV).
61. From 2 Cor. 5:17 (KJV).
62. [Anderson's note 12:] Traits of the Aborigines of America, pp. 161, 162. [Editor's note:] See 157–58 for the full text of the part of the poem devoted to Brown.
63. From the opening of the lecture David Brown presented in multiple locations across New England in 1823–1824; see Brown, "Address of Dewi Brown."
64. [Anderson's note 13:] Missionary Herald, vol. xx, pp. 345, 346. [Editor's note:] The preceding excerpt was rendered in a smaller font in the first edition.
65. From Isa. 35:1 (KJV).

Works Cited

A.B. "Concert of Prayer." *Panoplist, and Missionary Magazine* 11, no. 1 (1815): 19. Google Books.

"Adamant, *n.* and *adj.*" OED *Online*, Mar. 2012. Oxford University Press. http://www.oed.com/view/Entry/2071?redirectedFrom=adamant#eid.

Altman, Janet Gurkin. *Epistolarity: Approaches to a Form.* Columbus: Ohio State University Press, 1982.

Anderson, Rufus. *Memorial Volume of the First Fifty Years of the American Board of Commissioners for Foreign Missions.* Boston: American Board of Commissioners for Foreign Missions, 1861. Google Books.

Bannet, Eve Tavor. *Empire of Letters: Letter Manuals and Transatlantic Correspondence, 1680–1820.* Cambridge: Cambridge University Press, 2005.

Bellin, Joshua David. *Medicine Bundle: Indian Sacred Performance and American Literature, 1824–1932.* Philadelphia: University of Pennsylvania Press, 2008.

Benson, Mary S. "Graham, Isabella Marshall." In *Notable American Women, 1607–1950: A Biographical Dictionary*, vol. 2, edited by Edward T. James, Janet Wilson James, and Paul S. Boyer, 71–72. Cambridge MA: Belknap Press of Harvard University Press, 1971.

Bernardin, Susan. "The Authenticity Game: 'Getting Real' in Contemporary American Indian Literature." In *True West: Authenticity and the American West*, edited by William R. Handley and Nathaniel Lewis, 155–78. Lincoln: University of Nebraska Press, 2004.

Block, Sharon. *Rape and Sexual Power in Early America.* Chapel Hill: University of North Carolina Press, 2006.

Blodgett, Harriet. *Centuries of Female Days: Englishwomen's Private Diaries.* New Brunswick NJ: Rutgers University Press, 1988.

Bloom, Lynn Z. "'I Write for Myself and Strangers': Private Diaries as Public Documents." In *Inscribing the Daily: Critical Essays on Women's Diaries*, edited by Suzanne L. Bunkers and Cynthia A. Huff, 23–37. Amherst: University of Massachusetts Press, 1996.

Brooks, Joanna, ed. *The Collected Writings of Samson Occom, Mohegan: Leadership and Literature in Eighteenth-Century Native America.* New York: Oxford University Press, 2006.

Brooks, Lisa. *The Common Pot: The Recovery of Native Space in the Northeast.* Minneapolis: University of Minnesota Press, 2008.

Bross, Kristina, and Hilary E. Wyss. Introduction to *Early Native Literacies in New England: A Documentary and Critical Anthology,* edited by Kristina Bross and Hilary E. Wyss, 1–13. Amherst: University of Massachusetts Press, 2008.

Brown, Candy Gunther. *The Word in the World: Evangelical Writing, Publishing, and Reading in America, 1789–1880.* Chapel Hill: University of North Carolina Press, 2004.

Brown, Catharine. "Cherokee Mission." *Religious Intelligencer* 6, no. 17 (1821): 264–65. Google Books.

———. "Cherokee Mission." *Religious Intelligencer* 6, no. 47 (1822): 741–42. Google Books.

———. "Cherokee Mission." *Religious Remembrancer* 29 (Mar. 11, 1820): 116. American Periodical Series.

———. "Cherokee Nation." *Guardian, or Youth's Religious Instructor* 2, no. 10 (1821): 343–46. Google Books.

———. "Specimens of Indian Improvement." *Panoplist, and Missionary Herald* 15, no. 4 (1819): 170–71. American Periodical Series.

Brown, David. Letter to Lydia Sigourney. Nov. 6, 1822. Connecticut Historical Society, Hartford.

Brown, Dewi. "Address of Dewi Brown, a Cherokee Indian." In *Proceedings of the Massachusetts Historical Society: 1871–1873,* 30–38. Boston: Massachusetts Historical Society, 1873.

Bunkers, Suzanne L., and Cynthia A. Huff, eds. *Inscribing the Daily: Critical Essays on Women's Diaries.* Amherst: University of Massachusetts Press, 1996.

Campbell, Alexander. Letter to Unknown. July 11, 1824. CBP Item 24. Congregational Library, Boston.

Carney, Virginia Moore. *Eastern Band Cherokee Women: Cultural Persistence in Their Letters and Speeches.* Knoxville: University of Tennessee Press, 2005.

Casper, Scott E. *Constructing American Lives: Biography and Culture in Nineteenth-Century America.* Chapel Hill: University of North Carolina Press, 1999.

Cayton, Mary Kupiec. "Canonizing Harriet Newell: Women, the Evangelical Press, and the Foreign Mission Movement in New England, 1800–1840." In *Competing Kingdoms: Women, Mission, Nation, and the American Protestant Empire, 1812–1960,* edited by Barbara Reeves-Ellington, Kathryn Kish Sklar, and Connie A. Shemo, 69–93. Durham NC: Duke University Press, 2010.

———. "Harriet Newell's Story: Women, the Evangelical Press, and the Foreign Mission Movement." In *A History of the Book in America*, vol. 2, *An
Extensive Republic: Print, Culture, and Society in the New Nation, 1790–1840*,
edited by Robert A. Gross and Mary Kelley, 408–15. Chapel Hill: University of North Carolina Press, 2010.

Chamberlain, William. Letter to William Potter. Feb. 4, 1824. CBP Item 22.
Congregational Library, Boston.

Coleman, Michael C. "American Indian School Pupils as Cultural Brokers:
Cherokee Girls at Brainerd Mission, 1828–1829." In *Between Indian and
White Worlds: The Cultural Broker*, edited by Margaret Connell Szasz, 122–
35. Norman: University of Oklahoma Press, 1994.

Cornelius, Elias. *The Little Osage Captive, an Authentic Narrative: To Which Are
Added Some Interesting Letters, Written by Indians*. York PA: W. Alexander &
Son, Castlegate, 1824. Internet Archive. http://www.archive.org/stream/
littleosagecaptioocorniala#page/26/mode/2up.

Cowper, William. "O for a Closer Walk with God." In *Collection of Psalms and
Hymns, from Various Authors: For the Use of Serious and Devout Christians of
Every Denomination*, edited by Richard Conyer. York PA: Wilson, Spence,
and Mawman, 1772.

Crawford, Richard. "Music of the Federal Era." Liner notes. New World Records 80299, 1994. http://www.newworldrecords.org/linernotes/80299.pdf.

Cumfer, Cynthia. *Separate Peoples, One Land: The Minds of Cherokees, Blacks,
and Whites on the Tennessee Frontier*. Chapel Hill: University of North Carolina Press, 2007.

Decker, William Merrill. *Epistolary Practices: Letter Writing in America before
Telecommunications*. Chapel Hill: University of North Carolina Press, 1998.

Dierks, Konstantin. *In My Power: Letter Writing and Communications in Early
America*. Philadelphia: University of Pennsylvania Press, 2009.

Ellis, Sarah Hoyt. Letter to William Potter. N.d. CBP Item 17. Congregational
Library, Boston.

Fawcett, John. *Hymns Adapted to the Circumstance of Public Worship*. Leeds,
England, 1782.

Field, Delilah. Letter to Miss G. *Christian Repository* 1, no. 16 (1821): 63. American Periodical Series.

Gaul, Theresa Strouth. "Ann Paine's 1820 Travel Narrative: Comments on
Slavery and Observations of the Cherokees." *LEAR: Literature in the Early
American Republic* 4 (2012): 113–73.

———. "Cherokee Catharine Brown's Epistolary Performances." In *Letters and
Cultural Transformations in the United States, 1760–1860*, edited by Theresa
Strouth Gaul and Sharon M. Harris, 139–60. Burlington VT: Ashgate, 2009.

———, ed. *To Marry an Indian: The Marriage of Harriett Gold and Elias Boudinot in Letters, 1823–1839.* Chapel Hill: University of North Carolina Press, 2005.

Giddings, Edward Jonathan. *American Christian Rulers: Or, Religion and Men of Government.* New York: Bromfield, 1889–1890. Google Books.

Gilbreath, Polly. "Biographical Sketch." N.d. CBP Item 20. Congregational Library, Boston.

"Good Effected." *Religious Remembrancer* 45 (July 1, 1820): 177. American Periodical Series.

Hall, Moody. "Cherokee Mission." *Religious Remembrancer* 5 (Sept. 26, 1818): 19–20. American Periodical Series.

———. Letter to Jeremiah Evarts. 14 Feb. 1824. ABCFM Papers 18.3.1, vol. 3. Houghton Library, Harvard University, Cambridge MA.

Harris, Paul William. *Nothing but Christ: Rufus Anderson and the Ideology of Protestant Foreign Missions.* New York: Oxford University Press, 1999.

Hewitt, Elizabeth. *Correspondence and American Literature, 1770–1865.* New York: Cambridge University Press, 2004.

Hicks, Brian. *Toward the Setting Sun: John Ross, the Cherokees and the Trail of Tears.* New York: Atlantic Monthly Press, 2011.

Hill, Sarah H. "Weaving History: Cherokee Baskets from the Springplace Mission." *William and Mary Quarterly*, 3rd ser., 53, no. 1 (1996): 115–36.

Hoyt, Ard. Letter to Samuel Worcester. Mar. 2, 1820. ABCFM Papers 18.3.1, vol. 3. Houghton Library, Harvard University, Cambridge MA.

Huhndorf, Shari M. *Mapping the Americas: The Transnational Politics of Contemporary Native Culture.* Ithaca NY: Cornell University Press, 2009.

"Huntsville, Alabama." *American Sunday School Magazine* 5 (Nov. 1828): 327. Google Books.

"The Indian Cause." *Christian Watchman* 5, no. 19 (1824): 74. American Periodical Series.

Johnson, Nan. *Gender and Rhetorical Space in American Life, 1866–1910.* Carbondale: Southern Illinois University Press, 2002.

Johnston, Carolyn Ross. *Cherokee Women in Crisis: Trail of Tears, Civil War, and Allotment, 1838–1907.* Tuscaloosa: University of Alabama Press, 2003.

Justice, Daniel Heath. *Our Fire Survives the Storm: A Cherokee Literary History.* Minneapolis: University of Minnesota Press, 2006.

Kagle, Steven E. *American Diary Literature, 1620–1799.* Boston: Twayne, 1979.

Kagle, Steven E., and Lorenza Gramegna. "Rewriting Her Life: Fictionalization and the Use of Fictional Models in Early American Women's Diaries." In *Inscribing the Daily: Critical Essays on Women's Diaries,* edited by

Suzanne L. Bunkers and Cynthia A. Huff, 38–55. Amherst: University of Massachusetts Press, 1996.

Kidwell, Clara Sue. *Choctaws and Missionaries in Mississippi, 1818–1918.* Norman: University of Oklahoma Press, 1995.

Kilcup, Karen L., ed. *Native American Women's Writing, 1800–1924: An Anthology.* Malden MA: Blackwell, 2000.

Konkle, Maureen. *Writing Indian Nations: Native Intellectuals and the Politics of Historiography, 1827–1863.* Chapel Hill: University of North Carolina Press, 2004.

Kouffman, Avra. "Women's Diaries of Late Stuart England: An Overview." In *Recording and Reordering: Essays on the Seventeenth- and Eighteenth-Century Diary and Journal,* edited by Dan Doll and Jessica Munns, 65–101. Cranbury NJ: Rosemont, 2006.

Krupat, Arnold, ed. *Native American Autobiography: An Anthology.* Madison: University of Wisconsin Press, 1994.

———. *The Voice in the Margin: Native American Literature and the Canon.* Berkeley: University of California Press, 1989.

Madsen, Deborah L., ed. *Native Authenticity: Transnational Perspectives on Native American Literary Studies.* Albany: State University of New York Press, 2010.

Martin, Joel W. "Almost White: The Ambivalent Promise of Christian Missions among the Cherokees." In *Religion and the Creation of Race and Ethnicity: An Introduction,* edited by Craig R. Prentiss, 43–60. New York: New York University Press, 2003.

———. "Crisscrossing Projects of Sovereignty and Conversion: Cherokee Christians and New England Missionaries During the 1820s." In *Native Americans, Christianity, and the Reshaping of the American Religious Landscape,* edited by Joel W. Martin and Mark A. Nicholas, 67–89. Chapel Hill: University of North Carolina Press, 2010.

———. Introduction to *Native Americans, Christianity, and the Reshaping of the American Religious Landscape,* edited by Joel W. Martin and Mark A. Nicholas, 1–20. Chapel Hill: University of North Carolina Press, 2010.

———. *The Land Looks After Us: A History of Native American Religion.* New York: Oxford University Press, 2001.

———. "Visions of Revitalization in the Eastern Woodlands: Can a Middle-Aged Theory Stretch to Embrace the First Cherokee Converts?" In *Reassessing Revitalization Movements: Perspectives from North America and the Pacific Islands,* edited by Michael E. Harkin, 61–87. Lincoln: University of Nebraska Press, 2004.

Martinson, Deborah. *In the Presence of Audience: The Self in Diaries and Fiction.* Columbus: Ohio State University Press, 2003.

McClinton, Rowena, ed. *The Moravian Springplace Mission to the Cherokees.* Vol. 2, *1814–1821.* Lincoln: University of Nebraska Press, 2007.

McLoughlin, William G. *Cherokee Renascence in the New Republic.* Princeton NJ: Princeton University Press, 1986.

———. *The Cherokees and Christianity, 1794–1870: Essays on Acculturation and Cultural Persistence.* Edited by Walter H. Conser Jr. Athens: University of Georgia Press, 2008.

———. *Cherokees and Missionaries, 1789–1839.* New Haven CT: Yale University Press, 1984.

"Memoirs [*sic*] of Catharine Brown." *Recorder and Telegraph* 10, no. 28 (1825): 112. American Periodical Series.

Miles, Tiya. "'Circular Reasoning': Recentering Cherokee Women in the Antiremoval Campaigns." *American Quarterly* 61, no. 2 (2009): 221–43.

———. *The House on Diamond Hill: A Cherokee Plantation Story.* Chapel Hill: University of North Carolina Press, 2010.

"Miscellaneous Notices Relative to Religion and Missions." *Panoplist, and Missionary Herald* 16, no. 5 (1820): 232–33. Google Books.

"Mission and School at Brainerd." *Panoplist, and Missionary Herald* 14, no. 9 (1818): 431. Google Books.

"Missionary Dramas." *Religious Intelligencer* 3, no. 49 (1819): 792. American Periodicals Series.

Motz, Marilyn Ferris. "The Private Alibi: Literacy and Community in the Diaries of Two Nineteenth-Century American Women." In *Inscribing the Daily: Critical Essays on Women's Diaries,* edited by Suzanne L. Bunkers and Cynthia A. Huff, 189–206. Amherst: University of Massachusetts Press, 1996.

Moulder, M. Amanda. "Cherokee Practice, Missionary Intentions: Literacy Learning among Early Nineteenth-Century Cherokee Women." *College Composition and Communication* 63, no. 1 (2011): 75–97.

Moulton, Gary E. *John Ross, Cherokee Chief.* Athens: University of Georgia Press, 2004.

Murray, David. "Translation and Mediation." In *The Cambridge Companion to Native American Literature,* edited by Joy Porter and Kenneth M. Roemer, 69–83. Cambridge: Cambridge University Press, 2005.

Nelson, Joshua B. "Integrated Circuitry: Catharine Brown across Gender, Race, and Religion." *American Indian Culture and Research Journal* 30, no. 1 (2006): 17–31.

Noley, Homer. "The Interpreters." In *Native American Religious Identity: Unforgotten Gods,* edited by Jace Weaver, 48–60. Maryknoll NY: Orbis Books, 1998.

Nord, David Paul. "Benevolent Books: Printing, Religion, and Reform." In *A History of the Book in America*, vol. 2, *An Extensive Republic: Print, Culture, and Society in the New Nation, 1790–1840*, edited by Robert A. Gross and Mary Kelley, 221–46. Chapel Hill: University of North Carolina Press, 2010.

———. *Faith in Reading: Religious Publishing and the Birth of Mass Media in America*. New York: Oxford University Press, 2004.

Nussbaum, Felicity A. *The Autobiographical Subject: Gender and Ideology in Eighteenth-Century England*. Baltimore: Johns Hopkins University Press, 1989.

O'Connell, Barry. Introduction to *On Our Own Ground: The Complete Writings of William Apess, A Pequot*, edited by Barry O'Connell, xiii–lxxviii. Amherst: University of Massachusetts Press, 1992.

———. "Literacy and Colonization: The Case of the Cherokees." In *A History of the Book in America*, vol. 2, *An Extensive Republic: Print, Culture, and Society in the New Nation, 1790–1840*, edited by Robert A. Gross and Mary Kelley, 495–515. Chapel Hill: University of North Carolina Press, 2010.

Parker, Robert Dale, ed. *The Sound the Stars Make Rushing through the Sky: The Writings of Jane Johnston Schoolcraft*. Philadelphia: University of Pennsylvania Press, 2007.

Perdue, Theda. "Catharine Brown: Cherokee Convert to Christianity." In *Sifters: Native American Women's Lives*, edited by Theda Perdue, 77–91. New York: Oxford University Press, 2001.

———, ed. *Cherokee Editor: The Writings of Elias Boudinot*. Athens: University of Georgia Press, 1996.

———. *Cherokee Women: Gender and Culture Change, 1700–1835*. Lincoln: University of Nebraska Press, 1998.

———. *Slavery and the Evolution of Cherokee Society, 1540–1866*. Knoxville: University of Tennessee Press, 1979.

Perdue, Theda, and Michael D. Green, eds. *The Cherokee Removal: A Brief History with Documents*. Boston: Bedford Press, St. Martin's Press, 1995.

Phillips, Joyce B., and Paul Gary Phillips, eds. *The Brainerd Journal: A Mission to the Cherokees, 1817–1823*. Lincoln: University of Nebraska Press, 1998.

Potter, Laura. "Creek Path." *Religious Intelligencer* 6, no. 47 (1822): 742–43. American Periodical Series.

———. Letter to Jeremiah Evarts. Aug. 26, 1824. CBP Item 7. Congregational Library, Boston.

———. Letter to Jeremiah Evarts. Nov. [?], 1824. ABCFM Papers 18.3.1, vol. 4. Houghton Library, Harvard University.

Praigg, J. G. "Alabama." *Christian Observer* 96, no. 19 (1908): 12. American Periodical Series.

Reeves-Ellington, Barbara, Kathryn Kish Sklar, and Connie A. Shemo, eds. *Competing Kingdoms: Women, Mission, Nation, and the American Protestant Empire, 1812–1960.* Durham NC: Duke University Press, 2010.

Round, Phillip H. *Removable Type: Histories of the Book in Indian Country, 1663–1880.* Chapel Hill: University of North Carolina Press, 2010.

Ryan, Susan M. *The Grammar of Good Intentions: Race and the Antebellum Culture of Benevolence.* Ithaca NY: Cornell University Press, 2003.

Schneider, Bethany. "New England Tales: Catharine Sedgwick, Catherine Brown, and the Dislocations of Indian Land." In *A Companion to American Fiction, 1780–1865,* edited by Shirley Samuels, 353–64. Malden MA: Blackwell, 2004.

Schneider, Gary. *The Culture of Epistolarity: Vernacular Letters and Letter Writing in Early Modern England, 1500–1700.* Newark: University of Delaware Press, 2005.

Schultz, Lucille M. "Letter-Writing Instruction in 19th Century Schools in the United States." In *Letter Writing as a Social Practice,* edited by David Barton and Nigel Hall, 109–30. Philadelphia: John Benjamins, 2000.

Shoemaker, Nancy. Introduction to *Negotiators of Change: Historical Perspectives on Native American Women,* edited by Nancy Shoemaker, 1–25. New York: Routledge, 1995.

Sigourney, Lydia H. *Letters of Life.* New York: D. Appleton, 1866.

———. *Traits of the Aborigines of America: A Poem.* Cambridge MA: Cummings & Hillard, 1822. Google Books.

Simons, Judy. "Invented Lives: Textuality and Power in Early Women's Diaries." In *Inscribing the Daily: Critical Essays on Women's Diaries,* edited by Suzanne L. Bunkers and Cynthia A. Huff, 252–63. Amherst: University of Massachusetts Press, 1996.

Smith, Sidonie, and Julia Watson, eds. *Before They Could Vote: American Women's Autobiographical Writing, 1819–1919.* Madison: University of Wisconsin Press, 2006.

Sprague, William B. *Annals of the American Pulpit; Or, Commemorative Notices of Distinguished American Clergymen of Various Denominations, from the Early Settlement of the Country to the Close of the Year Eighteen Hundred and Fifty-Five,* vol. 4. New York: Robert Carter & Brothers, 1858. Google Books.

Szasz, Margaret Connell. Introduction to *Between Indian and White Worlds: The Cultural Broker,* edited by Margaret Connell Szasz, 3–20. Norman: University of Oklahoma Press, 1994.

"Teraphim, *n.*" *OED Online,* Dec. 2011. Oxford University Press. http://www.oed.com/view/Entry/199323?redirectedFrom=teraphim#eid.

"Visit of Indian Young Men." *Missionary Herald* 19, no. 1 (1823): 29–30. Google Books.

Vizenor, Gerald, ed. *Survivance: Narratives of Native Presence.* Lincoln: University of Nebraska Press, 2008.

Waddel, Moses. *Memoirs of the Life of Miss Caroline Elizabeth Smelt.* New York: Daniel Fanshawe, 1818. Google Books.

Walker, Robert Sparks. *Torchlights to the Cherokees.* New York: Macmillan, 1931. Reprint, Johnson City TN: Overmountain Press, 1993.

Warrior, Robert Allen. *The People and the Word: Reading Native Nonfiction.* Minneapolis: University of Minnesota Press, 2005.

———. *Tribal Secrets: Recovering American Indian Intellectual Traditions.* Minneapolis: University of Minnesota Press, 1995.

Watts, Isaac. *Divine and Moral Songs for Children.* London, 1715.

———. *Hymns and Spiritual Songs.* London, 1707.

Weaver, Jace. "From I-Hermeneutics to We-Hermeneutics: Native Americans and the Post-Colonial." In *Native American Religious Identity: Unforgotten Gods,* edited by Jace Weaver, 1–25. Maryknoll NY: Orbis Books, 1998.

———. *That the People Might Live: Native American Literatures and Native American Community.* New York: Oxford University Press, 1997.

Williams, Loring S. "Catharine Brown." *Pittsburgh Recorder* 6, no. 7 (1827): 26. American Periodical Series.

Woods, Leonard. *Memoirs of Mrs. Harriet Newell.* Boston, 1814.

Wyss, Hilary E. *English Letters and Indian Literacies: Reading, Writing, and New England Missionary Schools, 1750–1830.* Philadelphia: University of Philadelphia Press, 2012.

———. *Writing Indians: Literacy, Christianity, and Native Community in Early America.* Amherst: University of Massachusetts Press, 2000.

Yarbrough, Fay. "Legislating Women's Sexuality: Cherokee Marriage Laws in the Nineteenth Century." *Journal of Social History* 38, no. 2 (2004): 385–406.

To order or obtain more information on these or other University of Nebraska Press titles, visit www.nebraskapress.unl.edu.

CPSIA information can be obtained at www.ICGtesting.com
Printed in the USA
BVOW07s1544041113

335310BV00002B/2/P